WITHDRAWN

Playboys in Paradise

Masculinity, Youth and Leisure-Style in Modern America

Bill Osgerby

BERG

Oxford • New York

First published in 2001 by
Berg
Editorial offices:
150 Cowley Road, Oxford, OX4 1JJ, UK
838 Broadway, Third Floor, New York, NY 10003-4812, USA

Berg is an imprint of Oxford International Publishers Ltd.

Library of Congress Cataloging-in-Publication Data
A catalogue record for this book is available from the Library of Congress.

British Library Cataloguing-in-Publication Data
A catalogue record for this book is available from the British Library.

ISBN 1 85973 448 0 (Cloth)
1 85973 453 7 (Paper)

Typeset by JS Typesetting, Wellingborough, Northants.
Printed in the United Kingdom by Biddles Ltd, Guildford and King's Lynn.

Contents

List of Figures

Preface and Acknowledgements

Understanding gender categories as multiform and historically variable rather than monolithic and timelessly fixed has been a key theme to emerge from recent critical analyses of gender. Exemplifying this perspective has been the work of Judith Butler and her arguments that gender should not be conceived as a stable identity or an 'agency from which various acts follow', but instead should be recognized as 'an identity tenuously constituted in time, instituted in an exterior space through a *stylized repetition of acts*' (Butler, 1990: 140). In these terms, gender can be understood as a historically dynamic 'performance' – a 'corporeal style' that is fabricated and sustained through a set of performative acts and 'a ritualized repetition of conventions' (Butler, 1995: 31). Analyses of feminine identities have been prominent in highlighting the ways gender has been fabricated through 'performative' attributes and discursive practices, but a similar approach to the study of masculinity is relatively less developed.

In Britain, attention to the heterogeneity and variability of constructions of masculinity came to the fore during the 1990s. Much of this analysis focused on the figure of the narcissistic and self-conscious 'New Man' and an array of new, glossy lifestyle magazines with which he was associated. Authors such as Frank Mort (1988; 1996) and Sean Nixon (1996) mapped out what they interpreted as a new relationship between young men and the traditionally 'feminine' areas of commodity consumption. These developments, they argued, had generated a promotional culture whose visual codes worked to 'rupture traditional icons of masculinity', thus making space for a plurality of more provisional masculine identities (Mort, 1988: 194). In these terms, the growing interface between masculinity and consumer practice could be seen in a relatively positive light. In particular, the more overtly sexualized visual codes of the 'New Man' were interpreted as a 'loosening of the binary opposition between gay and straight-identified men', thereby extending 'the space available within the representational regimes of popular consumption for an ambivalent masculine identity' (Nixon, 1996: 202). Tim Edwards, however, has qualified this perspective. For Edwards, rather than being necessarily progressive, models of masculinity premised on consumption can also veer towards aspirationalism and conservative individualism – models of masculine consumerism being 'as equally personally destructive and socially divisive as they are individually expressive and democratically utopian' (Edwards, 1997: 2). Furthermore, Edwards contends, the narcissistic masculine consumer was not unique to the 1980s and 1990s but was constituent in a much longer history of men's active and overt practices of commodity consumption (Edwards, 1997: 92).

Debates about the nature of the relationship between masculinity and consumerism in contemporary Britain have influenced and informed the present study. But, while models of masculine consumerism may have become especially visible in Britain at the end of the twentieth century, it is argued that in the US the consuming male first emerged in the late nineteenth century, finding fuller form during the inter-war decades and then becoming increasingly pervasive amid the consumer boom of the 1950s and 1960s. Moreover, it is argued that the growing presence of narcissism and consumer practice in American masculine cultures did not, of itself, constitute an unequivocally progressive shift. Masculine identities premised on consumption certainly challenged and undermined established masculine codes and archetypes – especially the production- and family-oriented ideals associated with the traditional middle class. At the same time, however, models of masculine consumerism also elaborated a form of sexual politics that was, to a large part, reactionary and exploit-ative. Indeed, rather than being radical or transgressive, it is argued that the rise of the masculine consumer is better seen as part of wider developments in the fabric of American capitalism that saw the rise of a new middle-class faction whose habitus and value system was oriented around an ethos of youthful hedonism and leisure-oriented consumption.

Any discussion of class in the US is fraught with difficulty. Notions of class-based inequality go against the grain of America's 'official' ideologies. Social theorists, too, have often resisted bids to conceive the American social structure in terms of class-based socio-economic divisions. Instead, invoking the ideas of Max Weber, historians such as Daniel Snowman (1977) have presented the US as a 'status society', with the social hierarchy existing as a continuous gradation of 'status groups' marked out by the relative possession of social prestige. Certainly, crudely Marxist notions of 'class' as a system of relations characterized by inherent conflict and domination are inappropriate to an analysis of American society. But notions of 'class' can still be retained as a way of understanding the existence of distinct social groups distinguished by their differential possession of such attributes as wealth, income, authority and power.

In his survey of the formation of the American middle class, for example, Stuart Blumin (1985) opts for a notion of social class informed by the ideas of Anthony Giddens. In *The Class Structure of the Advanced Societies* (1981) Giddens argues that the concept of class is fundamental to an understanding of modern social structures – although it is a principle of social organization that varies in shape and strength between different societies. Deriving influence from both Marx and Weber, Giddens sees patterns of class relations as the outcome of overlapping processes of 'structuration'. In these terms, the clarity and salience of class relations within any given society is dependent on the degree of convergence that exists between the important 'structurating' processes of social mobility, the division of labour (together with its associated authority relationships) and the emergence of common patterns of consumption associated with particular 'distributive groupings'. For Blumin, this perspective offers a valuable framework for understanding patterns of class formation in the US because it recognizes both the overlapping categories of class-forming experience and the differential development of particular class groups at specific historical moments. Drawing on Giddens' approach, therefore, Blumin argues that amid the shifting social, economic and political contours of nineteenth-century America it is possible to identify 'a sufficient convergence of personal and social experience to give credence to the idea of an emerging middle-class way of life and to give at least preliminary support . . . to the hypothesis of middle class formation' (Blumin, 1985: 337). This study explores the emergence and subsequent evolution of this group, with special focus on the way concepts of masculinity, youth and consumption have figured within its patterns of development and transformation.

The discussion that follows draws upon a diverse range of historical sources, including newspapers, magazines and journals, official documents and reports, survey data, biography, autobiography, film and contemporaneous works of fiction. In Chapters 3 and 6 the analysis of contemporary magazines is especially prominent. The formal characteristics and distinctive themes of *Esquire* and *Playboy* are considered in some detail as texts that condensed and articulated a wide range of contemporary cultural preoccupations. These magazines, however, are not treated as a 'window on the world' – a straightforward embodiment or 'reflection' of the historical context in which they were produced. Instead, the emphasis is placed on the way these texts actively operated to explain and interpret the world, deploying particular textual codes and modes of address to suggest particular ways of making sense of cultural relations and patterns of social change. In so doing they presented their readers with a set of 'imagined identities' – representations of masculinity which offered men an avenue through which they could make sense of their place within a rapidly shifting cultural environment.

*

The author and publisher gratefully acknowledge the following for permission to reproduce material: Cluett, Peabody & Co. for Figure 2.3, Hart Schaffner & Marx for Figure 3.2, Curtis Publishing for Figure 4.1, MGM for Figure 5.3, Pictorial Press for Figure 7.2 and *Newsweek* for Figure 8.1. Every effort has been made to trace copyright holders. The author apologizes for any errors or omissions in the above list and would be grateful to be notified of any corrections that should be incorporated in the next edition or reprint of this volume.

This book would not have been possible without assistance from a legion of people. I am especially indebted to Kathryn Earle of Berg publishers for her original interest in my project and her patience while it was (slowly) coming together. For help in obtaining innumerable source materials I extend my gratitude to the staff of Southampton Institute Library, Mike and Mary Gallagher of Gallagher Paper Collectibles (New York) and Rick of Rin-Tin-Tin (Brighton). Elizabeth Wilson and Lyn

Thomas of the University of North London have both encouraged and facilitated my research, while Milly Williamson, Johnathan Wright, Des Freedman and Dave Phillips have all been great colleagues to work with. In the course of completing this project I was lucky enough to have help and encouragement from both my family and much valued friends. Anna Gough-Yates deserves huge thanks for her invaluable insights, support and friendship. My gratitude, too, to George Osgerby, Sean Gregory, John McIver, Dave Quinn, Clive Gilling and all the Surfin' Lungs. Alun Howkins also deserves thanks for letting me into university in the first place, and Andy Medhurst for always being ready with astute guidance and suggestions. Chris Bullar, Paul Cobley, Tim Edwards and Martin Evans also deserve a big vote of thanks. And huge thanks to Liz Davies for her ceaseless strength, patience and support. Thanks to everyone – mai-tais all round.

Chapter 1
Introduction: Young Men of Action and Acquisition

What strikes me about the whole thing is that this crime – its planning, execution, and the police action that followed – is a unique product of the times. It seems designed for the style and tempo of the mid-Sixties – a mass-media crime. Everything about it had a superficial kind of yé-yé glamour. The cast of characters – on both sides of the law – talked and acted as if they were part of a scenario for one of the now popular hard-bitten, jazzy movies or TV serials. The crime was sexy, it was athletic, it was cool, way out, and as they say, not to be believed. It was also pretty stupid when you think about it.

But who cares? The style was there. The crooks had a kind of *Man from U.N.C.L.E.* appeal; they were just – well – not *dowdy*. As you follow through the story, you can almost hear the beat of a souped-up musical score that might have been written for it by someone like John Barry (*Goldfinger*).

Jack Roth, 'The Beach Boy Caper', *Esquire*, September 1965: 118.

'THE BEACH BOY CAPER': MASCULINITY AND STYLE IN AN AGE OF AFFLUENCE

By any measure the robbery was audacious. In 1964, in the dead of a chill October night, thieves broke into the American Museum of National History in New York and made off with a small fortune in gems and precious stones – a haul that included the Star of India, the world's largest star sapphire. In itself the burglary was spectacularly newsworthy. Yet what was already one of the biggest news stories of the winter became a media frenzy when, several days later, FBI agents arrested three suspects in Miami.

The threesome – Roger Clark, Allan Kuhn and Jack Murphy – captivated the public imagination through both their looks and their dynamic lifestyle. The 'Beach Boys', as they were dubbed by the press, exuded flamboyant charisma. In their twenties, they were all good-looking, tanned and athletic and all seemed to boast dashingly glamorous occupations. Clark was a yacht skipper and swimming-instructor, Kuhn a skin diver and aspiring night-club singer, while Murphy – known as 'Murph the Surf' – was a professional surfer who claimed to have introduced the sport to Miami a few years earlier. The gang's history as thuggish, small-time criminals went almost unnoticed as the media conjured with images of winsome rogues living lives of adventure and extravagance around Miami's beaches and fashionable night spots. Readers of the *New York Times* were regaled with details of the group's high-rolling lifestyle of opulent leisure and beautiful women. Kuhn was said to own 'a white Cadillac, a two-masted yacht and a speed-boat' and to live in a $287-a-month luxury apartment (*New York Times*, 1 November 1964), while all three were portrayed as 'big spenders' who often carried over $20,000 in cash (*New York Times*, 3 November 1964). The American public seemed infatuated with the trio. Groups of teenage girls reputedly flocked to the Manhattan City Prison, trying to get a glimpse of 'Murph' or 'Allan', while crowds and television crews jostled for a view of the gang as they were released on bail and a Miami police chief reported problems with teenagers who 'looked up to these beach boys as heroes' (*New York Times*, 18 November 1964). Nor did the three men disappoint their fans. Revelling in their new status as media celebrities they brazenly announced their ambition to open a cocktail lounge called 'The Star of India'. 'It will be very nice', Kuhn jokingly assured a group of reporters, 'Very nice. No flophouse' (*New York Times*, 2 December 1964).

Outside the annals of American criminal history the case of 'Murph the Surf', the 'Beach Boy' gang and the Star of India was, in many ways, unremarkable. Most of the stolen gems were eventually recovered and the gang ultimately served prison terms after pleading guilty to the theft.[1] However, although the crime itself was of relatively little historical importance, the media fervour and public interest that the case elicited can be seen as a revealing barometer of the wider social and cultural climate. As Jack Roth observed in his ten-page feature on the events, penned the following year for up-market men's magazine *Esquire*, the affair was 'a unique product of the times', an episode almost 'designed for the style and tempo of the mid-Sixties' (1965: 118). As Roth explained, 'the *style* was there' – a style that struck a nerve in a society undergoing a range of profound cultural transformations. The image of young, carefree playboys who outwardly had time on their hands and money to burn seemed to crystallize important changes occurring in America's mores and values – and especially the shifts taking place within the masculine identities and lifestyles of the white middle class.

The significance of the Miami gang, therefore, lies not in their crime but in the way they embodied, for a brief historical moment, a wider celebration of a masculine universe of youthful pleasure, recreation and narcissism that became an increasingly prominent feature of American culture after 1945. To be sure, this was not the first time in American history that a powerful ideological nexus had existed between the cultural co-ordinates of youth, masculinity and leisure-oriented consumption. Since at least the late nineteenth century the existence of groups of young, upwardly mobile men with significant levels of disposable income had laid a basis for representations and mythologies in which the heady constituents of youth, masculinity, affluence and leisure were drawn together in a potent cultural configuration. However, while such a configuration was not unique to the post-war era, during the 1950s and 1960s it came into its own as a boom in domestic consumption transformed American social and economic life.

'WHAT SORT OF MAN READS PLAYBOY?' MYTHOLOGIES OF MASCULINITY, YOUTH AND CONSUMPTION

The changing and augmented patterns of consumption in post-war America had an intense impact on society as a whole, but had especially profound consequences for the lifestyles and culture of the white middle class. The 'traditional' middle class world that had originally emerged during the eighteenth and nineteenth centuries – with its emphasis on family life, the work ethic, moderation and probity – had been a powerful force, but by the 1920s was already losing some of its authority as American capitalism steadily prioritized consumption, leisure and immediate gratification. In the period after the Second World War these shifts accelerated and intensified, middle-class culture becoming more thoroughly permeated and under-pinned by a leisure-oriented consumer ethos. Moreover, amid these transformations there arose concepts of 'youth' and 'masculinity' whose associations with ideals of hedonism and consumption were more pronounced and fully formed than their predecessors. In particular, the 1950s and 1960s saw the 'footloose bachelor' and 'vibrant youth' emerge as prominent social constructs. Closely allied, and mutually reinforcing one another, these mythologized social types emerged as figureheads in middle-class America's embrace of lifestyles increasingly at ease with a credo of pleasure, self-expression and personal 'liberation' through consumption.

Separate and distinct social constructs, the concepts of masculinity and youth possess their own cultural lineage and trajectories of development. The mythologies surrounding masculinity and youth have, however, often complemented and informed one another. Moreover, at particular points in time – usually at moments of acute social and economic transformation – these elements of exchange and inter-action have become more accentuated. For example, at the turn of the century, amid the quickening pace of urbanization and the emergence of a modern consumer economy, there arose a recognizable 'bachelor subculture' (Chudacoff, 1999), its aura combining the vivacious autonomy of youth with the stylish panache of the affluent 'man about town'. The years of prosperity that followed the First World War, meanwhile, saw the embryonic relation between masculinity and youth consolidated as there emerged – especially within the white middle class – a more fully formed masculine identity predicated on the constellation of consumption, style and leisure. The Wall Street Crash and the years of depression that followed dealt a severe blow to the confidence of the American social and economic order. Yet the structures and ethos of the consumer economy survived surprisingly intact and during the 1930s the young man of style and affluence remained a figure who, perhaps more than any other, encapsulated the ideals and desires of a culture steadily oriented around the imperatives of commodity consumption.

Above all, however, it was during the late 1950s and 1960s that there developed the most intense and fully formed relationship between the mythologies of vivacious youth and those of hedonistic masculinity. As the dominant culture increasingly embraced an ethos of leisure-oriented consumption, images of youth and masculinity emerged as complementary, entwined emblems for American postwar prosperity and success – a synthesis of cultural signifiers that found its apotheosis in the image of the playboy. Prosperous and independent, virile and irrepressible, the suave and smooth-talking playboy arose during the 1950s and early 1960s as one of the defining icons of American vitality and modernity. The period saw the figure of the metropolitan playboy deified in an expanse of popular cultural texts, from films and television shows to lounge music and advertising campaigns, yet it was in the field of magazine publishing that he became most strikingly visible – marked, above all, by the rise of Hugh Hefner's *Playboy* magazine as a national institution. Launched in late 1953, and virtually an instant hit, *Playboy* magazine was a glossy eulogy to a young, masculine world of racy consumption, narcissism and leisure. In its obsession with style and ostentatious display, *Playboy* embodied the rise of a new American middle class for whom consumption, individuality and stylistic self-expression were becoming a way of life. More specifically, the magazine can be seen as safely steering its male readership through the provinces of visual pleasure and consumer practice – realms whose close associations with feminine discourse marked them out as precarious waters for articulations of masculinity keen to avoid any suggestion of unmanliness or effeminacy.

This masculine foray into the world of commodity consumption, however, was hardly unique to mid-century America. A significant body of research has justifiably highlighted the pivotal role of women in the emergence of the matrices of consumer culture.[2] Yet the impact of this work has tended to obscure the historical presence of men in the fields of fashionable display and consumer practice. In contrast, recent studies have begun to uncover a degree of masculine involvement in the development of commodity culture much greater than hitherto recognized. For example, Christopher Breward's (1999) survey of menswear retailing in Victorian London shows clearly that a relationship between masculinity, fashion and consumption can be identified even in the earliest manifestations of modern consumerism. As Breward himself points out, such research should not be seen as competing against, or overturning, established work on the historical construction of femininity, yet it certainly challenges any oversimplified account of fashionable consumption as an exclusively feminine domain (Breward: 1999: 8). In a similar vein (as Chapters 2 and 3 will demonstrate), the relation between men and commodity consumption has a long and connected history in America. It was, though, only during the 1950s and 1960s that masculine consumerism came into its own, the post-war explosion of the consumer economy drawing men more fully into the world of personal consumption.

Men's participation in the field of consumerism, however, has been fraught with conflicts and contradictions – feeding into perceptions of an ominous masculine 'crisis', which, as we will see throughout this study, have regularly punctuated the history of American masculinity. Masculine identities premised upon hedonism and conspicuous display have, for example, invariably conflicted with more conservative constructions of manhood rooted in ideals of hard work, thrift and moral self-discipline. Moreover, despite the history of a masculine presence in the realm of fashionable consumption, the arenas of stylistic pleasure and commodity consumerism remained – even during the 1950s and 1960s – closely bound up with feminine connotations. In post-war America, therefore, phenomena such as *Playboy* magazine can be seen as performing an important cultural role in the way they offered men an 'acceptable' avenue into the domain of self-conscious consumption. The inclusion of pornographic pin-ups served to mark out the magazine as avowedly masculine and heterosexual, allowing its male readers – secure in the knowledge that their heterosexual masculine identities would not be compromised – to cruise freely through its glossy features on furniture, interior decor, fashion and (sometimes quite sexualized) representations of men. *Playboy* also helped its readership negotiate their way through the tensions of post-war consumerism by regularly offering them reassuring and flattering self-images. Most obviously, from the late 1950s onwards, the magazine included a monthly promotional feature that asked readers (and potential advertisers) the rhetorical question 'What Sort of Man Reads Playboy?' Always, the tone of the answer was laudatory and inspiring. The *Playboy* reader was young, successful, adventurous and stylish – a young blade with a zest for living who showed expertise in the fields of fashion, furnishing and the spectrum of conspicuous consumption, yet who was also confident and assured in his heterosexual masculine identity.

Typical was the version that appeared in the magazine's November 1966 edition. Centred around a luxurious beach scene, the advertisement featured a young, muscular Adonis enjoying the fruits of the good life. Resplendent in jazzy Bermuda shorts, he shares an intimate moment of happiness with a beautiful young woman, the couple surrounded by an array of expensive scuba-diving equipment and a deluxe sports car. This, as the advertising copy explained, was the kind of lifestyle that distinguished the *Playboy* reader as a 'young man of action and acquisition' for whom 'the name of the game is fun' (*Playboy*, November 1966). This advertisement, then, captured the essence of the 'new masculinity' that had emerged in post-war America. With its accent on youth, glamour, fun and stylish hip, this was a construction of maleness tailored to the demands of the consumer society that blossomed in America during the 1950s and 1960s.

This is not, of course, to argue that post-war America was populated by millions of young men all living a life of lavish and sybaritic consumption. Theorists such as

WHAT SORT OF MAN READS PLAYBOY?

1.1 'For this young man of action and acquisition, the name of the game is fun' (*Playboy*, Vol. 13, No. 11, November 1966).

Elizabeth Wilson (1985: 246) and Jennifer Craik (1993: 50–1) point to the way in which style and fashion operate as vehicles for aspirational fantasies – and the images of hectic masculine consumption should be seen in this light. Nevertheless, while the lifestyles of 'vibrant youth' and the 'footloose bachelor' were always, to a large degree, mythologized fantasies constructed within the forms and texts of popular culture, such fantasies still connected with the material world in important respects. As Graham Dawson argues perceptively in his study of heroic figures and the popular imagination in inter-war Britain, it is important to recognize the way representations of masculinity figure as 'imagined identities' – idealized models through which con-sumers give meaning to their relationships with commodities and those around them:

> An imagined identity is something that has been 'made up' in the positive sense of active creation but has real effects in the world of everyday relationships, which it invests with meaning and makes intelligible in specific ways. It organises a form that a masculine self can assume in the world (its bodily appearance and dress, its conduct and mode of relating) as well as its values and aspirations, its tastes and desires . . . Representations furnish a repertoire of cultural forms that can be drawn upon in the imagining of lived identities. These may be aspired to rather than actually being achieved . . . [and] into this gap flows the elements of desire. The forms furnished by representations often figure ideal and desirable masculinities, which men strive after in their efforts to make themselves into the man they want to be. Imagined identities are shot through with wish fulfilling fantasies. (Dawson, 1991:118–19)

The figure of the 'young man of action and acquisition' for whom 'the name of the game is fun' should, therefore, be seen as an 'imagined identity' mobilized by (especially) middle-class American men after the Second World War. During the 1950s and 1960s, moreover, this 'imagined identity' achieved particularly strong cultural purchase as the ideologies and imperatives of consumer capitalism increasingly pervaded middle-class life, prompting men to adopt intelligible models of masculinity more attuned to the expectations and demands of a consumption-oriented society.

In these terms, then, the fantasy-world of stylish, fun-fuelled cool peddled in texts such as *Playboy* and constructed around events like the 1964 'Beach Boy Caper' was constituent in a broad cultural transformation that saw the American middle class acclimatize to an economic and social environment increasingly dominated by commodity consumption. As we shall see, this transformative sphere was always characterized by inconsistencies, tensions and contradictions. Yet, overall, it will be argued that this milieu performed a pioneering role on behalf of the dominant order. In his taste for unabashed pleasure seeking and less inhibited forms of (hetero) sexual expression, the 'young man of action and acquisition' initiated and experimented with new cultural forms and lifestyles that laid the basis for a middle-class habitus – a realm of cultural behaviours, attitudes and dispositions – reconciled with the demands of a modern consumer society.

'THE NAME OF THE GAME IS FUN': DISCOURSES OF MASCULINITY, CLASS AND LIFESTYLE

The history of masculinity is a relative newcomer to the academy. In some senses, of course, traditional scholarship has always been implicitly focused on men. Written by and about men, conventional historical narratives treated male experience as a universal norm, to the extent that women's lives have, until relatively recently, remained largely 'hidden from history' (Rowbotham, 1977). The pioneering work of feminist scholars, however, has both revealed and contested these assumptions. Since the early 1970s feminist historians have highlighted the centrality of gender relations in the shaping of social, economic and political life and have problematized the power structures seen to underpin them. Post-structuralist interventions, meanwhile, have further highlighted the relationship between power and knowledge, challenging any claim to over-arching or objective 'truth' within accounts of the past.[3] Influenced and informed by such critiques, a growing number of theorists have sought to interrogate the historical development of concepts of masculinity and, since the 1980s, an expanding body of historical work has sought to 'situate masculinities as objects of study on a par with femininities', these studies advancing notions of masculinity and male experience as 'specific and varying social-historical-cultural formations' (Brod, 1987: 2).[4]

Rather than being a set of timeless biological or psychological attributes, recent historiography has perceived masculinity as a collection of dynamic cultural codes and meanings. As a continually evolving socio-cultural construct, masculinity is seen as being profoundly embedded in the wider field of social, economic, political and cultural transformation (Stearns, 1990: 1–16).[5] This historical construction of masculine identities, moreover, has been understood as constituent in patterns of gender-based power relations that have often worked to sustain and reproduce male social and economic dominance (Kimmel, 1987a: 122). Many contemporary cultural theorists have, however, been keen to resist what they see as the totalizing and universalist tendencies inherent to notions of patriarchy. Instead, influence has been drawn from Michel Foucault's (1979) exploration of the way sexuality has been differentially constituted by historically specific discourses. Here, notions of gender and sexuality are seen as the outcome of a grid of social practices and power relations that provide frameworks for understanding the world. Such an approach recognizes the historical importance of gender inequalities, yet also acknowledges the plurality of gender-based power relations and the historical variation in the construction of gender identities (Nixon, 1997a: 300). In these terms, therefore, masculinity is not reduced to a unitary or coherent set of prescriptive ideals, but is conceived as a multiplicity of inconsistent and contradictory identity positions.

At any given historical moment, then, it is possible to find a range of competing articulations of masculinity – some dominant, some subordinate and some oppositional. Indeed, American society during the 1950s and 1960s can be seen in exactly this light – as a site where a variety of masculine identities existed alongside one another in a relationship of tension, conflict and struggle. The 'young man of action and acquisition', therefore, was one among a number of competing versions of masculinity. Yet, as this book will argue, it is one of deep historical significance for its challenge to – and partial displacement of – other, in some respects more conservative, masculine identities in which the pursuit of a life of pleasure was considered virtually the antithesis of respectable manhood.

Until the early twentieth century, production rather than consumption was considered, for the most part, the legitimate focus of middle-class men's energies. Finding their fullest expression in the cult of the 'self-made man', these production-oriented ideals have retained influence, representing one of the pre-eminent corner-stones of American culture. Yet from the beginning of the twentieth century there arose alternative models of middle-class masculinity that laid greater stress on the pleasures of consumerism. Already identifiable in nascent form by the 1900s, these consumption-oriented modes of masculinity began to take on greater social definition between the wars, though it was only amid the confident affluence of the 1950s and 1960s that they took centre stage in American middle-class life. In making sense of these transformations some illuminating insights can be drawn from the work of the French cultural theorist Pierre Bourdieu and his study of changes in the fabric of bourgeois culture in modern France.

In *Distinction* (1984), Bourdieu uses the notion of 'lifestyle' to denote patterns of taste and consumption used by social groups to distinguish themselves as distinct and coherent class formations. The concept of lifestyle was initially developed in the work of Max Weber, who argued that social stratification depended not solely on patterns of economic relation, but also on the degree of 'status' attached to the patterns of living and cultural preferences of different social groups. Bourdieu's painstaking survey of the shifting texture of bourgeois life in France after the Second World War combines this attention to status with a neo-Marxist analysis of class relations – Bourdieu arguing that cultural consumption represents a significant area of struggle in which symbolic hierarchies are established both between and within social classes (Bourdieu, 1984: 18). More specifically, Bourdieu contends that post-war France saw the rise of a new form of capitalist economy in which power and profits were increas-ingly dependent not simply on the production of goods, but also on the continual regeneration of consumer desires (Bourdieu, 1984: 310). To sustain its survival, therefore, this new economic order demanded the emergence of a new socio-cultural formation which championed the cause of commodity consumption and judged people 'by their capacity for consumption, their "standard of living" [and] their life-style, as much as by their capacity for production' (Bourdieu, 1984: 310).

For Bourdieu these processes of economic and cultural transformation had, by the late 1960s, laid the basis for the rise of a specific section of the French middle class, a group that he terms the 'new petite bourgeoisie' (1984: 311). Lacking the economic, cultural or social capital that distinguished the traditional petite bourgeoisie, this new class faction established its own distinctive status by colonizing new occupations based on the production and dissemination of symbolic goods and services – Bourdieu coining the term 'cultural intermediaries' to denote the new petit bourgeois cohort that rose to dominate fields such as the media, advertising, journalism, fashion and so on. Moreover, in its quest to secure its class position and status, the new petite bourgeoisie laboured to promote the legitimacy and prestige of the 'new model lifestyles' that characterized its membership. In these terms, then, members of Bourdieu's new petit bourgeois formation conceived of themselves as connoisseurs in 'the art of living' and sought to distinguish themselves as a distinct class formation by breaking away from the social values and attitudes of the traditional petite bourgeoisie, a group whose moral code had been based on:

> the opposition between pleasure and good [that] induces a generalized suspicion of the 'charming and attractive', a fear of pleasure and a relation to the body made up of 'reserve', 'modesty' and 'restraint', and [which] associates every satisfaction of the forbidden impulses with guilt. (Bourdieu, 1984: 367)

In place of the traditional 'morality of duty', Bourdieu contends, the new petite bourgeoisie increasingly elaborated a new 'morality of pleasure as a duty', in which it became 'a failure, a threat to self-esteem, not to "have fun"' (Bourdieu, 1984: 367). In this new 'art of living', therefore, a premium was placed on the 'ethic of fun' and the pursuit of expressive and liberated lifestyles – a cultural orientation defined by its preoccupation with personal gratification and individuality and established through the consumption of distinctive cultural goods and signifiers.

Bourdieu's original study was focused exclusively on developments within the French social structure during the late 1960s, but since the 1980s a growing body of authors have drawn on his work to analyse a broad range of contemporary cultural formations. For example, Paul Bagguley and his associates (1990), Mike Featherstone (1991) and Scott Lash and John Urry (1987) have all deployed Bourdieu's terms of analysis in their accounts of 'postmodern' cultures in the late twentieth century.[6] However, while these authors have focused their attentions on cultural shifts in contemporary Europe, it is also possible to see middle-class culture in America during the 1950s and 1960s as evidencing many of the qualities characteristic of Bourdieu's new petite bourgeoisie.

There are undoubtedly problems in transposing Bourdieu's account of the transformation of the French bourgeoisie during the late 1960s onto a post-war history of the American middle class. For example, in her comparison of the ways in which the contemporary French and American upper-middle classes use distinctive tastes to mark themselves out as discrete social groups, Michèle Lamont (1992) identifies some important cross-national differences. In France, for example, Bourdieu highlights the importance of cultural and socio-economic resources as the key markers of bourgeoisie cultural boundaries, whereas Lamont suggests that in America a more significant role is played by moral imperatives based around the qualities of honesty, hard work and personal integrity (Lamont, 1992: 4–5). More generally, Lamont contends that cultural perimeters are more strongly demarcated in France than in America, where the presence of powerful ideologies of egalitarianism has meant that such boundaries are weaker and more loosely defined. Nevertheless, though significant differences obviously exist between the national cultures of France and America, Bourdieu's account of a shift from a 'morality of duty' to an 'ethic of fun' remains a useful framework for understanding the transformation of American middle-class life.

As we shall see in more detail in the following chapter, the characteristic values of the American middle class as it took shape during the nineteenth century bear some marked similarities to those of Bourdieu's traditional petite bourgeoisie – whose repressive 'morality of duty' was complemented by an equally restrictive 'religious or moral conservatism often centre[d] on moral indignation at moral disorder, and especially the disorder of sexual mores' (Bourdieu, 1984: 367). The emergent middle class of nineteenth-century America also championed the qualities of diligence and probity, their cultural ethos characterized by an emphasis on self-discipline, thrift and an unswerving dedication to respectable family life. Constituent in this cultural formation, moreover, was a particular articulation of middle-class manhood. The nineteenth-century 'man of character' was marked out by his temperance and reserve, along with his ardent sense of civic duty and a devotion to hard-working industrious-ness. As the twentieth century progressed, however, notions of a masculinity defined by work and abstinence were undermined by an aggregation of social and economic changes. The reconfiguration of labour markets, the transformation of gender relations and the rise of mass consumption together unhinged many of the traditional certainties that had been at the heart of dominant conceptions of manhood. The broad contours of these changes were already evident during the 1920s and 1930s, yet it was after 1945 that their impact registered most strongly as middle-class culture adjusted to the growing levels of post-war affluence and prosperity.

There are, then, important temporal differences between the cultural changes that Bourdieu describes and those that took place in the American middle class. The kind of economic changes Bourdieu presents as the bedrock to the transformation of French bourgeois life during the 1960s were already manifest in the US during the early twentieth century. By the 1920s the American economy was no longer dependent simply on the production of goods, but increasingly relied on the continual re-invigoration of consumer demand. This economic framework was battered and bruised by the depression years of the 1930s, though in the wake of the Second World War commodity consumption not only recouped but further reinforced its position as a mainstay of the American economy. These shifts, therefore, predate those that Bourdieu identifies in France, yet are broadly congruent in terms of the growing economic role played by consumer demand. Moreover, alongside these economic developments there also took place a range of important cultural changes. Again, these were similar to those Bourdieu identifies in the French bourgeoisie, but occurred significantly earlier. During the 1950s and early 1960s the growing centrality of commodity consumption within the American economy was accompanied by the rise of an emergent middle-class group comparable to Bourdieu's 'new petite bourgeoisie'. Though Bourdieu's class faction did not fully take shape until the late 1960s, this new American middle class was recognizable as a distinct cultural formation by the mid-1950s, finding employment in the burgeoning realms of advertising, publishing, the media and the range of industries related to cultural production and circulation. Moreover, as with Bourdieu's 'new petite bourgeoisie', this new middle class faction were denoted by their skills in 'the art of living' – defining their social status and sense of cultural identity through distinctive, consumption-driven lifestyles, their values and codes of behaviour laying an accent on stylistic self-expression, self-conscious display and (to use Bourdieu's terminology) an 'ethic of fun'.

The Marxist influences underpinning Bourdieu's work inevitably lead him to identify socio-economic class as the pre-eminent force in the organization of relations of social distinction and cultural power. This position has drawn justifiable criticism from a number of theorists who have argued that it marginalizes relationships that might have an equally important bearing on configurations of taste and the mapping of cultural boundaries. John Frow (1995: 74), for example, has questioned the way such approaches privilege the determining role of class over that of gender and race, while Beverley Skeggs (1997: 16) criticizes Bourdieu's tendency to view gender as little more than a distributive mechanism operating within class groups. For Skeggs, greater recognition needs to be accorded to the influence of gender on the elaboration of cultural hierarchies and lifestyle constellations, gender identities bringing with them particular forms of cultural capital that both provide and restrict access to potential forms of social power (Skeggs, 1997: 10). Yet this critique need not lead to an abandonment of Bourdieu's analytical framework. As Leslie McCall (1992) maintains, the strength of Bourdieu's work in respect of gender may actually have been overlooked.[7] In Bourdieu's model, she argues, gender is seen as having a less immediately visible impact on social and mental structures – yet is still acknowledged as a crucial influence on the social structure (McCall, 1992: 851). According to McCall, therefore, Bourdieu's notions of taste as a marker of cultural boundaries offers a potentially profitable way of making sense of gendered social dispositions and symbolic practices.

From this perspective the consumption-oriented lifestyles that arose in America during the 1950s and 1960s can be seen as being mediated not only by factors of social class, but also by dimensions of gender. In fact one of the most significant dimensions to the reconfiguration of the American middle class after 1945 was the emergence of masculine cultures that fervently endorsed the 'morality of pleasure as a duty', embracing hedonistic consumption as an acceptable – indeed, highly desirable – focal point to their values, aspirations and social practices.

'Race' must also be acknowledged as a discursive field central to the development of these new cultural sensibilities. Black masculinity has long been highlighted as a site for the elaboration of powerful cultural mythologies, many theorists drawing attention to the history of racist stereotypes constructing black masculinity as 'hyper sexed', threatening and often predatory (hooks, 1991). Although seldom identified as such, white masculinity should also be considered as a cultural construction. As Richard Dyer (1997) argues, the power and authority of white culture has afforded 'whiteness' a quality of virtual invisibility – images and representations of white culture naturalizing themselves as the norm from which all others diverge. If 'whiteness' is to be dislodged from this position of centrality, Dyer contends, it 'needs to be made strange' (1997: 10). That is to say, critical scrutiny must reveal the ways in which 'whiteness' (like any other 'racial' category) has been historically fabricated. From this perspective, then, the 1950s and 1960s masculine archetypes of the 'footloose bachelor' and 'vibrant youth' can be seen as specifically *white* cultural motifs. However, whereas 'whiteness' has often been associated with the 'mind over body' qualities of 'tightness, . . . self control [and] self-consciousness' (Dyer, 1997: 6), these manifestations of white masculinity aspired to a relaxed hedonism through which they could be more at ease with the universe of bodily pleasures, more comfortable with the world of carefree fun. As we shall see, this world of 'effortless cool' certainly drew on signifiers of 'otherness' (for example, the music and styles of African American culture or the trappings of a stylized exotica) as a reference point and source of inspiration, but the 'young man of action and acquisition' was an unmistakably white cultural phenomenon.

*

The study that follows reviews the development of a masculine realm of youthful pleasure, recreation and narcissistic desire that has arisen as one of the defining features of American leisure style. In Chapter 2 the survey begins by examining the traditional models of bourgeois manhood that emerged in the nineteenth century and argues that, as these were destabilized by processes of socio-economic change, alternative masculine identities became more visible. A reaffirmation of rugged manhood was prominent, although also significant was the gradual emergence of a style-conscious masculine subject premised on consumption and hedonistic pleasure. Chapter 3, 'Lessons in "The Art of Living"', reviews the steady development of the masculine consumer during the inter-war decades. With a detailed analysis of the nature and significance of *Esquire* magazine, particular attention is given to the way masculine consumption was influenced by (and interrelated with) the simultaneous emergence of a leisure-oriented, middle-class youth culture. Chapter 4, '"People of Plenty"', assesses the profound contradictions that existed in gender relations during the Cold War. Despite powerful ideologies of conformity and 'domestic containment', it is argued that masculine identities remained heterogeneous, with models of masculinity based on consumerism and personal gratification increasingly coming to the fore as a new, 'consumption-friendly' middle-class faction began to take shape. The next chapter, '"The Old Ways Will Not Do"', highlights the prominence of youth in these processes, the rise of a 'teenage' leisure culture complementing and informing those models of middle-class masculinity that challenged traditional mores of puritanical conservatism. In Chapter 6, 'High-Living with the "Upbeat Generation"', an analysis of *Playboy* is used to explore the ascendance of the young, male consumer during the 1950s and 1960s – the success of the magazine testifying to the growing cultural purchase of a masculine identity based around conspicuous consumption and hedonistic nonconformity. Chapter 7, 'Bachelors in Paradise', continues the theme, examining the impact of the 'playboy ethic' throughout American cultural life during the 1950s and 1960s. Chapter 8 considers the relation between the counterculture and models of masculine hedonism, arguing that the bohemian ethos of libertine self-expression can be seen as complementary to (and constituent in) the transformation of the American middle class and its growing embrace of consumerist and leisure-oriented lifestyles.

This book argues that, as the middle class strove to adapt and reconfigure itself to the changing social and economic imperatives of the post-war world, it generated a range of new and forward-looking cultural identities geared around consumer desire and the practices of commodity consumption. In this respect articulations of masculinity were especially prominent – ideals of youthful hedonism, heterosexual pleasure and the 'ethic of fun' coming to play an increasingly significant role in the cultures of middle-class men. As these lifestyle formations and cultural identities took shape, however, they collided with the more staid and sober value systems of the traditional middle class. The struggles and contradictions that resulted marked an unsettling period for dominant systems of hegemony and, in some respects, helped open up cultural spaces in which radical political challenges could gain a foothold. Nevertheless, while the transformation of masculine identities by the 'ethic of fun' certainly marked a significant shift in middle-class value systems, ultimately it served to adapt dominant cultural codes to the new social and economic climate of the post-war world. Broadly speaking, therefore, class, 'race' and gender-based power relationships survived relatively intact and the social order was left (to borrow an apt phrase from the playboy lexicon) 'shaken, not stirred'.

NOTES

1   The trio's ambitions to become hosts of a swank night spot were never realized. On release from prison Roger Clark disappeared into obscurity. Allan Kuhn resurfaced in the early 1970s, advising the production of *Live a Little, Steal a Lot* (1975) – a feature film based on the robbery. Jack 'Murph the Surf' Murphy, meanwhile, slipped back into a life of crime and ultimately served a life sentence for murder – during which he was 'born again' and trained to become a Church minister. For an account of the burglary and the events that followed, see Messick and Goldblatt (1974: 201–9).

2 For key studies highlighting the relationship between consumerism and female identity see Abelson (1989), Leach (1984) and Walkowitz (1992).

3 For accessible accounts of the impact of postmodern and postructualist theory on modern historiography see Bentley (1999: 137–48) and Jenkins (1991: 59–70).

4 Dubbert (1979), Ehrenreich (1984) and Filene (1986) represent early, yet still deeply pertinent, attempts to engage with the historical construction of masculine identities in modern America. More recently, Bederman (1995), Chudacoff (1999), Kann (1991), Rotundo (1993), Stearns (1990) and White (1993) have all delivered excellent analyses of the changing conceptualizations of manhood in the US, while Kimmel's (1997) survey of the development of American masculinities is both encyclopaedic and highly readable. Fine anthologies of contributions to the field also exist in Brod (ed.) (1987), Carnes and Griffen (eds) (1990), Mangan and Walvin (eds) (1987) and Pleck and Pleck (eds) (1980), while Roper and Tosh (eds) (1991) draw together a range of studies related to a British context. Growing academic attention to the social and cultural construction of masculine identities is also attested to by the appearance of specialized scholarly journals such as *Men and Masculinities* (launched in 1998).

5 Admittedly, there exist other approaches to the study of gender that continue to stress essentialist imperatives. The conservative political climate of the 1980s, for example, saw a resurgence of socio-biological perspectives that interpreted a range of social and cultural behaviour as the outcome of intrinsic sex characteristics. The more populist writings of Robert Bly (1990), meanwhile, have presented manhood as a timeless psychological archetype. Recent work in the fields of social science, however, has generally viewed gender as a socially and culturally constructed category.

6 Authors such as Lury (1996) and Nixon (1997b) acknowledge that Bourdieu's study may be useful in understanding general relationships between class, taste and cultural distinction, but they contend that as yet there exists limited empirical evidence to demonstrate its general applicability to cultural contexts other than France. Several studies, however, have already made significant moves towards this. For example, investigations into middle class consumption patterns carried out by Savage and his associates (1992) point strongly to the existence of comparable processes of class formation in the UK during the 1980s.

7 Shi (2001) makes similar arguments.

Chapter 2
'This Side of Paradise': the Emergence of the Man of Style

Only Gatsby . . . was exempt from my reaction – Gatsby, who represented everything for which I have unaffected scorn. If personality is an unbroken series of successful gestures, then there was something gorgeous about him, some heightened sensitivity to the promises of life, as if he were related to one of those intricate machines that register earthquakes ten thousand miles away. This responsiveness had nothing to do with that flabby impressionability which is dignified under the name of 'creative temperament' – it was an extraordinary gift for hope, a romantic readiness such as I have never found in any other person and which it is not likely I shall ever find again.

F. Scott Fitzgerald, *The Great Gatsby* (New York: Scribner's, 1925: 8).

'RESTLESS IN THE MIDST OF ABUNDANCE': 'TRADITIONAL' MODELS OF MIDDLE-CLASS MASCULINITY

Arriving on American shores in 1831, Alexis de Tocqueville was struck by the difference in temperament he encountered compared to that he had left behind in Europe. For the young French nobleman, America was the incarnation of modern democratic principles, a society characterized by equality of opportunity and (compared to most European states) a relatively equitable division of power and property. Yet de Tocqueville was not only impressed by the American body politic. He was also fascinated by the American state of mind – in particular the peculiar sense of melancholy that led men to strive constantly for self-improvement and success. The American man, de Tocqueville argued, was 'restless in the midst of abundance', perpetually endeavouring toward greater achievement – to the extent that leisure became an irritating diversion and he would 'travel five hundred miles in a few days as a distraction from his happiness' (de Tocqueville, 1969: 693, originally published 1840).

Such industriousness transformed American economic life in the decades following independence. In 1710 net national product had stood at a value of barely $20 million, but by 1840 the figure had soared to around $1,530 million as social and economic growth was promoted through expanding trade, improvements in agriculture and manufacturing, demographic increase, urbanization and the development of transport and financial systems.[1] Yet de Tocqueville's impression of a society marked out by its equitable distribution of wealth and status was wide of the mark. In antebellum America there emerged wide inequalities in income and power as a relatively clearly bounded social hierarchy began to take shape.

Although an embryonic social structure was emerging in America by the beginning of the nineteenth century there was, as yet, no sense of a distinct middle class. The expression 'middle class' was, in fact, rarely used. Instead, the more nebulous terms 'middling sorts' or 'middling rank' denoted those of intermediate wealth and status. Only after the Civil War did there begin to take shape a recognizable 'middle class' distinguished by 'an unprecedented enthusiasm for its own forms of self-expression, peculiar ideas, and devices for self-discipline' (Bledstein, 1976: ix). The rise of this identifiable middle class was the outcome of a combination of economic and social factors.

The widening differences between the worlds of manual and non-manual work was crucial in the emergence of distinct class groups in America during the late nineteenth century. The growing scale and number of business firms brought a dramatic increase in the clerical workforce – from less than 70,000 in 1870 to more than 600,000 by 1900 (Blumin, 1985: 313). The entrance of women into office work accounted for a third of the increase, though the growth of men's clerical employment was also significant, rising at a rate three times faster than the expansion of the male workforce as a whole. Alongside the growth of the white collar sector, the character of clerical work was also changing – the increasing specialization of tasks steadily concentrating clerical employees in an office environment separated from the world of manual work. These shifting patterns of employment, then, played an important role in the emergence of discrete social groups by 'harass[ing] and entic-[ing] Americans into a permanent acceptance of a social division between hand workers and pen wielders, operatives and clerks, the blue collar and the white' (Warner, 1972: 77).

Patterns of urban growth were also important. In the mid-nineteenth century the US was still primarily a rural society, with just over 15 per cent of the population classed as urban in the 1850 census. By the beginning of the 1870s, however, this figure had climbed to nearly 21 per cent, reaching almost 46 per cent by 1910. In the spatial organization of the expanding towns and cities, moreover, visibly distinct social worlds began to take shape. In particular, the growing 'streetcar suburbs' figured as an important factor in processes of middle-class formation – daily life in a relatively homogeneous socio-economic community serving to strengthen both the substance and the boundaries of the middle class as a distinctive social group.[2]

Yet notions of the rise of a distinct and self-conscious middle class are not quite this clear cut. As Stuart Blumin (1985: 305) observes, there is little evidence to show that the nineteenth-century middle-class insisted on its identity as a 'class' and, in fact, usually avoided overt displays of class unity that might too obviously contradict the notions of *individual* agency central to its world view. The middle class, then, was certainly not 'class conscious' in terms of generating a collective and combative political identity. Nevertheless, Blumin argues, they were certainly 'class aware',[3] their personal and social experiences converging in a way that laid the basis for 'a specific style of living, and a specific social identity – a social world, in sum, that was distinct from others above and below it in the tangible hierarchy that was society' (Blumin: 1989: 297).

The developing middle-class world was distinguished, perhaps above all, by its distinctive patterns of family life. According to Mary Ryan 'the American middle class moulded its distinctive identity around domestic values and family practices' (1981: 15), with a new emphasis on smaller families and a greater investment of financial and emotional resources in the care and education of children. Central to this new model of family organization were systems of gender relations in which the middle-class home become a site of 'separate spheres'. According to this system of values the social realm was divided into two distinctly gendered realms, ranked unequally in terms of status and authority. Subordinate was the 'feminine' domain of private, idealized family life – women's identities oriented primarily around a 'cult of domesticity' in which they became the maternal guardians of the family and the home.[4] More dominant was the 'masculine' sphere of public life – middle-class men staking out their masculine identities through their occupational and civic activities and through providing for a household of dependants.

According to E. Anthony Rotundo, the middle-class man of the late nineteenth century was characterized by his determined self control in the pursuit of enterprise, productiveness and temperate respectability (Rotundo, 1993: 55). Within this general credo of productive effort and sober responsibility, however, Rotundo identifies two distinct ideals of middle class masculinity – the 'Christian Gentleman' and the 'Masculine Achiever' (Rotundo, 1987). The 'Christian Gentleman' was the more genteel, exhorting the moral imperatives of compassion, self-sacrifice and decency. The 'Masculine Achiever' gave more emphasis to the qualities of rugged individualism and personal autonomy – his reverence for hard work, competition and endeavour laying the basis for the powerful mythology of the 'self-made man'.

The figure of the 'self-made man' embodied the ceaseless quest for advance that de Tocqueville had seen as such an ingrained feature of American manhood. The term itself was originally coined in 1832 by Henry Clay in a Senate speech venerating the 'self-made' success of Kentuckian entrepreneurs and it quickly caught on as a descriptor of masculine achievement through individual energy and diligence.[5] During the mid-nineteenth century the cult of the 'self-made man' steadily took shape. Popular biographies such as John Frost's *Self Made Men in America* (1848), Charles Seymore's *Self Made-Men* (1858) and Freeman Hunt's *Lives of American Merchants* (1858) offered inspiring tales of men who had dragged themselves up from the gutter, scaling the dizzying peaks of private enterprise and public service through their dedicated toil. The launch of uplifting self-help magazines such as *Success*

(1897) and *World's Work* (1900), together with the popularity of Horatio Alger's 'pluck and luck' novels, confirmed the cultural purchase of the ethos and by the end of the nineteenth century the 'self-made man' had become a cornerstone in the rags-to-riches mythology of the American Dream.

Selfless devotion to work and diligent labour, then, became the trademarks of the upstanding middle-class man. He had his critics, however. Published in 1922, Lewis Sinclair's satirical novel, *Babbitt*, portrayed an image of hollow, middle class convention in the character of George F. Babbitt – a middle-aged, hard-nosed real-estate dealer. Rehearsing a critique of bourgeois conformity that would become commonplace thirty years later, Sinclair depicted a middle-class manhood that was stultifying in its fixation with work and the trappings of respectability. The satire touched a popular nerve and 'Babbittry' became a by-word for a middle-class masculinity made shallow and banal through its obsession with social standards.

Sinclair's critique followed two decades that had severely tested traditional conceptions of manliness. To contemporary eyes, the turn of the century was a time in which a range of dramatic economic and social changes conspired to rob men of their autonomy and status.[6] As Gail Bederman argues, although some critics have presented this period as representing a 'crisis' in American manhood, the nomen-clature of 'crisis' is misleading since the patterns of change never actually threatened the structures of masculine authority (Bederman, 1995: 11). Moreover, to suggest that manhood was in 'crisis' suggests a view of masculinity as 'a fixed essence that has its good moments as well as its bad, rather than an ideological construct which is constantly being re-made' (Bederman, 1995: 11). Rather than presenting American masculinity as a trans-historical category punctuated by moments of vigour and 'crisis', therefore, it is better to understand masculine identities as the outcome of ongoing processes of transformation and negotiation. At the same time, while the social construction of masculinity has been a continuous process, specific historical moments have marked especially significant points of transformation. And the late nineteenth century represented just such a moment, an aggregation of social, economic and cultural changes converging to transfigure dominant notions of masculinity and profoundly influence 'middle-class views of men's bodies, men's identities, and men's access to power' (Bederman, 1995: 11).

For the middle-class man, change was especially pronounced in the world of work. Economic development during the late nineteenth century brought a major restructuring of labour markets – the small-scale, competitive capitalism that had buttressed the culture of middle-class manliness all but disappearing by 1910. Between 1870 and 1910 the proportion of middle-class men who were self-employed dropped from 67 per cent to 37 per cent so that the typical middle-class man was no longer a small farmer or self-employed businessmen, but a corporate bureaucrat or clerical worker (Filene, 1986: 73).[7] Office and retail employment brought greater financial rewards and job security, yet also seemed to undermine the masculine ethos of autonomy and individual enterprise. A round of economic depressions during the late nineteenth century, moreover, brought thousands of bankruptcies and drove home the vulnerability of even the most hard-working entrepreneur. In the northern industrializing cities, meanwhile, the spectre of a developing labour movement, along with the arrival of increasing numbers of European immigrants and African American migrants, began to threaten the existing structures of social hegemony.

Changes in family life and gender relations also provoked unease. Between 1800 and 1900 the annual birth rate dropped by 40 per cent – the decline especially pronounced among white, native-born, Protestants, prompting eugenicist fears of 'racial suicide' (Filene, 1986: 11–12). Alarm was also occasioned by the rising divorce rate, which climbed from 7,000 in 1860 to 56,000 by the turn of the century (May, 1980: 2–7). The anxieties elicited by these shifts, meanwhile, were compounded by the dramatic transformations in women's lives. As the declining birth rate went some way toward freeing them from the burden of motherhood, an increasing number of middle-class women resisted the conventions of domesticity and struck out in the field of public affairs, the figure of the 'New Woman' coming to embody women's attempts to lay claim to the rights and privileges customarily accorded to men. Women's participation in the paid labour force, meanwhile, doubled between 1880 and 1900, growing by a further 50 per cent between 1900 and 1910 – by which time a quarter of the American workforce was female (Filene, 1986: 30). Although many women entered work through economic necessity, the shift further weakened 'conventional' gender expectations and gave many women an important taste of independence. In education, too, women were establishing a significant presence. In 1890 only one in fifty women aged between eighteen and twenty-one attended college, but by 1910 female college enrolments had trebled – the numbers doubling again in the subsequent decade (Filene, 1986: 26). In the bedroom, meanwhile, a more liberated female sexuality also seemed to register – social researchers reporting that, compared to their forebears, women who came to maturity after the turn of the century were much more likely to practice contraception and to have sex both before and outside marriage (Mintz and Kellog, 1988: 112).

By the beginning of the twentieth century, therefore, dominant notions of masculinity were beset by a sense of tension and unease. Urban, middle-class men, in particular, seemed besieged by the declining opportunities for individual enterprise, the rise of anonymous bureaucracies and the gradual transformation of family structures and gender relationships. These apparent challenges elicited diverse responses. Their numbers and influence were limited, but some men gave support to the feminist movement, backing the campaigns for women's suffrage and sexual reform.[8] More prevalent, however, was the drive for a virile reassertion of 'manly' qualities in response to the perceived 'feminization' of traditional masculine ideals. Here, the self-made man's emphasis on discipline and competition retained its importance, yet was combined with a pride in the qualities of robust physicality.

The quest for a restored sense of masculine verve registered in a host of cultural forms and social initiatives at the turn of the century. Popular literature was especially rich with themes of sturdy manhood. In 1902, for example, the publication of Owen Wister's *The Virginian* heralded the arrival of the modern Western and was followed by a succession of novels that cast the frontier life of the cowboy as the essence of rugged manliness. In the realm of magazine publishing, meanwhile, titles such as Bernarr Macfadden's *Physical Culture* and *True Story* won sizeable readerships through their emphasis on tough, male physicality and their lurid stories of sexual sensationalism. This field was led, however, by the *National Police Gazette*. Beginning in 1845 as a journal for specialized crime news, the *National Police Gazette* was revamped in the 1870s as a salacious scandal sheet combining spectacular crime stories, sports coverage and burlesque pin-ups. The readership of these magazines was largely working class, although a significant minority of middle-class male readers were also drawn to their universe of pugnaciousness and prurience. These readers manifested what Kevin White (1993: 7–10) describes as a trend towards 'underworld primitivism' – numbers of middle-class men identifying with the traits of toughness and aggressive sexuality that had once been the preserve of the lower orders. And beyond the fantasy world of popular literature 'underworld primitivism' also began to find a home in the saloon, the pool hall and other institutions once entirely antithetical to the values of middle-class manliness.

More respectable havens also existed for the elaboration of manful camaraderie. Some men sought to colonize the domestic environment, carving out part of the home as a private den or 'lair' – a distinctly male space from which the rest of the family was barred.[9] Outside the home middle class men also found sanctuary in the over 300 lodges and fraternal organizations that existed by the turn of the century (Carnes, 1989: 1). Fraternal orders such as the Odd Fellows and the Freemasons offered fellowship and social intimacy, while their mystic rituals and arcane ceremonies provided an avenue through which men could symbolically reinvent themselves as figures of pride and stature.[10] The growth of organized sport also partly stemmed from middle-class men's attempts to fashion a homosocial arena in which the values of virile manhood could be acted out and celebrated – hence spectator sports such as baseball, football and boxing all began to thrive, while athletics and bodybuilding were championed as ideal vehicles for the development of both physical prowess and moral fibre.[11]

The 'fighting virtues' were not only enacted on the sports field. The 1890s saw an exercise of national potency through a new era of imperialist expansion in the Pacific and South America. With Theodore Roosevelt's assumption of the presidency in 1901 this expansionism was sustained, Roosevelt's 'big stick diplomacy' embodying a reassertion of masculine vigour in the sphere of foreign policy. Indeed, Roosevelt himself personified the concept of a newly revitalized American manhood. Frail as a boy, an arduous regime of bodybuilding had transformed him into a model of manly action whose subsequent exploits in the Spanish-American War won national veneration. In both deeds and outlook Roosevelt epitomized the drive to reinvigorate American manhood. Most famously, 'Bull Moose' articulated the fear that 'over-civilization' was sapping the strength of the American male. Denouncing 'the soft spirit' of the age, Roosevelt insisted on the need for a return to 'the doctrine of the strenuous life', extolling the American people to 'boldly face the life of strife . . . for it is only through strife, through hard and dangerous endeavour, that we shall ultimately win the goal of true national greatness' (Roosevelt, 1900: 8, 20–1).

In his promotion of 'the strenuous life' Roosevelt singled out American youth for special attention. Under his aegis the Boone and Crockett Club, originally founded in 1888 to advance the sport of hunting, developed into an organization geared to building up the character of American boys. Indeed, *fin-de-siècle* anxieties regarding the state of American manhood were powerfully projected onto youth. Particularly strong concerns were voiced by G. Stanley Hall, the founder and president of Clark University. Fearing that middle-class men had lost the rugged qualities he saw as essential to civilization's continued development, Hall argued that boys should be encouraged to immerse themselves in 'primitive' physicality so they might 'evolve' into more powerful and more civilized men (Bederman, 1995: 77–120). Similar sentiments are detectable in the proliferation of movements using recreational programmes as a means to 'build character' in the rising generation of middle-class youth. Whereas the growing number of boys' clubs were geared towards the surveillance and control of working-class youngsters, groups such as the Young Men's Christian Association (YMCA) and the Boy Scouts arose primarily in response to concerns about the middle-class young.[12] According to alarmists, not only were respectable youths vulnerable to the corrupting influence of saloons, theatres and dance halls, but they were also being debilitated by sedentary living (Macleod, 1983: 47). Character-building movements such as the YMCA, the Scouts and smaller groups such as the Boys Brigades and the Men of Tomorrow, therefore, sought to redeem young men from the 'feminizing' influences of middle-class life, reviving and restoring their masculine vitality.

The myriad attempts to recreate a mythical culture of robust manhood, however, were far from all encompassing. Rather than absorbing themselves in a world of strident masculine physicality, some middle-class men assimilated themselves more fully into the realm of the home. Men, of course, had always played an important economic role in American family life. The 'separation of spheres' in the middle-class home had demanded of women commitment to homemaking and domesticity, but of men it required a dedication to providing for one's family. Between 1810 and 1820 the term 'breadwinner' began to be coined to denote this ideal of mature and respectable masculinity (Kimmel, 1997: 20) – the 'breadwinner ethic' promulgating values of sobriety and self-discipline in which men denied themselves in order to provide for their wives and families (Ehrernreich: 1983: 11).[13] The masculine breadwinner, then, had long been a cornerstone of middle-class respectability, but from the 1900s middle-class men's breadwinning responsibilities were increasingly combined with a greater involvement in domestic relationships.

During the early twentieth century the concept of the 'companionate family' emerged as a progressive alternative to the familial traditions of patriarchal authority and hierarchical organization. With its emphasis on companionship, mutual respect and emotional satisfaction, the ideal of the 'companionate family' proffered a 'new vision of middle class fatherhood' in which fathers found fulfilment through being integrated more thoroughly within family life (Griswold, 1993: 89–94).[14] For Margaret Marsh these developments represented the rise of a new model of 'masculine domesticity' in which conformity to the breadwinner ethos was combined with greater assimilation into the domestic sphere (Marsh, 1988, 1989, 1990: 74–83). The middle-class family remained a site of gender-based power inequalities, yet fathers were increasingly drawn into the family unit and 'although they did not routinely sweep and dust, domestic men nevertheless were expected to center their lives around their homes and families' (Marsh, 1988: 513). The companionate family represented, moreover, the linchpin of a new, suburban, domestic ideal. Notions of 'family together-ness' were institutionalized in the developing suburbs where architectural designs gave spatial manifestation to ideals of domestic bliss. The gendered divide between the 'feminine' space of the parlour and the 'masculine' space of the study steadily gave way to open-floor plans that emphasized family unity. Exemplary were the 'prairie house' designs of Frank Lloyd Wright (himself a staunch supporter of the American family) whose flowing interior spaces emphasized notions of a secure and solidly integrated nuclear family (Marsh, 1988; 1989).

Middle-class family life was also integral to the rising consumer economy. After the 1860s American economic performance had entered a phase of sustained improvement – the growth in industry's productive power combining with a gradual increase in levels of disposable income to lay the basis for an increasingly consumer-oriented economy.[15] Commodity consumption became a feature of life across the social scale, yet the suburban home emerged as an especially important market for the burgeoning range of commercially produced goods and services, the traditional middle-class values of puritanical thrift giving way to a greater acceptance of materialism (Horowitz, 1985: 68). The participation of the white-collar breadwinner in the new universe of consumerism, however, was driven not by personal gratification but by the needs and desires of his family. And attaining the goods increasingly regarded as essential accoutrements to respectable family life was not easy. Indeed, for many among the growing army of officeworkers and professionals, the material demands that came with a life of 'masculine domesticity' were a heavy burden and a frequent source of marital conflict (May, 1978, 1980: 137–56).

By the beginning of the Progressive Era, therefore, the pace of economic and social development was generating a range of contradictory responses within the cultures and value systems of middle-class men. On one hand, the period saw a strident reassertion of robust manhood in the face of what were perceived as 'feminizing' changes in labour markets and gender roles. On the other, the rise of a new model of 'masculine domesticity' saw some men play a more contributive role within family life. From the turn of the century, however, there also emerged a third archetypal response – one geared around a youthful culture of heterosocial recreation and hedonistic pleasure.

DAWN OF THE DUDE: CONSUMPTION, STYLE AND THE URBAN BACHELOR

Middle-class morality underwent considerable change in America at the beginning of the twentieth century. To many contemporaries it seemed as if the established conventions of respectable probity were breaking down as young men and women began mixing more freely in the new dance halls, cinemas and other ventures in the growing constellation of commercial leisure. These developments, however, did not necessarily represent an emancipatory liberation from a Victorian order of sexual repression. Indeed, as Michel Foucault (1979) shows, the late nineteenth century had actually been marked by a proliferation of public discourses about sexuality. Christina Simmons argues that the notion of Victorian repression was actually a myth generated during the 1920s and 1930s in the writings of white, liberal commentators who sought to win acceptance for a modified form of sexual regulation that 'rehabilitated male sexuality and cast women as villains if they refused to respond to, nurture, or support it' (1989: 158). From this perspective, rather than representing the dawn of sexual liberation, the new promotion of sexual behaviour as a natural and healthy aspect of social life can be seen as a strategy of male sexual control 'better adapted to a world where single women of the middle class were asserting a more active sexuality and where men were pressed to legitimate theirs' (Simmons, 1989: 158). Nevertheless, though gender inequalities remained pronounced in the 'new morality' of the 1920s, this should not obscure those dimensions of empowerment that were beginning to open up for women.

The links between the developing world of consumer business and the growth of women's cultural freedoms were ambiguous. Women's new economic opportunities, for example, were often more apparent than real, many women finding employment only in low-skilled occupations or in deskilled jobs previously done by men. At the same time, however, greater educational opportunities and the expansion of the clerical and retailing sectors offered at least some women the possibility of a career and a more autonomous life, while the rise of department stores and the growth of shopping provided a degree of public freedom. For some women these changes offered the possibility for the articulation of a more independent feminine identity –

one encapsulated in the image of the youthful flapper. With her jaunty clothes, short bobbed hair and breathless lifestyle, the flapper was the epitome of chic modernity. Carefully worked out in advertisers' narratives, the flapper was to a large part a consumer fantasy. Yet, as Martin Pumphrey (1987) argues, the ambiguities of this fantasy offered women enticing possibilities, the flapper's air of confidence and emphatic nonconformity posing a potential challenge to traditional constructions of feminine submissiveness and domesticity.[16]

The flapper stands as an enduring motif for the growing role of leisure and style in American culture during the 1920s. Yet a greater accent on consumption and pleasure was not restricted to the lives of young women. At the apex of the social scale, men of substance had, from the late nineteenth century, already shown a willingness to celebrate their cultural ascendance through proud displays of wealth in the spheres of fashion, leisure and social ritual. In the world of the metropolitan *nouveaux riches*, Thorstein Veblen (1899) identified an American 'leisure class' intent on mimicking the lifestyles of the European aristocracy through displays of 'conspicuous consumption', deploying consumer goods (luxurious furnishings, clothes, jewels) as markers of their social prestige. Beyond the 'leisure class' elite, moreover, there began to emerge other configurations of masculinity also distinguished by their predilection for hedonistic consumption.

Masculine identities premised on leisure and narcissistic display were not unprecedented. In the early nineteenth century, for example, the rapier wit and elegant poise of Beau Brummell and his fellow dandies had enthralled fashionable English society. Among Parisian arcades, meanwhile, there had meandered the *flâneur*.[17] A social type sketched by mid-nineteenth century social commentators, the *flâneur* was a nonchalant (and perhaps allegorical) 'spectator' of the modern world – a smartly dressed gentleman depicted as strolling through, observing and appropriating the pleasures of the modern cityscape. And, towards the end of the century, cities in northern America began to identify their own version of the urbane, masculine spectator – 'the dude'.

Distinguished by his affectation of stylish panache, the dude was in some ways comparable to the European *flâneur*. A stock character in popular humour by the turn of the century, the dude was generally conceived of as a young man, upwardly mobile and debonair, who sauntered through the throbbing streets of the growing city. A sense of ambivalence was, however, central to the original concept of the dude. In some respects the term was used as a jocular, almost amiable, epithet. Through his good looks and dapper clothes, for example, President Chester Arthur (holding office between 1881 and 1885) became known as 'The Dude President', while the turn of the century saw dilapidated Western cattle farms turned into 'Dude Ranches' – fashionable resorts where wealthy Easterners played at being cowboys. Often, though, the dude was constructed as a more negative stereotype. Probably stemming from German-American usage, the term itself was a likely derivation of

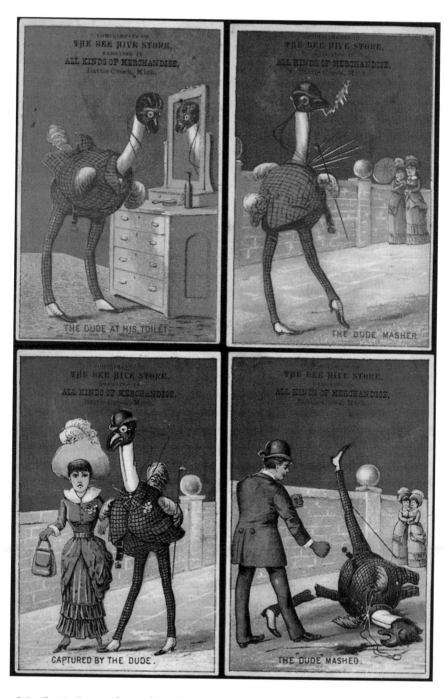

2.1 The 'Dude' as a figure of popular humour (trade cards advertising a Michigan general store, 1880s).

the expression *duden-kopf*, meaning idiot or blockhead. Amid the period's wider 'crisis' of masculinity, the dude's flamboyance was configured as absurd and effeminate. A subject of suspicion and ridicule, he was a caricature generally derided as an unmanly 'pussyfoot' (Paoletti, 1985; White, 1993: 16).[18] Over time, however, the dude's brand of style-conscious élan was to become more acceptable as the middle class became increasingly permeated by the forces of commercialism and commodity consumption.

After 1900 American cities steadily developed into centres of commercial leisure and mass consumption. Alongside the dance halls, spectator sports, saloons and movie theatres a deluge of new consumer goods was released onto the market, while the burgeoning advertising industry imbued mass-produced goods with intangible values that went far beyond their utilitarian function.[19] The rise of this modern consumer economy was grounded on a socially diverse urban market yet, as Howard Chudacoff (1999) persuasively argues, the demand generated by an extensive 'bachelor subculture' was especially significant.

By the turn of the century urban America was home to a veritable army of young bachelors. In 1890 Chicago alone counted a population of over 170,500 single men between the ages of fifteen and thirty-four. More widely, the national marriage rate (the number of marriages per 100,000 population) dropped from ninety-eight to ninety-one between 1870 and 1890, census figures for 1890 showing that 41.7 per cent of all males over the age of fifteen were unmarried – the highest proportion recorded until the late twentieth century (Chudacoff , 1999: 47–55). Several factors contributed to this trend. In some instances postponement of marriage may have been a response to economic hardship. Yet Chudacoff shows that marriage actually remained strongest among the most economically disadvantaged social strata (the immigrant and native working classes), while rates of bachelorhood were highest among the better-off, white, middle and upper classes (1999: 64). More significant were demographic shifts, differential migration patterns possibly causing an imbalance in sex ratios and an excess of single men in rapidly growing urban communities – though many cities with high proportions of bachelors also had a comparable surplus of single women (Chudacoff, 1999: 56–61). Rather than economic or demographic trends, Chudacoff argues, the decisive forces behind the growth of an urban bachelor subculture were patterns of socio-cultural change. Most crucially, the ascendance of the new commercial leisure industries threw into disarray traditional patterns of social relation and laid the basis for 'a new heterosocial culture, one that brought together young, unattached men and women in social and sometimes sexual relationships that minimized personal commitment' (Chudacoff, 1999: 67).

In the new urban centres men were drawn into a diverse field of commercial entertainment. At the seamier end of the scale were brothels, blood sports and the other illicit pleasures of 'underworld primitivism'. But also significant were an array of business concerns geared to the demands of young, single men – from eating houses, barber shops and saloons to dance-halls, billiard parlours and vaudeville theatres (Chudacoff, 1999: 106–45). Unfettered by family responsibilities, the urban bachelor represented an especially lucrative market and the developing consumer industries scrambled for his custom. Moreover, while working class men undoubtedly figured in these trends, the greatest economic muscle was wielded by their middle-class peers – a growing number of city bars, tailors, tobacconists, theatres and other commercial ventures thriving on the patronage of affluent, young 'men about town'.

2.2 The 'New Bachelor'. (Box for New Bachelor cigars, c. 1890s).

Important elements of suspicion and unease, however, still surrounded codes of indulgent leisure. These found their fullest voice in the prohibition movement's crusade against alcohol and its view of drink as the baleful corrupter of national morality. In 1916 twenty-three states were already officially 'dry' and that year's national elections returned a Congress dominated by prohibition sympathizers. By January 1919 ratification had been given to the Eighteenth Amendment to the Constitution outlawing the manufacture and sale of intoxicating liquors and, with the passage of the Volstead Act the following year, the Prohibition era began. Yet Prohibition was always more of an ideal than a reality since Congress and the state legislatures were reluctant to fund more than token enforcement. Opportunities for disregarding the law, therefore, remained legion and in the city nightlife of speak-easies and cabarets a culture dominated by the pleasures of stylish consumption continued to grow. And against this backdrop there appeared a new masculine archetype who encapsulated both the allure and the perceived dangers of the developing consumer society – the gangster.

America boomed in the 1920s. Driven forward by the expansion of consumer industries, gross domestic product rose by nearly 40 per cent between 1922 and 1929, accompanied by a 45 per cent rise in wages. Film stars and other glamorous celebrities of the age embodied the sense of prosperous good times, showcasing the possibilities for fulfilment and display offered by the new consumerism. The gangster can be seen as performing a similar role – the public enemy being defined not simply by his violent criminality, but also by his lavish lifestyle. With his expensive suits, tuxedos, spats and jewellery, his luxurious mansion and taste for fashionable nightlife, the gangster was, David Ruth argues, 'an oversized projection of the urban America seduced by the promises of consumption' (1996: 69). According to Ruth, throughout the 1920s and 1930s the gangster image was used by writers and film makers (not to mention their audiences) as an avenue through which to explore the abundance of goods that had transformed their society – the gangster's stylish extravagance offering a glimpse of the new paths to individual fulfilment apparently opened up by the mass-consumption economy. As well as embodying the promise of the new consumerism, however, the gangster also signalled its dangers. The gangster's prodigious wealth seemed to suggest that economic mobility was blurring distinctions of class, while the ease with which he mixed with leading citizens in restaurants, bars and night-clubs suggested an effacement of conventional distinctions between the respectable and the disreputable (Ruth, 1996: 81–5). The image of the 1920s gangster, then, offered an ambivalent commentary on the rise of consumerism. Commodity consumption was constructed as offering the potential for sensual pleasure and individual fulfilment, though at the risk of undermining traditional value systems and social structures.

The gangster's combination of ostentatious display and deviant criminality underlined the anxieties that still surrounded consumerism during the 1920s. Yet the popular fascination with his image and style also attested to a gradual acceptance of masculine identities predicated on consumer desires. The earlier archetype of the dude had often been an object of scorn, his commitment to fashion and the comforts of city life seen as effeminate and unmanly. But, as the twentieth century progressed, forms of masculinity began to emerge in which personal gratification and hedonistic leisure were valued and sought after. Alongside the quest for a revived sense of robust manhood and the rise of a family-oriented 'masculine domesticity', then, there also took shape a masculine identity at ease with the developing realm of commodity consumption. In contrast to the 'producer ethos' that had venerated hard work and censured consumption, this form of masculinity found fulfilment in distinctive goods and the trappings of style – a system of values that came to play a pivotal role in 'reorient[ing] the blossoming American consumer culture . . . in the direction of youth and the individual, rather than toward the family' (Chudacoff: 1999: 19).

'FLAMING YOUTH': GENDER, GENERATION AND LEISURE IN THE JAZZ AGE

Like masculinity, notions of youth can be seen as socially and culturally constructed. Rather than an immutably fixed stage in human physical and psychological development, the concept of 'youth' has been dynamic and multi-faceted – the outcome of interconnected social, economic and political processes that have varied across time and between cultures.[20] In the US the modern system of age stratification was the product of shifts in demographics and labour markets that, during the late nineteenth and early twentieth centuries, combined with developments in the fields of legislation, family organization and education to mark out young people as a distinct social group associated with particular social needs and cultural characteristics (Chudacoff, 1989). From the 1870s, notions of childhood were steadily institutionalized through the growth of compulsory schooling and the introduction of minimum age labour laws, and in the decades that followed other generational groups were given form and substance through the course of social and economic change.

The concept of adolescence as a distinct period in human development was first given systematic 'scientific' formulation in G. Stanley Hall's rambling opus, *Adolescence: Its Psychology and Its Relations to Physiology, Anthropology, Sociology, Sex, Crime and Education* (1904). For Hall, adolescence represented a discrete phase of bio-psychological transformation that began with puberty and ended in mature adulthood – an innately volatile period of identity formation that he portrayed as inherently troubling for both young people and wider society. Though now largely disowned by the scientific and professional communities, at the time of their publication Hall's ideas were profoundly influential in the fields of psychology and pedagogy where they helped mark out adolescence as a life stage demanding special attention and supervision.

Developments in the realm of psychological theory were not alone in enhancing the social profile of youth during the early twentieth century. Shifts in demography and family structure were also significant. In 1790 (the year of the first American census) average family size was 5.8 persons, but by 1920 this figure had shrunk to 4.3 – a decline of almost 25 per cent (Seward, 1978: 73). This decrease in family size was especially pronounced within middle-class households where children were given a new prominence in family affairs, parents investing more time and money in the care of the individual child. As the parent-child bond intensified, youngsters remained emotionally and economically dependent on their parents for a longer period – this extension of parental provision allowing young people to remain within the world of education for a greater stretch of time (Fass, 1978: 85).

The early decades of the twentieth century were a time of reorganization and growth in American education. Between 1900 and 1930 the number of high school students grew by 650 per cent so that, by the beginning of the 1930s, close to 60 per cent of the high school-age population were enrolled. This shift had important cultural ramifications, high school attendance giving young people massive exposure to a culture oriented around their peers rather than their family. Indeed, in their classic study of small-city life in the mid-1920s, Robert and Helen Lynd were struck by the degree to which adolescents' social lives revolved around their school friends, so that school had become 'a place from which they go home to eat and sleep' (1929: 121). Yet the world of the high school remained circumscribed by adult supervision and it was in college and university life that there began to develop the most visible and influential forms of peer-based youth culture. Once limited to a relatively small elite, colleges and universities saw a threefold increase in enrolments between 1900 and 1930, nearly 20 per cent of the college-age population attending some kind of educational institution by the end of the 1920s (Fass, 1978: 124). And among this growing student body there developed a new cultural universe distinguished by its own styles, interests and attitudes.

At the centre of the newly developing peer culture was the network of fraternities and sororities that controlled campus social life. Fraternities had existed in American colleges since the 1820s, though developed rapidly after the Civil War. Aided by loyal alumni, fraternities began to build residences and lodges for their meetings and played an increasingly active role in student life through the sponsorship of sports competitions, dances and all manner of social events. Dramatic expansion followed during the twentieth century. Able to provide accommodation and dining services for the proliferating numbers of students, fraternities and sororities were encouraged to grow by college administrators so that by 1912 there were 1,560 national chapters, their number surging to 3,900 by 1930. At many colleges during the 1920s as many as 35–40 per cent of students belonged to fraternities or sororities and on some campuses the figure reached as high as 65 per cent (Fass, 1978: 143–4). Offering young adults a means of social identification and peer acceptance, fraternities allowed college life to crystallize into a distinct social experience. While certainly influenced and informed by wider, adult society, this peer-oriented milieu is seen by Paula Fass (1978: 122) as marking the rise of the first modern American youth culture, college students increasingly sharing their own set of cultural styles and social rituals that were played out at dances, parties, movie theatres, cafeterias and an array of campus hangouts.

A new emphasis on heterosocial interaction was a cornerstone within this developing peer culture. Distinct boundaries still existed as to what constituted permissible erotic behaviour, but there evolved new codes of dating and petting that introduced a measure of casual informality to rituals of courtship.[21] Cinemas and restaurants were important focal points to the new culture of heterosocial recreation, though it was the growing number of public dance halls and nightclubs that were pivotal. And whereas the older, ballroom dance styles were characterized by controlled and regular motion, new dances such as the Charleston and the Blackbottom were more daring. Borrowing heavily from African American social dances such as the Cakewalk and the Turkey Trot, the new dance steps incorporated bodily movements that were more relaxed and expressive. Music, too, was adopted from African American culture. First emerging in New Orleans at the turn of the century, jazz quickly took hold in the black enclaves of Chicago and New York and from there filtered into the subcultures of white nightlife. During the 1920s the volume, exuberance and sensuality of jazz found resonance in the developing cultures of white, urban leisure – black music and dance offering a taste of risqué pleasure to those who sought to break through the boundaries of prim decorum and step boldly into the new age of hedonistic modernity.

In the field of fashion a sense of forward-looking change also registered – especially in clothing for men. From the 1890s sportswear became popular for casual attire, shirt styles previously worn for sports replacing more formal garb as a new, leisure-oriented aesthetic surfaced within male fashion. Indicative of this transformation was the 'Arrow Man' who became a fixture of advertisements for Arrow shirts from 1905 onwards. A model of well-groomed and chiseljawed masculinity, the 'Arrow Man' became the first in a series of youthful and stylish masculine archetypes whose virile muscularity guaranteed a fashionability untainted by suspicions of effeminacy (White, 1993: 26). The

2.3 The 'Arrow Man'. (Advertisement for Arrow collars and shirts, 1913 – courtesy of Cluett, Peabody & Co.)

Progressive Era also saw an identifiable 'collegiate' or 'Ivy League' style of dress take shape. Clothing firms such as Campus Leisure-wear (founded in 1922), together with the movie, magazine and advertising industries, gave coherence to this smart-but-casual combination of button-down shirts, chino slacks, letter sweaters, cardigans and loafers – a leisure-style that steadily reached out from the campus into the wider male population.

The rise of leisure-oriented sensibilities in male fashion was also reflected in the development of a multi-million dollar swimwear industry. Between 1900 and 1920 beach-going established itself as major facet of American leisure and the firms of Jantzen, Catalina and Cole (all former specialists in underwear and sweater manufacture) emerged as 'the Ford, Chrysler and General Motors of the swim-wear trade' (Lencek and Bosker, 1989: 44). Jantzen's growth was especially prolific, its sale of 600 bathing suits in 1917 leaping to 4,100 in 1919 and then spiralling to over 1,500,000 by 1930 as the firm secured its position as the market leader in beach attire. Moreover, swimwear for both men and women gradually became not just more comfortable but more 'emancipated' in design. During the 1920s the tubular maillot (a two-piece swimsuit of vest and shorts manufactured for both men and women) became increasingly streamlined, exposing more and more bare flesh, while the arrival of men's swimming shorts and trunks in the 1930s underlined the way that athleticism and youthful sex appeal had become central values of male appearance.

During the 1920s the ideal of a young and vibrant masculinity also figured as a recurring leitmotif in American literature. The mood of zestful, affluent youth was captured most obviously in the work of F. Scott Fitzgerald. In *This Side of Paradise* (1920) Fitzgerald caught the essence of an American generation struggling to define itself, the novel's lead character – Princeton undergraduate Amory Blaine – rebelling against his staid, Midwestern upbringing in a quest for sexual and intellectual enlightenment. Similar themes surfaced in *The Great Gatsby* (1925). Fitzgerald's most famous novel was an exploration of the power and pitfalls of the American ideals of self-creation and success. Yet, in the enigmatic Jay Gatsby, Fitzgerald also created a character who personified many of the shifts taking place in the dominant culture of 1920s America. In his palatial home, fabulous parties and expensive clothes Gatsby was emblematic of America's growing fascination with consumption, glamour and opulent leisure, the character embodying the emergence of a new masculine style that was defined by a sense of youthful hedonism. Fitzgerald's chronicle of the new generation and its ethos was both perceptive and seductive, the author himself coming to personify the lush, fast-paced lifestyles his novels described. Nor was Fitzgerald alone in glorifying a new generation of vivacious young men and women. Percy Marks in *The Plastic Age* (1924) and Floyd Dell in his autobiographical trilogy (*Moon-Calf*, 1920; *The Briary-Bush*, 1921 and *Souvenir*, 1929) also struck a chord with their depictions of young lives of hectic leisure, while respectable opinion was shocked by *Flaming Youth* (1923) – Warner Fabian's tale of torrid passions among the young of upper-class suburbia.

Outside the pages of *Gatsby*-esque fiction, middle-class youth culture also took on a radical hue, although it was not political activism that stoked the fires of rebellion. Attempts were made to mobilize young people politically – with liberal and socialist clubs formed at many colleges and universities – but they developed little momentum and attracted only a minority of students. During the 1920s the middle-class young were, for the most part, conservative in their political orientations. Rather than politics, it was style that energized the radicalism of youth. As Fass puts it, campus culture was '"naughty" not angry' – young people proudly conceiving of themselves as modern in dress, manners and attitude and opposing 'all attempts to return American life to an impossible past that would condemn their new liberties in sex, thought, and interest' (Fass, 1978: 375–6). Rather than politics, then, it was matters of style and individuality that were crucial within the developing campus peer culture and, while the political radical existed as a marginal and somewhat eccentric figure, 'a man who drank gin, shimmied and petted was fashionably "naughty"' (Fass, 1978: 360).

*

As America developed into a modern consumer society, therefore, new articulations of a youthful, style-conscious and desiring masculine subject began to take shape – these standing in stark contrast to Victorian ideals of masculinity that had prized diligence, thrift and self-control. Amid the opulence of the Jazz Age, a young, hedonistic and narcissistic masculine archetype gradually coalesced – the term 'playboy' increasingly being coined to denote this easygoing and self-indulgent *bon vivant*.[22] Within this matrix of leisure-oriented masculine consumption, moreover, youth was a pre-eminent theme. Synonymous with the new horizons of commercial leisure, the peer-culture of white, middle-class college youth was increasingly looked upon as the cutting edge in fashion, music and stylistic expression. And as young people adjusted to the shifting patterns of inter-war life – generating new patterns of gender relations and consumption-driven lifestyles – they gradually drew the rest of the middle class with them. Amid the excitements of a rapidly changing world, the young 'had come to represent modernity, the impulse toward adjustment, and even the promise of twentieth century life' (Fass, 1978: 128).

NOTES

1   More detailed surveys of American economic growth during this period can be found in Licht (1993) and Olsen and Rockoff (1994).

2 The classic account of these processes is provided in Warner (1962). For other informed overviews of suburban growth in nineteenth-century America, see Fishman (1987) and Jackson (1985).

3 Blumin's distinction between 'class consciousness' and 'class awareness' is influenced by Anthony Giddens' insistence that 'The difference between class awareness and class consciousness is a fundamental one, because class awareness may take the form of a denial of the existence or reality of classes. Thus the class awareness of the middle class, in so far as it involves beliefs which place a premium upon the individual responsibility and achievement, is of this order' (Giddens, 1959: 111).

4 The term 'cult of domesticity' was originally coined by Kraditor (1968). Further discussion of constructions of femininity in nineteenth-century America can be found in Cott (1977) and Sklar (1973), while an overview of historical literature dealing with the notion of 'separate spheres' is provided by Kerber (1988). Although their work deals with developments in England rather than America, Davidoff and Hall (1987) also offer valuable observations regarding the role of gender relations in the formation of middle class identities during the nineteenth century.

5 The seminal studies of the concept of the 'self-made man' were elaborated by Wyllie, (1954) and Cawelti (1965). A recent attempt to revise their insights is offered by Decker (1997). For the most thoroughgoing account of the shifting contours of middle-class masculinity in nineteenth century America, see the work of Rotundo (1983, 1987, 1993).

6 This *fin de siècle* sense of masculine anxiety has been mapped out by, among others, Dubbert (1980), Filene (1986), Higham (1970), Kimmel (1987a) and White (1993).

7 See also Kimmel (1997: 103), Rotundo (1993: 248–51) and Stearns (1990: 149–50).

8 Notable examples were the Greenwich Village radicals who, believing that reform of gender relations was the imperative adjunct to socialist revolution, worked to bring about sexual equality in both public and private life. See Kimmel (1987a, 1987b, 1997: 112–6).

9 As Kimmel notes, solid oak panelling, deep leather furniture, smoking paraphernalia and a smattering of hunting trophies on the walls 'all made it clear that man was not in the least feminized by returning to his lair, his den, after hunting in the corporate jungle all day' (Kimmel, 1997: 111). See also Rotundo (1993: 227).

10 The fullest historical accounts of fraternal orders in America are provided in Carnes (1989) and Clawson (1989).

11 The role of competitive sport in masculine cultures at the turn of the century is discussed in Filene (1986: 95), Higham (1970) and Rotundo (1993: 239–44).

Detailed histories of the development of prize-fighting, baseball and athletics can be found in, respectively, Reiss (1990), Smith (1990) and Gorn (1986).

12 Originally founded in England in 1844 as a moral guide to young tradesmen, the YMCA was brought to Boston in 1851. The character of the American organization changed significantly after 1886 when Luther Gulick took over its directorship. Under Gulick the promotion of physical culture became a paramount concern in the YMCA's programme, the organization seeking to instil among its members the 'Muscular Christian' principles of a healthy mind, body and spirit. Another import from England, the Boy Scouts were originally launched by Lord Baden-Powell in 1908. Two years later the Boy Scouts of America were founded by Ernest Thompson Seton and within four years more than 100,000 boys had enrolled, followed by nearly twice that number by 1917. For a detailed history of the development of the YMCA, the Boy Scouts and similar youth movements see Macleod (1983).

13 Additional accounts of the rise of the 'breadwinner ethic' are provided in Gordon (1980), Griswold (1993: 10-33), Kann (1991: 198) and Mintz and Kellog (1988: 50–5).

14 For further discussion of the rise of the companionate family and changes within notions of middle-class fatherhood during the early twentieth century see Mintz and Kellog (1988: 107–32).

15 There exists much debate regarding the emergence of modern patterns of consumption. Historians such as Cipolla (1980) suggest it is possible to locate the origins of modern consumerism as early as the Middle Ages. Appleby (1978) argues that the acquisitive mindset characteristic of the modern consumer can be identified in the seventeenth-century Anglo-American world, while British scholars have highlighted the late eighteenth century as marking the onset of the 'consumer revolution' (McKendrick, Brewer and Plumb, 1982). America also exhibited many features associated with modern consumerism by the end of the eighteenth century, although historians have generally cited the late nineteenth and early twentieth centuries as the crucible of recognizably modern forms of mass consumption. See Fox and Lears (eds) (1983) and Strasser (1989).

16 For further discussion of changes in the lives and culture of women during the 1920s and their possible challenge to traditional constructions of femininity, see Freedman (1974) and Latham (2000).

17 Walter Benjamin's (1983) analysis of Charles Baudelaire's nineteenth century social commentaries has played a large part in popularizing the concept of the *flâneur*. Comprehensive accounts of the nineteenth century dandy and *flâneur* can be found in, respectively, Moers (1960) and Tester (ed.) (1994).

18 The sense of unease regarding the 'degeneration' of American manhood also transformed attitudes towards the gay subcultures that, by the 1850s, had emerged in cities such as New York, San Francisco, Boston and Philadelphia.

These had once existed relatively easily alongside the heterosexual mainstream, but at the turn of the century they became subject to greater hostility. For histories of the development of gay culture in nineteenth century America see Chauncey (1994) and D'Emilio and Freedman (1997: 121–30).

19 The development of mass production and distribution in this period is discussed in Chandler (1980), Hounshell (1984) and Scranton (1991). Accounts of the rise of commercial entertainments in the early twentieth century are provided in Erenberg (1981), Peiss (1986), May (1980) and Nasaw (1993).

20 For a more detailed discussion of 'youth' as a socially and historically constructed discourse see Austin and Willard (eds) (1998: introduction). According to these authors, conceptions of youth are always historically specific and any study of youth culture must carefully 'locat[e] young people and the representations of their lives in a complex and changing historical network of institutions, economic structures, state policies, adult initiatives, and youths' self-activities' (1998: 3).

21 See Bailey (1988: 25–57), D'Emillio and Freedman (1997: 256–60), Modell (1987) and White (1993: 146–64).

22 The term 'playboy' was already in usage by the early twentieth century, evidenced by the production, in 1907, of *The Playboy of the Western World* – playwright John Millington Synge's droll satire on Irish braggadocio. In America, however, the term passed into much wider circulation during the 1920s. During the late 1920s, for example, New York City's flamboyant mayor, James J. Walker became known as 'The Playboy of New York' (as well as the 'Night Mayor') through his predilection for speakeasies and chorus girls. For a lively account of Walker's intriguing rise and ignominious fall see Mitgang (2000).

Chapter 3
Lessons in 'The Art of Living': the 'Playboy Ethic' Takes Shape

The new deal has given leisure a new economic significance, and the five-day week has become not merely every man's right but virtually every man's duty.

More time to read, more time to indulge in hobbies, to play, to get out of town – more time, in short, to think of Living as an art, as well as a business.

Men have had leisure thrust upon them. Now they've got it, they must spend it somehow. Many of them – perhaps even the majority – haven't the faintest idea how to go about it.

What more opportune occasion for the appearance of a new magazine – a new kind of magazine – one that will answer the question of What to do? What to eat, what to drink, what to wear, how to play, what to read – in short a magazine dedicated to the improvement of the new leisure.

That magazine is *Esquire* . . . Esquire means simply Mister – the man of the middle class. Once it was the fashion to call him Babbitt, and to think of him as a wheelhorse with no interests outside of business. That's very outmoded thinking, however. For today, he represents the New Leisure Class.

Arnold Gingrich, 'The Art of Living and the New Leisure Class', promotional pamphlet for the launch of *Esquire* magazine, 1933.

HISTORICIZING 'THE NEW LEISURE CLASS': GENEALOGIES OF THE CONSUMING MALE

During the 1920s and 1930s the mores and fashions of collegiate youth culture heralded the rise of a middle-class masculinity formed around consumerist desire and youthful hedonism. This, however, contrasts with historical accounts that present consumption-oriented models of masculinity as only arriving amid the economic boom of the 1950s and 1960s. Barbara Ehrenreich, for example, has been especially influential in her arguments that the traditional 'breadwinner ethos' of sober, family-based masculinity first began to crumble during the 1950s, giving way to a new 'playboy ethic' more in step with the pace and trajectory of post-war socio-economic change (Ehrenreich, 1983: 170–1). For Ehrenreich the figure of the 1950s playboy represented a new model of self-indulgent masculinity which refused to succumb to the fetters of domesticity and instead prioritized a quest for personal gratification in a sparkling world of endless leisure, luxury and lascivious indulgence (1983: 41). The preceding chapter demonstrated, however, that the distinguishing features of Ehrenreich's 'playboy ethic' had actually begun to condense long before the 1950s – existing in embryonic form in the metropolitan bachelor subcultures of the late nineteenth century and finding fuller form in the campus culture of the Jazz Age.

For some theorists the origins of the 'playboy ethic' can be traced back even further. According to Paul Hoch (1979), since antiquity the history of Western masculinity has been underwritten by a series of fluctuations between two dominant paradigms of manhood. On the one hand Hoch identifies the puritan, who is 'hard-working, hard-fighting . . . [and] who adheres to a production ethic of duty before pleasure' (1979: 118). Juxtaposed to the puritan, Hoch argues, there stands the playboy – who 'lives according to an ethic of leisure and sensual indulgence', denoted by his 'extravagances of dress, lifestyle and sexual affairs' (1979: 118). For Hoch, the oscillation between these two masculine poles has been determined by levels of economic prosperity – the rise of a playboy archetype being contingent on the existence of 'sufficient economic surplus, and a sufficient class polarization, so that the necessary wealth to pursue the life of pleasure can exist at the top of society' (1979: 118).

Hoch's broad historical brush strokes, however, dictate that his analysis lacks precision. Certainly, parallels exist between the playboy figure of the mid-twentieth century and earlier manifestations of the masculine consumer – for instance, the *flâneur* of nineteenth-century Europe, or the bachelor subcultures of the *fin de siècle* American metropolis. But Hoch's ambitious survey of over three thousand years of human history overreaches itself, leading him to identify such diverse figures as the patrician courtier of the Roman Empire and the chivalrous noble of renaissance Europe as prototype playboys. Such claims are too vague and epochal in their terms of reference, blurring across cultural forms from hugely divergent cultural and temporal contexts. Instead, a more historically grounded analysis highlights the roots of the 'playboy ethic' as lying in the consumer society that took shape at the end of the nineteenth century – the style-conscious, male consumer gradually given greater cultural definition and legitimacy during the inter-war years as he was steadily codified and courted by the institutions of the expanding commercial market.

'A MAGAZINE FOR MEN ONLY': *ESQUIRE* AND THE CODIFICATION OF MASCULINE CONSUMPTION

The mid-1920s saw the middle class, male consumer begin to come into his own – offering rich pickings to those who could successfully tap into his tastes and desires. And the partnership of David Archibald Smart and William Hobart Weintraub succeeded with aplomb. Smart (a publisher of advertising brochures) and Weintraub (an executive in clothing sales) joined forces in Chicago in 1926 to launch *The Man of Today* – a trade journal for the men's fashion industry. With minimal editorial content, *The Man of Today* functioned as a promotional catalogue for high-class clothing stores who gave complimentary copies to their charge account customers. The scheme proved hugely popular and by the end of 1928 the journal – its name quickly changed to *Gentleman's Quarterly* – had a print run of around 180,000 and was being shipped to over 200 men's clothes stores all over the country. The scale of success prompted Smart and Weintraub to follow up with the launch of additional catalogues aimed at a variety of men's clothes retailers – *The Observer, The Etonian* and (the seasonal) *Gifts for a Gentleman* featuring more formal and sophisticated attire, while *Club and Campus* catered to leisure styles and the rising college market. The aspirations of upwardly mobile male consumers, then, seemed to offer entrepreneurs like Smart and Weintraub a rosy future – although this looked like it might be cut short following the stock-market crash of October 1929.

While no historical consensus exists on the complex causes of the slump in American share prices, it seems likely that the collapse was at least partly rooted in the nature of the 1920s economic boom.[1] Increases in consumer demand had been stunning, but by the mid-1920s modest economic downturns were already suggesting the scale of growth could not be sustained indefinitely. In agriculture falling prices badly hit farmers who had financed improved productivity through heavy bank loans, while in industry large profits and the mechanization of production had encouraged manufacturers to extend their output to levels the market was increasingly unable to absorb. Confidence in the economy stumbled briefly in both 1924 and 1927, but in 1929 the Wall Street Crash announced its almost total collapse. The depression that followed was a body-blow to the consumer-oriented economy that had taken shape during the preceding decades. Between 1929 and 1933 gross national product fell in real terms by roughly 30 per cent and industrial production was nearly halved, with the consequence that nearly 13 million people were unemployed by 1933. These four years, then, saw a dramatic breakdown of consumer demand as real income fell by 36 per cent. In such a climate virtually no consumer industry survived unscathed. Those that had catered to the masculine universe of style and leisure were no exception. Between 1929 and 1933, for example, the dollar volume of sales by men's clothing retailers dropped by 49 per cent, while the number of actual stores plummeted by 40 per cent (Corbin, 1970: 340).

The Great Depression meant abject hardship and broken dreams for many. For men whose status and identity were premised on their role as breadwinner, unemployment was an especially crushing, even emasculating experience. Many came to see themselves as humiliated failures as forces beyond their control robbed them of the ability to support their families (Griswold, 1993: 46–50). It is important to remember, however, that even during the darkest days of the Depression not everyone was queuing at the soup kitchens.

The American economy was certainly on its knees during the early 1930s, but some sectors of the business world remained confident. The publishers of *Time* magazine, for example, were shaken by the stock market crash, but in February 1930 resolved to push ahead with the launch of *Fortune* – a sumptuous magazine dedicated to corporate affairs. Their optimism proved well placed and (despite its unprecedented cover price of a dollar) *Fortune's* monthly circulation rose from 34,000 to 139,000 within six years, while its advertising revenues tripled – a success that attested to the significant disposable income retained by some sections of the population. Indeed, for a lucky few, affluent high living remained a possibility and continued to represent a lucrative market for men of enterprise.

David Smart and William Weintraub were just such men. As the Depression bit into the sales of their clothes catalogues, the duo looked for money-making alternatives. In 1930 they developed a scheme in which they sold exclusive photographs of opening-night Broadway celebrities to provincial clothing stores interested in promoting local sales through the display of the glitterati's latest styles. Smart and Weintraub's venture, however, raised the hackles of competitors and the leading trade paper, *Men's Wear*, charged that many of the 'candid' photos had been deliberately staged. Nonplussed by the accusations, Smart and Weintraub drafted in the help of Arnold Gingrich (chief editor of their catalogues) and resolved to hit back by launching a trade magazine of their own. Hence the first edition of *Apparel Arts* appeared in September 1931, with an initial print run of 7,500 copies. Its style of presentation consciously modelled on *Fortune*, the new magazine was a lavish quarterly that combined high-class fashion pictorials with evocative editorial features and the occasional documentary photo spread. Popular as both a trade paper and as a catalogue for clothes retailers, *Apparel Arts* also proved a hit with store clientele – customers sometimes walking off with copies after leafing through their pages. Encouraged by this response, the Smart/Weintraub/Gingrich team discontinued (the by then ailing) *Gentleman's Quarterly* and began to envisage a magazine more squarely aimed at the store customer. Titles initially considered for the new project included *Trend*, *Beau* and *Trim*, although all these had already been copyrighted. Instead, the trio settled on an idea triggered by a letter from their attorney addressed to Arnold Gingrich Esquire.[2]

The first edition of *Esquire* magazine appeared in Autumn 1933 – a year in which a quarter of the American workforce were unemployed. Yet the popularity of *Esquire* testified to the survival of an upmarket consumer ethos among many of those who had escaped the blight of the Depression. The magazine's high production values and large, glossy, colourful format ensured a hefty cover price of fifty cents, but *Esquire* defied industry expectations and became a success almost immediately. Of the initial printrun of 105,000 copies, 100,000 were shipped to fashion retailers to be sold from their counters, the remainder going to news stands where they sold so well many of the store copies had to be re-called to replenish stock. The scale of success was overwhelming and, though originally projected as a quarterly, *Esquire* went monthly with a second edition that sold 400,000 copies, circulation soaring to more than 728,000 by the beginning of 1938 (Merrill, 1995: 45; 51).

The secret of *Esquire*'s triumph lay in the way it constructed itself as the peerless arbiter of good taste. At the editorial helm, Arnold Gingrich crafted the magazine into the premier exponent of cosmopolitan finesse. At the centre of the formula was a reverence for stylish elegance. Alongside the advertisements for high-class mens-wear, *Esquire* featured its own detailed, colour illustrations of the fashionable man in his natural habitat ('A Day at the Anglers' Club, Key Largo'; 'To Palm Beach via the French Riviera') – the sharp captions and crisp text (mostly furnished by Gingrich himself) trumpeting the latest trends in masculine attire.[3] Around this core of sartorial *savoir faire*, *Esquire* elaborated a wider universe of taste and refinement, the regular features on foreign travel, cuisine and interior decor underlining the magazine's appeal to a readership of middle class men who aspired to urbane and educated sophistication. Prominent, too, were *Esquire*'s literary pretensions, its first issue including contributions from (among others) John dos Passos, William McFee, Erskine Caldwell, Manuel Komroff and Dashiell Hammett, while subsequent editions featured bylines from a catalogue of Pulitzer and Nobel prizewinners. Regular contributions from F. Scott Fitzgerald, meanwhile, further emphasized *Esquire*'s spirit of lush opulence and its dedication to the notion of 'living as an art'.

From the outset *Esquire* made it clear that leisure-oriented consumption was at the top of its agenda. Promotional material penned by Gingrich announced the magazine as the spokesman for a 'New Leisure Class', while the premier edition included a lead feature by Nicholas Murray Butler (then president of Columbia University and a respected public figure) celebrating a dawn of 'The New Leisure' which was set to extend the 'opportunity to learn the art of living' (*Esquire*, Autumn 1933). In a similar vein *Esquire* not only accorded routine coverage to the more exclusive avenues of relaxation (golf, motoring, fishing and so on), but also included a regular 'shopping' department – 'Talking Shop With *Esquire*' – with advertisements for pipes, ties, ice-buckets and a variety of trinkets and novelties. Above all, though, it was through its attention to the pleasures of imbibing that *Esquire*'s mood of nonchalant indulgence became most tangible. The release of the magazine's second edition in December 1933 coincided with the repeal of Prohibition (a decision itself partly a consequence of federal attempts to kick-start consumer spending) and the liquor industry quickly accounted for a large portion of *Esquire*'s advertising revenue. And, just as the magazine's style coverage was virtually a seamless extension of its fashion advertising, *Esquire*'s regular features on martini etiquette and the intricacies of the highball served to augment and reinforce the interpellation of a debonair and upwardly mobile male consumer.[4]

As Tom Pendergast (2000) recognizes, *Esquire* was not the first American magazine that addressed itself to a consuming male subject. During the late nineteenth century magazines such as *McClure's*, *Munsey's* and the *Saturday Evening Post* had initially been based around the Victorian masculine ethos of hard work, thrift and production, though Pendergast argues that these titles tentatively began to embrace new models of masculinity that constructed men in terms of consumption, self-realization and personality. The first decades of the twentieth century, meanwhile, saw magazines such as *Vanity Fair* (originally launched in 1892) and *New Success* (1918) offer visions of masculinity based even more explicitly around a consumerist agenda in which men were encouraged to think of themselves 'not as objective cores of values but as . . . malleable potentialities, capable of achieving multiple expressions through the goods they purchased and the way they presented themselves' (Pendergast, 2000: 140–2). For Pendergast, the significance of *Esquire* lay in the way it successfully pulled together these earlier fragments of masculine consumerism into 'a coherent representation of a modern masculine ideal' (Pendergast, 2000: 28).

Since the nineteenth century mass-circulation magazines (other than those specifically targeted at a female market) had generally assumed a masculine readership. *Esquire*, however, was the first to acknowledge openly the gender-specific basis of its audience appeal – the magazine expressly billing itself as 'A Magazine for Men Only' (*Esquire*, Autumn 1933). Though Gingrich himself professed to have drawn inspiration from classy general-interest magazines like *Vanity Fair* and *New Yorker* (launched in 1925), in truth *Esquire's* recipe of gendered fashion, fiction and consumption-oriented features shared more in common with chic women's titles such as *Harper's Bazaar* (1867) and *Vogue* (1892).[5] To have acknowledged such parallels, however, would have fatally compromised the resolutely masculine and heterosexual universe that *Esquire* sought to generate. As we saw in the preceding chapter, masculine identities predicated on commodity consumption and a devotion to style had already begun to evolve during the early twentieth century. Yet the realms of fashion and consumption remained uncertain territory for American men. Times had certainly changed since the caricature of 'the dude' had caustically ridiculed the style-conscious male as unacceptably effete, but the fields of fashionable consumption and display continued to have markedly feminine associations. As M.M. Lebensburger observed in 1939 in his *Selling Men's Apparel Through Advertising*:

> Because women are so obviously and notoriously interested in personal appearance and style there is a feeling common among men that any demonstration of this same interest on their part is an indication of effeminacy [and] . . . an outward manifestation of distaste for style or indifference to style is, therefore considered the mark of masculinity. (cited in Merril, 1995: 32)

Esquire not only potentially jeopardized its readership's masculine self-image by venturing into fields closely associated with feminine social roles – fashion, cookery and home furnishing. The assiduous eye its style-spreads cast over the male form also risked charges of homo-eroticism. Authors such as Denise Kervin (1991) have contended that it was only in the 1980s that the male body was constructed as an erotic spectacle in fashion advertising and features. Yet, while the visual codes deployed by *Esquire* and its advertisers in the 1930s may not have fetishized the male body quite as overtly as their 1980s counterparts, the male form was nevertheless constructed as the object of a voyeuristic gaze that threatened to rupture the hetero-sexual assumptions central to dominant articulations of masculinity. Indeed, this was something that *Esquire's* editorial team were well aware of and, in creating the magazine's format, they went to great lengths to include elements that were (as Gingrich later euphemistically put it) 'substantial enough to deodorize the lavender whiff coming from the mere presence of fashion pages' (Gingrich, 1971: 81).

There always existed potential for *Esquire's* representations of the spectacle of the male body to be co-opted by a homo-erotic gaze, but Gingrich and his associates worked hard to limit the possibilities. Despite its interest in fashion and style, the first edition of the magazine made it patently clear to readers that it 'never intend[ed] to become, by any possible stretch of the imagination, a primer for fops' (*Esquire*, Autumn 1933). Instead, the publishers asserted that through their editorial judgements over content and presentation they intended to allow *Esquire* 'to take on an easy natural masculine character – to endow it, as it were, with a baritone voice' (ibid.). As Kenon Breazeale (1994: 1) astutely observes, *Esquire's* grand strategy was to 'organize a consuming male audience' – but in order to transform its readers into desiring male subjects the magazine had to maintain a status as unquestionably masculine and heterosexual. Throughout the 1930s, therefore, *Esquire* incorporated a range of 'baritone' elements in an effort to 'displace all the woman-identified associations so firmly lodged at the center of America's commodified domestic environment' (Breazeale 1994: 6).

Esquire was hardly a full-blooded advocate of the 'strenuous life'. Yet, while the magazine was always more at home in the cocktail lounge than the great outdoors, it was careful to signpost its credentials to sturdy manhood. Significantly, for example, the cover of the first edition made virtually no overt reference to matters of style or fashion. Instead, a water-colour tableau depicted two flying-suited adventurers embarking on an exciting hunting expedition, the pilots passing their gun cases and fishing gear to local guides as they stepped from the pontoons of their sea-plane to a waiting canoe. *Esquire's* sports coverage also bolstered its claims to solid manliness – with regular features on boxing and baseball complemented by articles on the daredevil challenge of big-game hunting, shark fishing and bullfighting. Rugged masculine imagery also surfaced in many of the magazine's general articles and short-stories – not least in those written by Ernest Hemingway, one of *Esquire's* most prominent contributors throughout the 1930s. Hemingway's reputation as a literary tough guy had already been well established with the publication of *The Sun Also*

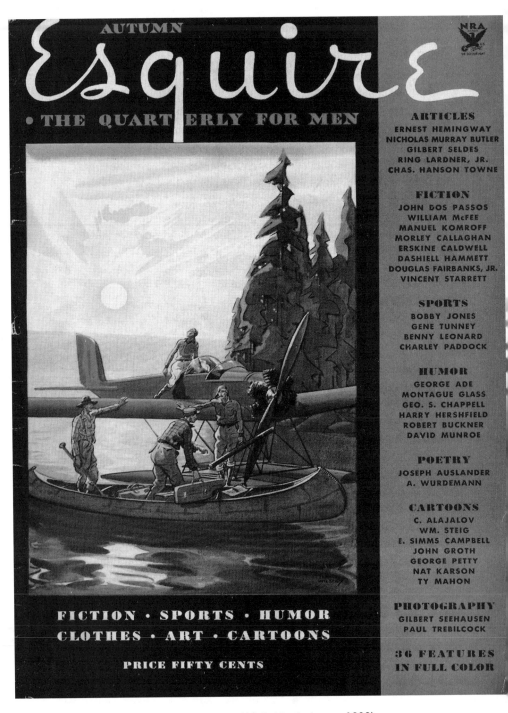

3.1 'The Magazine For Men' (*Esquire*, Vol. 1, No. 1, Autumn 1933).

Rises (1926), *A Farewell to Arms* (1929) and *Death in the Afternoon* (1932) and Gingrich was ecstatic when the author agreed to contribute to the new magazine. Hemingway's first article, 'Marlin Off the Morro' (an account of his Marlin-fishing exploits in Cuba) was proudly featured in *Esquire*'s premier edition and the author went on to contribute no less than thirty-two further pieces – including the highly regarded short story, 'The Snows of Kilimanjaro'. Indeed, Hemingway was considered such an important asset to the magazine that David Smart presented the writer with one thousand shares of *Esquire* stock in 1937 (Merril, 1995: 35).

Even more than its interest in rough-hewn machismo, it was through its treatment of women that *Esquire* marked itself out as unequivocally 'baritone'. In the pages of the magazine women were coded in two principal ways – both decidedly misogynistic. On one hand women were used as 'a foil against which a superior male taste could be posited' (Brezeale, 1994: 8). Here, regular satirical features constructed women as woefully inept in the art of good living – contributor Dick Pine, for example, laconically explaining why 'Women Can't Cook' and agitating for a 'revolt against the unholy brew prescribed by lady columnists and humorously labelled "food"' (*Esquire*, September 1939). Alongside these jibes at feminine taste, however, women were also presented as the passive objects of a sexualized male gaze. Since the late nineteenth century sexually provocative material had been produced on the margins of the American magazine industry, while *National Police Gazette* had regularly featured pin-ups of burlesque and vaudeville stars. But *Esquire*'s version of 'cheesecake' (as it was known in the industry)[6] owed more to the tradition of the 'Gibson Girl'. Originally developed in Charles Dana Gibson's drawings for *Life* and *Collier's* magazines, the Gibson Girl was an ideal of sprightly yet sensuous femininity that became a stock image in popular culture at the turn of the century. *Esquire*'s 'updated' version of the Gibson Girl appeared in the form of paintings by commercial artist George Petty. Sleekly air-brushed and coquettishly flirtatious, the 'Petty Girl' first appeared in *Esquire*'s premier edition and was included with growing frequency throughout the 1930s, Petty's drawings given added prominence from December 1939 when they began to feature as double-page fold-outs. The Petty Girl figured as the key element in a wider universe of sexually coded representations of femininity that functioned to establish heterosexuality as an incontrovertible 'given' within *Esquire*'s mode of address. With its identity firmly anchored around the co-ordinates of heterosexual masculinity, therefore, the magazine was free to court its readers as a group of unabashedly style-conscious, male consumers.

The inclusion of erotic material also allowed *Esquire* to invest a risqué sexual allure in both itself and its advertisers' products. At the same time, however, the titillating content had to be carefully negotiated if the magazine was to avoid being seen as salaciously vulgar. *Esquire* maintained its air of classy discernment partly by locating its sexual images within a 'classic' tradition of racy pictorials going back to the Gibson Girl of the 1890s, but more generally though its use of humour. *Esquire* successfully positioned itself as playfully daring rather than tastelessly lewd by creating a mood of comic revelry personified in Esky, the magazine's mascot. A diminutive but well-heeled gent with huge eyes and an enormous walrus moustache, Esky became a fixture of *Esquire's* covers throughout the 1930s, his eyes popping out farcically as he leered towards a bevy of female companions. Inside, the theme continued, with suggestive cartoons featuring voluptuous women ogled by lecherous peeping-toms, and doe-eyed belles succumbing to the charms of wolfish Lotharios. Other magazines had already carved out a niche for off-colour humour – for example, Wilford H. Fawcett's pocket-sized *Captain Billy's Whiz Bang* (launched after the First World War) and *Smokehouse Monthly* (1926), together with Dell's *Ballyhoo* (1931) – but their pitch was boorishly down market. In contrast, *Esquire* affected a wit that was roguish, yet refined. The work of talented cartoonists such as E. Simms Campbell and Howard Baer was allotted a whole page to itself (a first in the American magazine industry) and presented with a luxuriant, full-colour gloss that ensured connotations of polished sophistication.

The inclusion of 'muscular' outdoor features, 'cheesecake' pin-ups and ribald humour, therefore, served to legitimate *Esquire's* style coverage and fashion advertising as 'acceptably' masculine. But to configure itself as the trend-setting spokesman for contemporary manhood, the magazine needed a further ingredient. For this it looked to the world of youth.

America's young had been hard hit by the Depression. Young people represented 27.5 per cent of those unemployed in 1930, and by 1937 at least 3,923,000 youngsters aged fifteen to twenty-four (representing 16 per cent of the total youth population) were still out of work (Reiman, 1992: 143). The high level of unemployment among the rising generation was seen as an especially dangerous threat to American social and political stability, and as a consequence youth figured prominently in the attempts to stimulate economic recovery that followed the inauguration of President Franklin Roosevelt in 1932.[7] Roosevelt's New Deal initiatives went some way toward boosting youth employment, although many young people continued to face significant hardship. Even those from relatively well-to-do backgrounds were hard hit – this reflected in the 10 per cent decline that took place in college enrolments between 1932 and 1934 (Reiman, 1992; 59). Nevertheless, the campus peer culture that had developed in the 1920s remained buoyant, still representing an attractive market for manufacturers such as Arrow, Campus and a legion of competitors – whose advertisements still evoked an image of college life as a world of natty fashions and fraternity high-jinx.

Esquire was keen to associate itself with the vibrant and lively ideals that continued to surround campus culture throughout the Depression era. While much of the magazine's content assumed a relatively mature audience, *Esquire* also carefully cultivated a younger readership of men in their early twenties – a potentially lucrative market that attracted advertisers throughout the 1930s. *Esquire* kicked off its coverage of student style in its very first issue, with a feature spotlighting the 'elegant indolence' of undergraduates at Princeton ('the fountainhead of young men's fashions'), together with a double-page spread of college fashion that featured camel-hair polo coats, snap-brim Homburgs, polka-dot bow-ties and the full wardrobe of clothes and accessories that were 'dominant on every campus where attention to the niceties in the matter of dress is the rule rather than the exception' (*Esquire*, Autumn 1933). This attention to the finer points of student style continued with fashion spreads that appeared throughout the 1930s. Every autumn, meanwhile, *Esquire* would include a 'Going Back to School' feature previewing the latest trends for the dapper undergraduate returning to his studies – sometimes accompanied by a section on 'University Liveables', where advice was offered on all the other requisites essential to a successful academic semester (phonographs, portable radios, closet-sized refrigerators and so on).

In charting the minutiae of middle-class student style, *Esquire* not only acquired a cachet with the profitable market represented by 'Joe College'.[8] The strategy also afforded the magazine an aura of youthful dynamism.

3.2 'Initiation – nothing! I caught this worm wearing my new Hart Schaffner & Marx suit'. (Advertisement for Hart, Schaffner & Marx Suits, 1939 – courtesy of Hart Schaffner & Marx.)

Association with the world of campus culture endowed *Esquire* with connotations of high-spirited verve and allowed it to pose as the spokesman for a rising generation of young, male consumers. And, though the lean years of the Depression were not especially conducive to the growth of an ethos of hedonistic masculine consumption, neither did they present an insurmountable obstacle. Especially if the profitability of *Esquire* was a gauge – the magazine turning an annual profit of around $1.5 million by the mid-1930s and making a small fortune for its publishing team (Merril, 1995: 54).[9]

L'après-midi d'un crew haircut . . .

SHORT on hair but long on fashion is the gags-eyed undergraduate at the left, wearing a typical university model suit in Devon cord, a new fabric for country and campus wear and heir apparent to the popular Covert cloth tradition. The suit is single breasted, with three-button front, notched lapel and narrow trousers. The raincoat is of lightweight cotton with raglan shoulders, military collar and stitching at the bottom. A new shoe for both campus and country wear is the ankle high reverse calf chukka in nutting color, with crepe soles and heels. He also wears brown and white chevron wool hose, flannel shirt in brown check effect with cutaway collar and red wool tie in Paisley design. In his hand is the small shape checked tweed varsity cap. Don Juan de la Hamburger wears a Lovat green Shetland tweed jacket. Note the four-button front, revival of an old college fashion. Accessories include a white oxford button-down collar-attached shirt, worn with a striped silk crochet tie, grey flannel slacks and light brown snapbrim hat. Shoes are brown wing-tip brogues with red rubber soles and heels, the hose, district check wool.

(For answers to all dress queries, send stamped self-addressed envelope to Esquire Fashion Staff, 366 Madison Ave., N.Y.)

3.3 'L'après-midi d'un crew haircut . . .' (*Esquire*, Vol. 12, No. 3, September 1939: 154).

Esquire's publishers enjoyed their wealth and began to live out the lifestyle proselytized in their magazine. David Smart did so with particular relish, moving into a plush bachelor apartment (appointed with a huge, circular bed) and working in an opulent penthouse office where he was surrounded by chartreuse leather divans and pigskin-covered walls. Such extravagance was, of course, well beyond the reach of most middle-class, young men of the time – even the 'elegant indolents' of Princeton. Yet *Esquire's* aspirational fantasies were still important in the way they furnished upwardly mobile, male consumers with a repertoire of cultural codes and meanings – or an 'imagined identity', to use Dawson's (1991:118) term – which made intelligible their relationship with style, desire and commodity consumption. In this way *Esquire* served both to organize and to legitimate a consumption-oriented masculine self that had existed in nascent form since the beginning of the century, but which became more discernible and fully formed during the 1920s and 1930s. It was, though, only with the economic growth associated with the Second World War and its aftermath that the modern leisure styles of the hedonistic, male consumer began to assume their pivotal position within American cultural life.

'READY TO FIGHT AT THE DROP OF AN *ESQUIRE*': MASCULINITY AND SOCIAL CHANGE DURING WORLD WAR TWO

President Roosevelt's assured rhetoric carried him to re-election in 1936, but the New Deal's performance was less auspicious than its reputation. The Federal government's relief measures and pragmatic recovery programmes helped the economy stagger back to its feet, but the revival was neither strong nor sustained. Ultimately, it was only the demand generated by rearmament that restored economic confidence. The outbreak of World War Two was a vital stimulus to American economic recovery; between 1939 and 1941 the gross national product rose by roughly 30 per cent and personal consumption by a little more than 12 per cent – although full employment was not finally achieved until 1943.

The war not only served to re-energize the American economy. It's impact on social and cultural life was also tremendous.[10] In some respects the experience of wartime can be seen as allowing a return to patterns of social relation predominant before the Depression. The war, for example, saw a substantial rise in the number of marriages. This was partly prompted by the uncertainties of wartime life and the prospect of long periods of separation – but the economic revival was also important. Young people who had delayed marriages and postponed childbirth during the Depression began to establish families, contributing to a sudden surge in both the marriage and birth rates. Between 1940 and 1946 3 million more Americans married than could have been expected had marriage rates remained at pre-war levels and by 1943 the birth rate was the highest in twenty years (Mintz and Kellogg, 1988: 154). And, despite shortages of housing, food and clothing, the war was a time of relative comfort for the average American family – their income rising by 28 per cent between 1941 and 1944. Nevertheless, while the war years certainly promoted marriage and allowed for a regeneration of the nuclear family, in other respects it worked to accelerate and intensify the changes in gender identities and relations that had been underway since the beginning of the century.

During the 1930s the huge number of jobless men had discouraged employers from hiring women. The war years, however, saw millions of women recruited to replace men serving in the Forces and between 1941 and 1944 the female labour force jumped from 14.6 million to 19.4 million, while as many as one in four married women held a job outside the home by 1945. During the war itself shifts in the sexual division of labour provoked limited social anxiety – women's increased paid employment generally being accepted as a temporary response to the exceptional conditions of wartime. Yet the degree of social and economic autonomy gained by women during the war would prove difficult to reverse and in peacetime the shifting boundaries of gender roles occasioned increasing unease.

Wartime migration also dislocated the established patterns of social life. Over 15 million civilians moved during the war, intensifying long-term trends towards urbanization. Migration to centres of industrial production saw cities such as Detroit develop into enormous urban sprawls, while California's expanse of shipyards and aircraft plants brought exponential growth – state population increasing by 3.7 million during the 1940s. As millions of men and women – many of them young – were uprooted from their families and communities by military service or employment in the war industries, traditional restrictions on sexual behaviour were displaced. As a consequence, the war represented an important moment in the formation of public gay and lesbian cultures. These had existed in America since at least the 1890s, but World War Two marked 'something of a nation-wide "coming out" experience' (D'Emilio, 1983: 24) – the growth of various sex-segregated, non-familial institutions allowing greater opportunities for the development of same-sex relationships, while the 1940s saw the emergence of gay and lesbian community networks that included bars, social clubs and incipient political organizations.

Wartime migration was also a liberating experience for many heterosexuals. Movement from the stifling confines of small-town parochialism to the relative freedoms of metropolitan life dislodged many sexual constraints and promoted a universe of new erotic opportunities and representations. During the war years the birth-control movement gained official acceptance as an aid to family stability – although the wider availability of contraception was also constituent in a general easing of restraints on sexual behaviour. The social transformations wrought by the war provided an environment conducive to greater sexual liberalism and levels of pre- and extra-marital sexual activity grew as a consequence.[11] However, while a greater measure of sexual freedom was enjoyed by both men and women, sexual relations continued to be governed by an important 'double-standard' – male sexual behaviour and desires being accorded greater legitimacy, while those of women remained less acceptable and relatively taboo. Significant gender inequalities, therefore, under-pinned the 'permissiveness' of the war years, with the greatest sexual freedom extended to heterosexual men. In fact the patterns of wartime social change may have registered their greatest impact on the realm of *male* sexuality by providing a climate favourable to the development of a masculine identity in which heterosexual desire figured more prominently (indeed, was often celebrated with gusto). This was an articulation of masculinity addressed by a commercial market where the more explicit sexual objectification of women underlined the gender-based inequalities of the new sexual 'freedom'.

Developments at *Esquire* magazine were part agent and part reflection of the emergence of more libertine masculine sexual values. After reaching a peak of 728,000 at the end of 1937, *Esquire*'s circulation dipped dramatically to 453,000 by June 1938 as the magazine's novelty wore thin (Gingrich 1971: 141). In response, publisher David Smart began to take a firmer hand in *Esquire*'s editorial direction, gradually edging out Gingrich – the magazine's founding editor – who eventually retired to Switzerland in 1946. Under Smart's influence, the literary features and articles favoured by Gingrich were given less prominence and instead the 'cheese-cake' elements – the Petty Girls, gate-fold pin-ups and blue cartoons – were given greater billing. Difficulties arose, however, when George Petty demanded better terms for his work, refusing to supply *Esquire* with its regular 'Petty Girls' from mid-1940 until the beginning of 1941. Though ultimately resolved, the dispute prompted

Smart to search for an artist who could supplant Petty. In Alberto Vargas he found his alternative. Peruvian by birth, Vargas had already carved out a career as a successful illustrator and commercial artist. Impressed by Vargas' art nouveau style, Smart contracted him to work for *Esquire*, the first of Vargas' many erotic depictions of women appearing in the October 1940 issue. A shrewd operator, Smart ensured that Vargas' work appeared under the title 'The Varga Girl' – with the final 's' omitted from the artist's surname. Smart argued this made for a more resonating moniker, though the slight change in spelling also allowed *Esquire* much greater copyright control over the images.

During 1941 the work of Petty and Vargas both featured regularly in *Esquire*, but it was the 'Varga Girl' who grabbed the limelight. While there were superficial similarities between the two artists' work, the art deco streamlining of Petty's characters gave them a demure, almost ethereal, quality. The Varga Girl, in contrast, was powerfully eroticized. Drawn in warm flesh tones and depicted in strikingly seductive poses, she was voluptuously curved and buxom, anticipating an image of feminine beauty that became more fully established in American popular culture after the war – exemplified by the physique of stars such as Ava Gardner, Marilyn Monroe and Jane Russell. An immediate hit, the Varga Girl played a big part in *Esquire*'s revival, Vargas' work prominently featured not only in the magazine's promotional material but also in its merchandising. Rushed out in time for Christmas 1940, *Esquire*'s 'Varga Girl Calendar' sold 325,000 copies at a quarter each and was followed by the release of 'Varga' playing cards and date books – their success prompting the launch of Esquire Buy-Products as the magazine's merchandising subsidiary (Merril, 1995: 93). But it was not just the Varga Girl that gave *Esquire* magazine a new lease of life. The war also played an important role.

During the 1940s American news-stands were graced by a growing number of sexually oriented pin-up magazines. Publishers such as Robert Harrison (more famous during the 1950s as the reviled owner of Hollywood scandal-sheet, *Confidential*) began to garner profits from titles such as *Beauty Parade* (launched in 1941), *Eyeful* (1943) and *Wink* (1945) – magazines that evoked a burlesque tradition through their garishly coloured, suggestive covers and their combination of light-hearted editorial and revealing pictures of showgirls and models. Pin-up magazines prospered during wartime partly as a consequence of the general loosening of sexual morality and partly as a result of the burgeoning market for such material among the growing ranks of servicemen. In the belief that pin-up magazines were healthy for troops' morale, the US military endorsed their circulation, even creating its own publication – *Yank* – which included regular (although fairly restrained) pin-up features. Uncle Sam also gave his support to *Esquire*. Always ready to exploit an opportunity, David Smart persuaded army top brass that *Esquire* could play a strategic role in the war effort and – alongside *Reader's Digest* and *Life* – his magazine was accorded privileges as a publication vital to the fortitude of GI morale. On the back of the military market *Esquire* flourished. By 1943 the magazine's circulation had climbed back to more than 600,000, with servicemen accounting for 69,000 subscriptions while a further 30,000 copies were sold to post exchanges for distribution to army bases in Europe. Additionally, 100,000 issues of a special, 'military' edition of *Esquire* (printed without advertising) were distributed free to troops (Merril, 1995: 93).

The military market was also big business for Esquire Buy-Products. Of the 300,000 copies of the 1943 'Varga Girl Calendar' sold by mail-order, 49 per cent were shipped to servicemen (Merril, 1995: 93). The Varga Girl herself became a phenomenon among American forces – Vargas' artwork not only adorning barrack-room walls but also figuring in the 'nose art' decorating the fuselage of many American fighter-planes and bombers.[12] Indeed, in some senses the Varga Girl (and *Esquire's* wider universe of prosperous good living) represented for many servicemen the ideals they were fighting for – not simply the virtues of democracy, but also the comforts and pleasures of modern consumerism.[13] In these terms, then, there was a modicum of truth to comedian Bob Hope's wartime quip that 'Our American troops are ready to fight at the drop of an *Esquire*' (cited in Merril, 1995: 93).

Despite its journey deeper into the world of 'cheesecake', *Esquire* also maintained its commitment to sartorial panache. In 1942 the rigours of war were beginning to register in the field of men's fashions as the War Production Board introduced restrictions on fabric usage. Men's suits were forbidden from including an extra pair of trousers, shorter jackets and narrow lapels were encouraged and dinner-jackets could only be single-breasted. But *Esquire* put a brave face on the situation, arguing that government restrictions were actually in line with the styles of the day – fewer fancy details, narrow trousers and less elaborate evening wear. The magazine also applauded the growing military influence on men's fashion as battle jackets with flap pockets came into vogue and the bush jacket made a comeback. *Esquire*, then, put its shoulder patriotically behind the war effort, but the magazine also maintained its bid for adventurous nonconformity. This it achieved partly through cultivating a relationship with the 'otherness' of jazz.

Esquire was always pitched fairly exclusively at a white readership. By giving laudatory coverage to black jazz musicians, however, it gleaned kudos as a magazine with its finger on the pulse of a buzzing, creative 'underground'. During the 1940s American popular music was largely dominated by (white) big band swing, but *Esquire* eschewed the likes of Glenn Miller and Tommy Dorsey in favour of what it presented as the more 'authentic' sounds of New Orleans jazz – thereby securing a reputation as both intellectually informed and daringly left field. *Esquire's* attention to jazz had begun as early as 1934, but picked up pace during the early 1940s as Gingrich developed a passion for the music. In 1943 the editor hit upon the idea of imitating the *Collier's* magazine gimmick of annually selecting a star-studded 'All-American Football Team'. But Gingrich's version had a twist – *Esquire* would pick an 'All-American Band' drawn from the ranks of the country's premier jazz players.

The magazine's first jazz poll (conducted among a panel of *Esquire* aficionados) appeared in 1944, the winners including Louis Armstrong, Billie Holliday, Artie Shaw and a retinue of jazz luminaries who received their 'Esky' Awards at a gala reception held in New York's Metropolitan Opera House. For the next three years *Esquire* remained virtually the only mainstream American magazine promoting jazz and, in 1947, added to its regular coverage with the publication of an annual *Esquire Jazz Book* featuring articles, discographies and biographies of its poll winners.[14]

Esquire's reverence for black jazz musicianship belied the intensification of racial tensions during the war. Government moves against segregation gradually opened up opportunities for African Americans in both industry and the military, but inequality remained pronounced. In the south Jim Crow remained alive and well, while in the north and west many employers discriminated against African- and Mexican American workers. Racial hostility erupted into violent confrontation on numerous occasions. The summer of 1943 saw particular violence as racial friction sparked disorders in Detroit and New York, while Los Angeles witnessed a series of racist attacks that the press dubbed 'zoot suit riots'.

Zoot suits – flamboyant outfits featuring broad, tapered jackets and pleated, baggy trousers, tight at the ankle and sometimes accompanied by a wide-brimmed hat and gold watch chain – had been sported by young Mexican Americans (as well as some black and a scattering of poor white youths) in several American cities since the beginning of the 1940s. The style was loaded with cultural meaning. Zoot suits were a badge of defiance for socially and economically marginalized youths who 'refused to concede to the manners of subservience' (Cosgrove, 1984: 78). In donning the zoot suit, groups of subordinate youth appropriated the symbolic language of affluent display formerly the exclusive province of wealthy whites. The zoot suit, therefore, represented a flagrant challenge to dominant expectations – its swaggering show of conspicuous consumption raising an insolent middle finger to assumptions that members of a subordinate group should necessarily exhibit that subordination through their appearance. Nor was this gesture of resistance lost on white society. While conspicuous consumerism was gradually establishing its acceptability within the white middle class, black displays of hedonistic materialism were recognized as a flagrant challenge to the social order. Hence the brazenness of the zoot suit roused particular enmity among working-class whites who were affronted by the flaunting of ostentatious consumption by those they regarded as social inferiors. With the introduction of wartime clothing restrictions, the zoot suit incited particular bitterness – its rebellious connotations exacerbated by (in white eyes) an outrageous lack of regard for the war effort. In June 1943 white anger boiled over. For over a week gangs of off-duty servicemen roamed the streets of Los Angeles assaulting zoot-suited Mexican Americans. The youths were brutally beaten and ritually striped of their garb in a series of attacks that spread throughout California, similar incidents being reported from as far afield as Detroit, New York and Philadelphia.[15]

The sensational news coverage surrounding the 'zoot suit riots' also fed into a wider climate of anxiety about youth culture. Between the wars youth culture had often been admired as the exciting herald to a prosperous future. During the 1940s, however, youth was increasingly vilified as the deplorable evidence of social decay. Working-class youth was the main target, the media running lurid stories about the violence of urban street gangs – official statistics seeming to confirm an epidemic of juvenile lawlessness. Young women's sexual behaviour also occasioned unease, fears cohering around 'Victory-' or 'V-girls' – young women whose 'free and easy' liaisons with servicemen were interpreted as evidence of a breakdown in national morality. Contemporary diagnoses of these problems stressed the social disturbance of wartime – absent fathers and (especially) working mothers cited as undermining the family structures central to social cohesion. But while wartime conditions certainly disrupted patterns of family life – with, for example, an 11 per cent increase in the divorce rate (Adams, 1994: 123) – there was no clear link between these changes and the rising indices of delinquency. In fact, statistical data suggesting an explosion in delinquency was, itself, dubious. Anticipated and watched for by expectant social agencies, the wartime 'rise' in juvenile crime was duly identified – a classic example of self-fulfilling prophecy. Indeed, in 1944 a Senate sub-committee investigating the causes of delinquency concluded that, although juvenile crime was a serious issue, there was little hard evidence of a wartime escalation (Gilbert, 1986: 36).

What had changed, though, was young people's spending power. The labour demands of the wartime economy drew more young people into the workforce, partially reversing trends towards extended schooling and dependency on parents. In 1944, Census Bureau statistics indicated that over two in five young men aged between sixteen and seventeen were gainfully employed – 35 per cent of these having left school altogether to enter full-time work (Modell, 1989: 165-6). As a consequence, greater disposable income was delivered into young hands. By 1944 American youth was believed to account for a spending power of around $750 million, much of it discretionary (Adams, 1994: 127). This economic muscle not only helped crystallize notions of young people as possessing unprecedented cultural autonomy but also provided the basis for a significant expansion of the commercial youth market which (as we shall see in Chapter 5) continued apace after 1945, feeding into shifting patterns of gender relations and influencing the wider development of lifestyles based around hedonistic modes of commodity consumption.

*

Middle class models of pleasure-oriented masculine consumption did not wither away during the Depression. If anything, the 1930s saw a growing acceptance of men as stylish consumers. The 1920s image of the flamboyant gangster had been tarnished by its criminal associations, while there was always something unsettling about Jay Gatsby's fixation with the superficial accoutrements of success. During the 1930s, however, masculine archetypes more at ease with consumerism and an ethos of pleasure gradually came to the fore. Indicative was *Esquire* magazine's codification of a chic and insouciant masculine consumer. Allied with the developing culture of campus youth, this inter-war version of the 'playboy ethic' accrued connotations of dynamism and modernity and won a significant cultural foothold for practices of self-conscious masculine consumption.

The wartime acceleration of social and cultural change, however, prompted anxiety within the more conservative elements of the dominant order. Trends towards sexual liberalism were especially disconcerting and were subject to particular opprobrium as traditional bourgeois culture struggled to maintain its hegemony. Before the war, obscenity laws and the media's practices of self-censorship had begun to relax. But during the early 1940s a rearguard action was fought on behalf of traditional morality by the American Postmaster General – Frank C. Walker. Prompted by local protest groups, Walker began to deny discount (second-class) postal rates to dozens of detective, adventure and 'pin-up' magazines that he deemed obscene.[16] Initially his efforts focused on pulp titles geared to working-class readers, but he soon set his sights on *Esquire*. From January 1941 each issue had to be submitted to the Post Office for approval – *Esquire*'s editorial team making changes to anything deemed unacceptable. But in 1943 Walker stepped up his crusade. Arguing that *Esquire* included material of an 'obscene, lewd and lascivious character', Walker threatened to withdraw the magazine's postage concessions. With the loss of reduced postal rates *Esquire*'s prospects for financial survival would have been bleak, and so the magazine strenuously resisted the cancellation. Initial Postal Board hearings found in favour of the magazine, but the decision was overruled by Walker – the imperious Postmaster pushing ahead with the revoking of *Esquire*'s mailing privileges. A series of appeals saw the legal battle drag on for three more years, ultimately reaching the US Supreme Court in 1946. Here, a unanimous decision finally vindicated *Esquire* and ruled as unconstitutional any attempt by the Post Office to exercise powers of censorship.

The protracted legal case gave *Esquire* a mountain of publicity, while the Supreme Court's ruling limited federal powers to control the tide of 'cheesecake' magazines that flooded onto the market during the 1950s. The significance of the case, however, went further than this, indicating a broader set of social trans-formations. Postmaster General Walker can be seen as the figurehead of a traditional bourgeois morality striving to maintain its authority in a period of cultural flux. Growing up in Montana, Walker came from working-class stock, though had made his fortune in a variety of business ventures and during the 1920s emerged as one of Roosevelt's closest advisors. An ardent and influential Roman Catholic, Walker was not only one of Roosevelt's wealthiest confidants, he was also one of the most conservative. To a man like Walker, therefore, *Esquire*'s ethos of hedonism and sexual licence was anathema. The magazine's world of consumer desires and sensual pleasures starkly contrasted with traditional bourgeois notions of manhood rooted in hard work and moral self-discipline – and this contradiction accounted, at least partly, for Walker's fervent campaign.

The codes of hedonistic masculinity espoused by *Esquire* broke away from traditional bourgeois value systems, but this did not amount to a radical transgression. Rooted in the values of free-market capitalism, and to a large part premised on the sexual objectification of women, the axioms of masculine consumerism sought to adapt rather than overturn the existing social order. Yet the ethics of personal gratification and hedonistic consumption still represented an important challenge to traditional middle-class sensibilities. The conflict between the two sets of cultural ideals would reverberate for decades to come, but after 1945 the young, style-conscious male consumer gradually gained the upper hand as a reinvigorated American economy laid the foundation for the rise of a middle-class culture more fully oriented around the pleasures and desires of commodity consumption.

NOTES

1   For summaries of the relationship between patterns of economic growth in the 1920s and the subsequent depression see McElvaine (1993: 25–50) and Potter (1974: 59–89).

2   Accounts of the early history of *Esquire* magazine can be found in Gingrich (1971), Merrill (1995) and Peterson (1956: 260–5).

3   An illustrated survey of *Esquire*'s fashion features during the 1930s and 1940s is provided in Hochswender and Gross (1993).

4   Alongside its monthly tips on the essentials of good barmanship, the late 1930s also saw the publication of *Esquire's Liquor Intelligence* – the magazine's first manual offering readers guidance on 'how to drink like a gentleman and know it'.

5   Indeed, these similarities were not lost on contemporary commentators. A few years after *Esquire* first appeared, for example, *Time* magazine suggested it could be considered 'Vogue for men' (*Time*, 4 September 1939).

6   The term 'cheesecake' entered the lexicon of American slang in roughly 1915 as a term denoting mass-produced and publicly acceptable 'pin-up' images of semi-nude women. Accessible – although disconcertingly celebratory – histories of the genre are provided by Gabor (1985; 1996).

7   The National Youth Agency, launched in 1935, spearheaded New Deal programmes geared to generating youth employment.

8   The term 'Joe College' was increasingly used during the inter-war period as a euphemism for the average, male undergraduate.

9 *Esquire*'s success prompted imitations from rival publishers. In 1937, for example, Fawcett launched *For Men*, a pocket-sized magazine pitched at a market of middle class males. Heavy on text, however, it lacked the lively pizzazz of *Esquire*. Closer to *Esquire*'s brand of glossy fashion and opulent leisure was *Bachelor*, also launched in 1937. However, while *Bachelor* claimed it was 'mirroring the varied interests of the discerning cosmopolite [*sic*]' (April 1937), it eschewed most of the 'baritone' elements with which *Esquire* secured its heterosexual status. Much more open in its homo-erotic coding, *Bachelor* can be seen as an early (though short-lived) attempt to tap into the gay consumer market.

10 Overviews of the impact of World War Two on the American home front include Adams (1994), Jeffries (1997) and Winkler (1986).

11 For a survey of the impact of World War Two on sexual behaviour in the United States see D'Emilio and Freedman (1997: 260–1, 288–9).

12 An illustrated history of World War Two American aircraft 'nose art' – including many Vargas-inspired designs – can be found in Valant (1987).

13 More generally, Adams suggests that commercial interests often constructed the war as a struggle to defend the free market – the ideological significance of the war becoming vulgarized as American business 'identified the Axis as enemies primarily of free enterprise and equated victory with the renewal of consumer choice' (Adams, 1994: 130).

14 The same year, however, saw *Esquire*'s reputation as the authoritative champion of American jazz seriously blemished. In 1947 the organization of the poll had been handed to Ernest Anderson (publicist for Eddie Condon, a guitarist associated with white jazz players) and under his aegis the ranks of award winners were dominated by white musicians. As a consequence a group of thirty-three previous 'Esky' winners protested to the editors and the magazine was sued by one of its own jazz experts who had been barred from involvement in the poll. *Esquire* settled out of court and the jazz poll never took place again. See Merril (1995: 121–2).

15 Full accounts of the history and significance of the wartime 'zoot suit riots' are provided in Cosgrove (1984), Escobar (1996) and Mazón (1984).

16 The Postal Act of 1879 allowed lower postal rates for the mailing of publications, but gave the Post Office the power to deny these privileges to material judged obscene. This was a clause that Frank Walker applied with zealous frequency. Appointed as Postmaster General in 1940, within his first two years of office he had cited twenty-three magazines as obscene and denied mailing privileges to sixty-two publications. See Merril (1995: 106).

Chapter 4
'People of Plenty': Constructions of Masculinity in the Promised Land

What has happened to the American male? For a long time, he seemed utterly confident in his manhood, sure of his masculine role in society, easy and definite in his sense of sexual identity. The frontiersmen of James Fenimore Cooper, for example, never had any concern about masculinity; they were men, and it did not occur to them to think twice about it . . . [But] by mid-century, the male role had plainly lost its rugged clarity of outline. Today men are more and more conscious of maleness not as a fact but as a problem . . . The recovery of identity means, first of all, a new belief in apartness. It means a determination to resist the over-powering conspiracy of blandness, which seeks to conceal all tension and conflict in American life under a blanket of locker-room affability. . . . The achievement of identity, the conquest of a sense of self – these will do more to restore American masculinity than all the hormones in the test tubes of our scientists.

Arthur Schlesinger Jr., 'The Crisis in American Masculinity', in *The Politics of Hope* (London: Eyre and Spottiswoode, 1962: 237–46, originally published in *Esquire*, November 1958).

'THE BEST YEARS OF OUR LIVES'?: CONFLICT AND CONTRADICTION IN POSTWAR AMERICA

Released in 1946, *The Best Years of Our Lives* is often regarded as a film that captures the buoyant hopes of American society after World War Two. Both critically acclaimed and commercially successful, the film focuses on the lives of returning servicemen and their families – a generation of Americans looking forward to their 'best years' in a new era of peace and prosperity. The film's up-beat title and happy resolution, however, belie the turbulence at the heart of its narrative, the veterans facing pain and trauma as they adjust to the shifting social and cultural terrain of the postwar world. This contrast between the film's veneer of positive optimism and the inner turmoil of its characters can be seen as symbolic of the wider tensions in American society after 1945. Beneath a patina of assured confidence, postwar America was shot through with uncertainty, stress and discord. Indeed, contrary to popular perceptions of the late 1940s and fifties as a time of stability and cohesion, recent historiography suggests the period is better understood as 'an era of conflict and contradiction, an era in which a complex set of ideologies contended for public allegiance' (Biskind, 1983: 4).[1]

As we have already seen, processes of flux and fragmentation have been endemic to the history of American public and private life. After World War Two, however, the US entered a period of especially profound social upheaval. The global tensions of the Cold War, the resurgence of domestic consumption, changes in gender roles and the gradual emergence of civil rights activism and other movements of popular protest all contributed to a climate of apprehension. As in previous periods of intense transformation, the sense of generalized uncertainty found coherence around specific objects of concern. Disquiet particularly focused on issues of sexuality and gender identity. As Jeffrey Weeks (1985: 44; 1989: 254) argues perceptively, debates about sexuality and gender invariably possess an important symbolic dimension. Touching on crucial social boundaries and provoking intimate questions about personal identity, these issues often condense wider concerns about the nature and pace of social transformation. This was especially evident in postwar America where anxieties about the general climate of social change were given acute focus in debates surrounding sexual behaviour and the changing character of gender relations.

'AMERICA'S GREATEST ASSET': THE FAMILY, CONSUMERISM AND SUBURBAN 'CONTAINMENT'

Though popularly regarded as a model of 'traditional' domestic life, the nuclear family of the 1950s was an historical anomaly. During the mid-century years Americans married younger, divorced less often and had more children than ever before (or than they would in future decades). By 1956 the median age for first marriage had slipped to a record low of twenty-two for men and twenty for women (compared to medians of twenty-four for men and just over twenty-one for women in 1940). The divorce rate also declined. During the 1930s it had been relatively low, at around 10 divorces per 1,000 marriages, though rose steeply to 24 per 1,000 in 1946, but then fell to 15 per 1,000 in the mid-1950s. The wartime baby boom, meanwhile, continued apace – the birth rate rising from 19.4 to 26.6 per 1,000 of population between 1940 and 1947 and hovering at around 24 per 1,000 throughout the 1950s (Bremner, 1982: 28). Demographic indices, therefore, attest to the postwar era as being the high-water mark in the history of family life, young Americans turning to marriage and parenthood with apparent enthusiasm.[2]

The postwar vitality of the nuclear family was indebted to several factors. For many people, keen to leave behind the hardships of the Depression and the disruptions of wartime, marriage seemed to promise happy fulfilment. Moreover, against an unsettling background of rapid social change and the looming threat of nuclear war, many men and women eagerly embraced marriage and parenthood as 'a source of meaning and security in a world run amok' (May, 1999: 18). Domesticity, then, undoubtedly had its attractions and was not simply imposed from 'above' on a hapless population. At the same time, however, the postwar reaffirmation of family life was charged with ideological significance.

The ascendance of the nuclear family after 1945 was closely bound up with the wider political culture of the era. The end of the war was followed by a new sense of crisis and uncertainty, the optimism of peace quickly overshadowed by the Cold War and the possibility of nuclear destruction. Social life was also plagued by doubts and anxieties as wartime disquiet about sexual morality was reignited.[3] Already manifest by the late 1940s, popular concern about changing sexual values and gender roles were further intensified by the publication, in 1949 and 1953, of Alfred Kinsey's reports into the sexual behaviour of men and women. The Kinsey reports had a seismic impact on American culture.[4] Thrusting sex into the forefront of the national consciousness, Kinsey pointed to a vast, clandestine world of sexual experience sharply at odds with publicly espoused norms of probity, fidelity and heterosexuality. Kinsey's revelations further stoked existing perceptions of impending sexual chaos, these anxieties steadily fusing with fears of communist expansionism and domestic subversion to form an atmosphere of insecurity and suspicion that dominated the American cultural landscape throughout the postwar era. It was in this context, then, that foreign policies geared to the 'containment' of communist influence in Europe and Asia found their parallel in the domestic arena. During the Cold War America's cultural agenda became infused by paradigms of containment – literature, cinema and the spectrum of popular culture deploying narratives that 'functioned to foreclose dissent, preempt dialogue, and preclude contradiction' (Nadel, 1995: 14).

At the heart of these ideologies of containment stood the image of the prosperous, middle-class family. In her comprehensive study of postwar domesticity, Elaine Tyler May (1999) contends that family life was configured as a vision of reassuring certainty in an unpredictable and threatening world. As the superpowers squared up, pressures for social stability intensified and nonconformity – whether in political, cultural or sexual terms – was increasingly perceived as a threat to American security. Amid this ambience of anxiety and distrust, May argues, strategies of 'domestic containment' promoted marriage and home-making as fundamental to the strength and vitality of democratic life – and deviation form these norms risked charges of abnormality, even deviance (May, 1995: 127–34, 1999: xxv, 82).

Representations of contented family life were ubiquitous in American culture during the Cold War. Academics, politicians and the mass media all championed the family as both the cornerstone of American liberty and as a panacea to the perceived social and sexual dangers of the day. In magazines like *Life*, depictions of the middle-class family embodied a confident sense of national identity, while television series such as *Ozzie and Harriet* (1952–66), *Father Knows Best* (1954–63) and *Leave It to Beaver* (1957–63) all presented an idealized family life of cheerful tranquillity.[5] Professionals were also conspicuous in their enthusiasm for the family. In 1948 a conference of representatives from over a hundred national organizations met in Washington, taking as their theme 'The Family – America's Greatest Asset', while in the sphere of social science the arch-functionalist Talcott Parsons proclaimed the nuclear family the mainstay of stability in modern societies (Parsons, 1949; 1955). The proliferation of nuclear family life, meanwhile, was effectively underwritten by federal government through the provision of a host of financial incentives – from tax exemptions for dependent children to subsidies for suburban home ownership (Coontz, 1992: 76–7; May 1995: 137–8).

The green-lawned environs of suburbia gave spatial manifestation to ideologies of containment. After 1945 demand from dislocated war workers and returning service-men intensified the wartime housing shortage and spurred a vast new construction programme. Billions of government dollars were pumped into mortgage loan schemes managed by the Veteran Administration (VA) and the Federal Housing Administration (FHA), while new building methods (especially the techniques of mass-produced prefabrication pioneered by developers such as William Levitt) allowed for a surge in housing construction to meet pent-up demand. Growth was concentrated in sub-urbia. Of the 13 million new homes completed between 1948 and 1958, 85 per cent were built in the suburbs, so that by 1960 suburbia was home to as many Americans as the central cities.[6] The suburbs' significance, however, went beyond simple demographics. It was, for example, no accident that the centrepiece of the American National Exhibition in Moscow during 1959 was a life-size model of a six-room ranch-house stocked full of American consumer goods. As Vice President Richard Nixon and Nikita Khrushchev toured the exhibit, Nixon lectured the Soviet Premier on how the social order in the US approached perfection, insisting that 'American superiority in the Cold War rested not on weapons, but on the secure, abundant family life of modern suburban homes' (May, 1999: 12). Indeed, the 'ranch-style' architecture of the suburbs was, itself, a monument to American prosperity. Echoing the open-plan layouts developed earlier in the century by Frank Lloyd Wright, the postwar 'ranch-house' brought together the family in a setting that combined the certainties of traditionalism with all the comforts of modern consumerism. Suburbia, then, possessed powerful symbolic connotations during the Cold War. A comfortable and reassuring universe of station wagons, backyard barbecues and Little League ball games, the suburban vision represented a powerful affirmation of the vitality and virtue of American free-market capitalism.[7]

Indeed, for millions of people, the phenomenal success of America's postwar economy actually did bring unprecedented affluence. Increases in wartime production laid the groundwork for a staggering postwar boom – overseas exports doubling in value between 1945 and 1957 and gross national product soaring by 250 per cent between 1945 and 1960. The escalation of military spending during the Korean War was partly responsible for pushing the economy forward, the Defense Department budget leaping from $14.3 billion to $49.3 billion between 1950 and 1953 (Jezer, 1982: 119). Also vital, however, was the massive growth in consumer demand. With the cessation of hostilities, wartime savings provided the initial fuel for a postwar buying spree that was sustained across two decades by a steady growth in national purchasing power.[8] In the fifteen years after 1945 (itself a boom year) per capita income grew by 35 per cent and, by 1960, 31 million of the nation's 44 million families owned their own home, 87 per cent had a television and 75 per cent possessed a car (Coontz, 1992: 24–5). America had become a fully fledged consumer society.

But not everyone had a stake in the good life. The FHA's exclusionary zoning and 'redlining' policies kept suburban enclaves racially segregated so that the suburban idyll was essentially a phenomenon of white America. Moreover, disparities of wealth and income remained pronounced and throughout the postwar era millions of Americans continued to live in poverty.[9] By the end of the 1960s the persistence of inequality had become glaringly apparent amid a tumult of social and political conflict – but during the 1950s the scale of growth gave credence to notions of a whole nation bathing in the glow of affluent abundance. Indeed, during the Cold War, mythologies of prosperous consumption figured as one of the most powerful warheads in America's ideological stockpile.

Richard Nixon was not alone in deploying domestic consumption as evidence of American capitalism's global superiority. In 1954 David Potter presented Americans as a 'People of Plenty' whose access to economic abundance had afforded them 'a capacity for independent decision and self-reliant conduct' – Potter contrasting this (perhaps with a sidelong glance at the Soviets) to the traits of 'submissiveness, obedience and deference' he saw as characteristic of 'the economy of scarcity' (Potter, 1954: 204–5). Above all, however, it was W.W. Rostow who gave scholastic kudos to the ideological discourse surrounding America's consumer affluence. Widely regarded as America's leading theoretician of modernization, Rostow had completed work on his 'Non-Communist Manifesto' just four months before Nixon delivered his 'kitchen debate' homilies. In *The Stages of Economic Growth* (1960), Rostow offered a blueprint of economic development consciously modelled as an alternative to Marxist hypotheses. According to Rostow, economic growth could be conceived as a progression through key historical stages culminating in an 'Age of High Mass-Consumption' – the point at which societies could reap the fruits of economic maturity through the mass availability of consumer goods. Rostow recognized that the Soviet Union was a mature economy, but argued that its political system precluded progression into the final furlong of development. The US, on the other hand, had blazed a trail into the ultimate phase of growth and could confidently stand as a model for the developing world.[10] In Cold War America, therefore, consumption became a totem of modernity and progress – the US posing as a promised land where the mechanics of economic prosperity had been successfully combined with the institutions of democratic freedom.

Within this discourse, the suburban family was promoted as consumer capit-alism's brightest beacon. Indeed, in 1954 it seemed only natural that *Life's* special issue on US growth should spotlight 'The Boom Time Family Picture' – the magazine profiling five average families, all with rising incomes that had allowed 'the purchase during the year of some luxury, something beyond ordinary needs which helped make 1953 for most of them, as for the rest of the US, the best economic year of their lives' (*Life*, 4 January 1954).[11] The affluent, suburban home and family-centred consumption, therefore, came to define the virtues of the American Way. Yet the values of family consumption were still solidly rooted in a traditional ethos of rationality and rectitude. Rather than being geared to hedonistic or indulgent desires, the goods purchased by the middle-class family – a modern refrigerator or a gleaming station wagon – fostered more conservative values, reinforcing home life and upholding traditional gender roles (May, 1999: 148).

The 1950s ideal of suburban domesticity powerfully rearticulated notions of the 'companionate family' that had first surfaced at the beginning of the century. Just as the original 'companionate' model had advocated mutual involvement in domestic life, the 1950s ideal ascribed 'complementary' gender roles within the family. Social scientists like Parsons, for example, argued that the ideal family structure exhibited a measure of equality between husbands and wives, though with a distinct division of labour in which 'the man takes the more instrumental role, the woman the more expressive' (Parsons, 1955: 23). Parson's view was matched by popular depictions of the American family. In May 1954, for example, the editors of *McCall's* magazine coined the term 'togetherness' to denote a modern style of emotionally satisfying family life oriented around the home, and throughout the 1950s 'togetherness' became a byword for a family ideal of shared parental responsibilities – though with men and women fulfilling differently prescribed marital roles (Weiss, 2000: 115–39).

For women, this role was firmly located in the home. Though accepted as a wartime necessity, women's increased participation in the labour force was viewed with growing ambivalence. Women's greater sexual independence, meanwhile, was often interpreted as a challenge to traditional gender roles. Peacetime, therefore, saw pervasive moves to promote an ideology of femininity rooted in marriage and family life. A battery of popular texts and academic opinion (especially within the emerging sphere of child development) combined to advocate the role of housewife and mother as natural and fulfilling. In Hollywood the representations of emancipated and glamorous women, conspicuous during the 1930s (and exemplified in the persona of Mae West), gave way to more homely and submissive constructions of femininity (May, 1999: 33–4, 56–7). A more vitriolic attack on female autonomy, meanwhile, registered in the fields of psychology and psychiatry. Ferdinand Lundberg and Marynia Farnham's 1947 best seller, *The Modern Woman: The Lost Sex*, was especially venomous. According to Lundberg and Farnham, the *raison d'être* of female sexuality was 'receptivity and passiveness, a willingness to accept dependence without fear or resentment, with a deep inwardness and readiness for the final goal of sexual life – impregnation', and those who failed to conform to this ideal were pathologized as 'the array of the sick, unhappy, [and] neurotic, [who are] wholly or partly incapable of dealing with life' (Lundberg and Farnham, 1947: 237). Nor were these views safely confined to the pages of pseudo-scientific potboilers. Carol Warren (1987) shows how refusal or inability to adjust to the homemaker role could result in women being labelled neurotic or schizophrenic – a diagnosis which sometimes led to electro-shock therapy or institutionalization.

The ideal of prosperous family life was, therefore, central to the exercise of 'domestic containment' during the Cold War. Images of affluent suburbia were pivotal to the ideological strategies through which American capitalism asserted its claims to economic and moral supremacy, while the promotion of family-oriented gender roles sought to reign-in and safely corral the cultural changes perceived as threatening the social order. For women this meant conformity to an ideal of home-making domesticity. But men were also objects of containment – the dominant ideal of domestic femininity finding its counterpart in an equally powerful ideology of family-oriented masculinity.

The ordeal of the 1930s Depression had shaken the breadwinner ethic, but after 1945 its status was restored. As the provider of the affluent family life central to America's Cold War ideological arsenal, the breadwinner archetype was promoted with as much vehemence as the feminine home-maker. In the social sciences Morris Zelditch toed the functionalist line, emphasizing the importance of the nuclear family and its demarcated gender roles in his argument that 'the American male, by definition, must "provide" for his family . . . His primary area of performance is the occupational role, in which his status fundamentally inheres; and his primary function in the family is to supply an "income", to be the "breadwinner"' (Zelditch, 1955: 339). Lundberg and Farnham also waded in with a characteristically scathing critique of men who refused to conform to this ideal – the bilious psychologists arguing that not only should 'bachelors of more than thirty, unless physically deficient, . . . be encouraged to undergo psychotherapy', but that they should also 'be subjected to differential tax rates so that they at least might enjoy no economic advantage over married men and fathers' (Lundberg and Farnham, 1947: 370–1). This suspicion of bachelors and vigorous affirmation of fatherhood was, at least partly, informed by contemporary fears surrounding homosexuality – gay men figuring prominently in the McCarthyite demonology of spectres threatening national security.[12] Indeed, as Ehrernreich observes, in both the psychiatric literature and popular culture of the period 'the image of the irresponsible male blurred into the shadowy figure of the homosexual' (1983: 24).

Intrinsic to the postwar renaissance of the breadwinner was a renewed emphasis on the ideals of 'masculine domesticity'. In 1954 *Life* announced the arrival of 'the new American domesticated male', with fathers taking on new responsibilities as 'baby tender, dish-washer, cook, [and] repairman' – the magazine averring that 'probably not since pioneer days . . . have men been so personally involved in their homes' (*Life*, 4 January 1954). In its celebration of family 'togetherness', meanwhile, *McCall's* enthused that the old-fashioned father – the 'disciplinarian and bogeyman' – had been 'pretty well replaced by the father who's pal and participator', the magazine featuring a model of 'a modern American husband and father' who devoted himself to making a home for his wife and children (*McCall's*, May 1954). Celebrated in popular texts such as *Ozzie and Harriet and Father Knows Best*, the domesticated male was also enshrined in new, family-oriented pastimes and practices. Most obvious was the rise of the weekend barbecue as a national institution. Presided over by Dad, the barbecue was an arena where men could act out their role as beneficent family figurehead, exhibiting a domestic proficiency that was safely reconciled with their sense of masculine self – because the barbecue took place in the 'great outdoors', whereas the kitchen remained clearly designated as a space for Mom (Levenstein, 1993: 132).

The postwar ideal of participatory fatherhood, therefore, possessed considerable currency. As the affluent, suburban family was configured as the backbone to American democracy, the domestic breadwinner was venerated as a steadfast pillar of the nation's moral integrity and economic security. Indeed, as early marriage and family life were promoted as antidotes to the range of cultural forces perceived as threatening American social stability, the breadwinner model was proclaimed as an obligation and a duty. To stray from this norm was to court suspicion. Failure to conform to the breadwinner ethic could cast doubts on both a man's sexual identity and his social status and, as Ehrernreich argues, during the early 1950s 'there was the firm expectation . . . that required men to grow up, marry and support their wives. To do anything else was less than grown up, and the man who wilfully deviated was judged to be somehow "less than a man"' (1983: 11–12). While powerful, however, these ideals were never all-pervasive and during the fifties they steadily fragmented – 'contained' America increasingly perceived as lacking the verve, dynamism and independence of spirit needed if the US were to remain the backbone of the 'free world'.

TROUBLE IN PARADISE: THE CRISIS OF CONFORMITY AND THE 'DECLINE OF THE AMERICAN MALE'

Dominant ideological discourse constructed post-war America as paradise on earth. The reality for many, however, was dramatically different. By the early 1960s the limits of American prosperity were being revealed, studies such as Michael Harrington's widely read *The Other America* showing how many Americans had 'proved immune to progress', Harrington estimating that between 40 and 50 million

The Saturday Evening

POST

September 13, 1958 — *15¢*

A SUPERB NEW NOVEL:

SO LOVE RETURNS

By Robert Nathan

I CALL ON ZSA ZSA GABOR

By PETE MARTIN

2/-

4.1 The ideal of the suburban breadwinner. (*Saturday Evening Post*, Vol. 231, No. 11, 13 September 1958 – courtesy of Curtis Publishing.)

people (equivalent to about 25 per cent of the population) lived in poverty (Harrington, 1962: 6). The racial tensions of wartime, meanwhile, escalated further as the slow pace of civil rights reform prompted more concerted action against segregation and racial inequality. Even at the heart of the American Way misgivings were beginning to register – cracks quickly appearing in suburbia's facade of happy abundance.

By the end of the 1950s the postwar revival of mass consumption, initially celebrated as a benchmark of American progress and modernity, was prompting unease. McCarthyite red baiting worked to silence those who questioned the economic or political basis of American society, but critics of American *cultural* life largely escaped the witch hunts. During the Cold War, therefore, it was possible for a gathering body of writers to criticize what they regarded as the malignant cultural fallout of the consumer boom.

Ensconced in Southern California, Herbert Marcuse saw the consumer culture proliferating around him as an elaborate system of indoctrination. For the Frankfurt School émigré, contemporary America represented the apotheosis of capitalist manipulation – a 'one-dimensional' society where people's consumer obsessions rendered them oblivious to their exploitation (Marcuse, 1964). As a radical Marxist, Marcuse's hostility was unsurprising – but he was far from alone in his antipathy. The late 1950s and early 1960s saw writers of all political hues decry the rise of a debased 'mass culture' they perceived as the corollary of modern consumerism. Published in 1957, liberal economist J.K. Galbraith's *The Affluent Society* provided a neat epithet for the era, though was deeply critical of the damage sustained to the quality of public life through the indulgent feast of private consumption. From a more conservative perspective, in his book *The Image* (1961), historian Daniel Borstein lamented what he saw as the shallow, mass produced culture made possible by modern technology. In a similar vein Dwight Macdonald, in a series of essays later collected as *Against the American Grain* (1962), criticized bitterly what he depicted as a cultural life increasingly drained of meaning and individuality through processes of cynical marketing and mass consumption.

Within this critique of cultural massification, the American suburb – once acclaimed as the lifeblood of freedom and democracy – was denounced as a principal harbinger of malaise. Suburbia was increasingly caricatured as a debilitating domain of dismal uniformity, social commentators stigmatizing the suburbs as the essence of shallow banality – a critique exemplified by Lewis Mumford's portrayal of:

> a multitude of uniform, unidentifiable houses, lined up inflexibly, in uniform distances, on uniform roads, in a treeless communal waste inhabited by people of the same class, the same income, the same age group, witnessing the same television performances, eating the same tasteless prefabricated food, from the same freezers, conforming in every outward and inward respect to a common mold manufactured in the central metropolis. (Mumford, 1961: 486)

A gathering body of opinion also questioned the mythologies of suburban family 'togetherness'. Themes of family turmoil and disintegration, for example, surfaced in the work of dramatists such as Arthur Miller (*Death of a Salesman*, 1949) and Tennessee Williams (*Cat on a Hot Tin Roof*, 1954). Popular attention, meanwhile, began to focus on the alienation of the suburban homemaker, *Newsweek* reporting in 1960 that the American wife was 'dissatisfied with a lot that women of other lands can only dream of. Her discontent is deep, pervasive, and impervious to the superficial remedies which are offered at every hand.' (*Newsweek*, 7 March 1960) In 1963 the publication of Betty Friedan's bestseller, *The Feminine Mystique*, gave powerful voice to this 'problem with no name'. It did not appear until the early 1960s, but Friedan's book was rooted in the previous decade and the disconsolate responses she received during 1957 while surveying the life experiences of her female peers from the class of '42. Women in postwar America were, according to Freidan, suffocated by the claustrophobic restrictions of domesticity. For Freidan, the gap between the ideal of the 'happy housewife' and the dreary reality of family life had generated feelings of confusion, self doubt and despair – the 'feminine mystique' – that prevented women from realizing their full potential and confined them to the 'comfortable concentration camp' of affluent suburbia.

The 1950s ideal of the suburban breadwinner also attracted powerful criticism. Indeed, as Friedan's biographer Daniel Horowitz observes, *The Feminine Mystique* can be seen as a feminist reworking of existing concerns regarding the impact of affluence on the lives of middle-class men (Horowitz, 1998: 207–8). Alongside the exaltation of responsible, breadwinning masculinity, the 1950s also saw a growing critique of the grip of domesticity and conformism on the lives of American men. In its 1957 special edition on 'The American Male', for example, *Cosmopolitan* conjectured that although America boasted 'the biggest, richest, healthiest male in history', the pace of social change had given him 'an insecurity he often finds it difficult to cope with' (*Cosmopolitan*, May 1957). A starker vision of masculinity in crisis was offered by *Look* magazine in 1958 with a series of articles subsequently published as the anthology *The Decline of the American Male* (1958). According to *Look's* contributors, the American male was 'no longer the masculine, strong-minded man who pioneered the continent and built America's greatness'. Instead, he had descended into 'a pit of subjection' (*Look*, 4 February 1958). *Look* presented a disconsolate portrait of the American male – downtrodden by his overbearing wife, mentally and physically exhausted by the corporate rat race and beaten into submission by relentless pressures to conform. The modern man, *Look* warned ominously, had now become 'too soft, too complacent and too home oriented to meet the challenge of other dynamic nations like China and the Soviet Union' (*Look*, 25 February 1958). At the cinema, too, the 'breadwinner' was looking less confident, Steven Cohan (1997: 1–34) showing how films such as *North by Northwest* (1959) can be read as a wry satire on the foibles of the breadwinning role model.

By the late 1950s, therefore, the breadwinner stood as a paradoxical figure. On one hand he was promoted as the nation's economic and moral bulwark – but, on the other, his domesticity and conformism were presented as debilitating afflictions. The title of Sloan Wilson's novel, *The Man in the Gray Flannel Suit* (1955), provided an enduring emblem for the bland miasma that many saw as the curse of American manhood – intellectuals from across the political spectrum joining the fray with a shelf of books and articles denouncing what was portrayed as a society drowning in a sea of insipid complacency. In *The Lonely Crowd* (1950a), David Reisman epitomized the stance. For Reisman, conformity amounted to a kind of emasculation, postwar America seeing the rise of an 'other-directed' man who blindly followed the lead of those around him in a desperate search to 'belong'. In a similar vein *Fortune* editor William Whyte's study, *The Organization Man* (1956), lamented the passing of rugged individualism and the emergence of a white-collar world that rewarded conformity rather than initiative, crushing the individual beneath the collective will of the organization. In various ways authors as diverse as C. Wright Mills (1951), Daniel Bell (1960) and Vance Packard (1960a; 1960b) all echoed these anxieties, elaborating critiques of a culture they saw as stifling individuality and freedom beneath a blanket of oppressive conformity.[13]

This identification of a repressive conformity at the heart of American life was a shocking thesis because it challenged assumptions central to the dominant ideologies of Cold War America. In the field of political science authors such as Hannah Arendt (1951), Zbigniew Brezinski (1956) and Carl Friedrich (1954) had refined the notion of 'totalitarianism' to denote authoritarian regimes that wielded overwhelming control of their citizens through the use of modern technology and state agencies. In these terms, therefore, both the Soviet Union and Nazi Germany were understood as examples of tyrannically regulated state monoliths. Filtering into popular discourse, this paradigm was a powerful ideological weapon as it not only equated Soviet society with the despotism of the Third Reich, but also cast Western democracy as the bastion of freedom. The idea that the US was itself becoming characterized by oppressive conformity and mechanical obedience, therefore, was an alarming prospect that reverberated through the national psyche. Amid the suspicions of the Cold War, however, any challenge to the institutions of corporate America risked charges of unpatriotic disloyalty. Instead, as both Barbara Ehrernreich (1983: 36) and Gail Dines (1998: 42) argue, critics found a softer target in the figure of the American woman.

America's perceived slide into the paralysing doldrums of massification and conformity was invariably configured in gendered terms. 'Mass culture' was presented as a sea of passive and repetitive 'feminine' banality that drowned out 'masculine' vigour and creativity.[14] Possibly the most mysogynistic version of the thesis appeared in Philip Wylie's *Generation of Vipers* – a book originally published in 1942, but with a cultural purchase that ensured its twentieth pressing by 1955. Coining the term 'momism', Wylie lambasted 'the perfidious materialism of mom' who, he claimed, smothered her sons with over protection, turning them into passive and effete weaklings (1955: 216). Throughout the 1950s Wylie continued his tirade against the 'dynasty of the dames' and the 'womanization of America', accusing women of not only undermining and debilitating the American male within the confines of the home, but also in the spheres of business and the arts.[15]

Nor was Wylie wildly out of step with contemporary thinking. The 1950s and early 1960s saw the modern woman routinely cited as the bane of American manhood. The widely touted 'crisis of masculinity' gave these themes their greatest currency. In 1956, for example, *Life* opined that the creeping rise in divorce rates was the consequence of a growing 'sexual ambiguity' in which men were becoming more 'passive and irresponsible' while 'the emerging American woman tends to be assertive and exploitative' (*Life*, 24 December 1956). Similar conclusions were reached in *Look* the following year, Robert Moskin drawing on a battery of empirical studies to argue that 'petticoat rule' was rendering men socially and culturally (and sometimes physically) impotent as women's increasing dominance set America 'drifting toward a social structure of he-women and she-men' (*Look*, 4 February 1958). *Cosmopolitan* offered a similar (though more tongue-in-cheek) picture in 1959,

Many husbands are made to feel as useless as a fifth wheel on the family car.

4.2 'Many husbands are made to feel as useless as a fifth wheel on the family car.' (*Cosmopolitan*, Vol. 147, No. 1, July 1959.)

rhetorically asking how it was possible for a man to 'remain manly . . . when his wife brings home a paycheque, beats him at poker, and drives him into what psychologists forebodingly call "sexual ambiguity"' (*Cosmopolitan*, July 1959).

Patterns of life in suburbia seemed to provide especially damning evidence of a 'crisis' in contemporary gender relations. The portrayal of the suburbs as a 'vast, communalistic female barracks' (Keats, 1956: 57) became widely established – critics claiming that the daytime absence of husbands allowed mothers to exercise a suffocating control over the home and children. Sons, especially, were seen as being enfeebled by life within the 'suburban matriarchy', while the father was presented as becoming 'soft' and ineffectual – the 'organization man' returning from the corporate treadmill to have his individualism further wrung from him by an oppressive and stultifying home life.[16] Anxieties about the vigour of American manhood, meanwhile, were further intensified by the wide circulation of Kinsey's findings that not only had many men admitted to homosexual experiences, but that female sexuality peaked late in life while male virility waned considerably earlier.[17]

By the close of the 1950s concerns surrounding American vigour were reaching critical mass. Towards the end of the decade economic growth faltered, while Soviet success in the space race (with the launch of Sputnik 1 in 1957) sent a shiver of apprehension through the country. It seemed as though America was becoming impotent – somehow losing its 'sense of national purpose' and stumbling into the troughs of social and economic ennui.[18] Against this background of bewildered uncertainty, John F. Kennedy's pledge to 'get America moving again' in the Presidential election of 1960 was a compelling overture. Kennedy's victory over Nixon (his Republican rival) was narrow, but JFK's administration captured the public imagination by seeming to usher in a new era of virility. In his metaphor of the 'New Frontier', Kennedy echoed earlier liberal attempts to couple the promise of economic prosperity with the cause of social justice – for example, the 'New America' motif of the 1952 Adlai Stevenson campaign and (most obviously) Roosevelt's New Deal. But Kennedy's political rhetoric also mobilized long-standing mythologies in which the frontier experience was cast as bestowing on the United States a uniquely robust spirit of liberty and self-reliance. By posing 'the question of the New Frontier', therefore, Kennedy sought to stamp a new seal of masculine authority on American politics and culture, JFK challenging the American people to make a choice 'between the public interest and private comfort; between national greatness and national decline; between the fresh air of progress and the stale, dank atmosphere of "normalcy"; between determined dedication and creeping mediocrity'.[19]

Kennedy's exhortation for a reclamation of American drive and assertiveness condensed themes that had become commonplace among contemporary critics. His vilification of 'private comfort' and the 'dank atmosphere of "normalcy"' drew on an established ideological discourse that configured America as becoming woefully 'feminized' through 'soft' suburban materialism and a rising tide of grey flannelled conformity. Kennedy offered to restore America's virility and reverse the drift towards 'femininity'. His public persona, moreover, furnished the breadwinner ideal a fresh sense of vitality – responsible fatherhood given a new aura of vigour through JFK's reputation as a courageous war hero. As May observes, 'With his stylish wife at his side and his two children, [Kennedy] seemed to embody the virtues of the American domestic ideal par excellence: the tough cold warrior who was also a warm family man' (May, 1999: 195).

Kennedy's private life, however, did not entirely accord with this public image. Indeed, under his presidency the White House was no stranger to the most sybaritic vagaries of 'private comfort'. Outwardly the sober national figurehead and upright family man, in private JFK pursued more indulgent interests – with a penchant for late night martini sessions, poolside carousing and a succession of mistresses and one-night stands.[20] In this respect the President can, himself, be seen as embodying many of the contradictions and inconsistencies intrinsic to dominant models of masculinity during the 1950s and early 1960s. Just as American foreign policy failed to 'contain' communist influence abroad, 'domestic containment' failed to exercise an iron grip over cultural life at home. Indeed, the sheer amount of effort invested in pressing down the lid of 'containment' suggests that many people (including the President) were pursuing practices and lifestyles markedly at odds with the ideals of family-oriented 'togetherness'.

May's concept of 'domestic containment' is, for the most part, acutely perceptive. Yet she overstates the case in arguing that after 1945 young Americans 'found that viable alternatives to the prevailing family norm were virtually unavailable' (1999: xxvi). Contradictions were germane to constructions of gender throughout the postwar period. Rather than being marked by straightforward conservative retrenchment, the Cold War was a time of tensions and transformations. The family-centred, suburban stereotypes wielded considerable ideological power, but there continued to exist a multiplicity of gender identities and ideals. For example, the experience of many women – especially those whose class or race excluded them from the 'comfortable concentration camp' of white suburbia – sharply contrasted to Betty Friedan's 'happy housewife' caricature. Despite efforts to return working women to the home, the proportion of women aged fourteen and older who were active in the labour force continued to grow – from 25.4 per cent in 1940, to 29 per cent in 1950 and 34.5 per cent in 1960 (Rupp, 1982: 36). Women's activism also remained wide ranging, encompassing trade unionism and the civil rights movement, as well as feminist causes and campaigns.[21] Popular representations, too, featured multiple constructions of femininity. Surveying popular women's magazines of the post-war era, for instance, Joanne Meyerowitz (1994) argues that images of women as independent, creative and nonconformist existed alongside (and competed against) the more conservative visions of submissive domesticity.

THE 'COMPLETE MALE' AND THE RESURRECTION OF RUGGED MANHOOD

Postwar America's diversity of feminine identities was matched by its range of masculinities. Dominant representations of the breadwinner fostered an impression of unity and cohesion, but masculinity was a deeply problematic and contested terrain. Ideals of masculine domesticity, for example, often attracted virulent criticism. Philip Wylie was, of course, especially vociferous in his contentions that domestic drudgery was robbing men of their dynamism. And Wylie's calls for a resurrection of sturdy maleness was paralleled in the realm of popular culture – an array of popular films, literature and magazines affirming a sense of rugged manfulness. In 1955 the first 'Marlboro Man' advertising campaign evoked an aura of masculine grit, while at the cinema the postwar revival of the Western (like Kennedy's political rhetoric) re-articulated frontier mythologies of masculine endeavour, John Wayne walking tall as an icon of strapping manhood. 'The Duke''s silver screen machismo was matched in the field of literature by Ernest Hemingway's enduring status as a literary man of action. Awarded the Nobel Prize for Literature in 1954 following the success of his novella, *The Old Man and the Sea* (1952), 'Papa' Hemingway was enshrined as a rock of authentic heroism amid an age of superficial materialism.[22] A more abrasive macho posture was struck by Mike Hammer, the hero of Mickey Spillane's popular detective novels. Beginning with *I, The Jury* in 1947, Spillane's first six novels sold over seventeen million copies by 1953 – Hammer personifying the ethos of the hairy-chested tough guy as he dealt out death and destruction to conniving (and frequently female) communist agents.

Perhaps the most uncompromising champions of hard-boiled masculinity were the numerous 'true adventure' pulp magazines. Heralded by the launch of Fawcett Publications' *True* magazine in 1936, the ensuing wave of 'true adventure' pulps were home to a world of two-fisted action. During the 1940s *True* was followed by titles such as *Sir!* (1943), *Saga* (1947) and *Stag* (1950), joined during the 1950s and early 1960s by a welter of magazines whose titles were a paean to hard-bitten machismo – *Action for Men, Man's Life, Man's Magazine, Male, Men, Man's Adventure, Man's Illustrated, Man to Man, Man's World, Man's Daring, ad nauseam*. Cheap and garish, these 'macho pulps'' stock in trade was a no-nonsense brand of ruggedly heterosexual masculinity. Purportedly 'true' tales of wartime heroics and the testing of manhood ('There Were Only 12 of Us – Against 5000 Nazi Beasts!'; '7 Bloody Hours That Saved Korea') appeared alongside 'glamour model' photospreads and prurient exposés of lascivious debauchery ('Exposed: The Truth About Love-Hungry Divorcees'; 'Are Nudist Camps Communism's Newest Stronghold?'), together with a range of fiction and feature articles dealing with crime-fighting, hunting, sport and other suitably 'manly' pursuits.

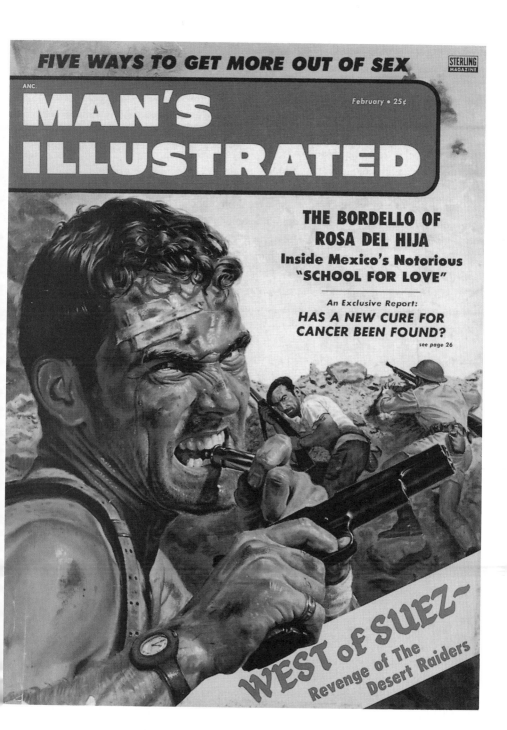

4.3 'True Adventures for Bold Men'. (*Man's Illustrated*, Vol. 2, No. 4, February 1957.)

Like Wylie, then, the 'macho pulps' fell over themselves to affirm masculine virility in the face of a perceived 'feminization' of American manhood. Indeed, in a 1956 commentary that could almost have come from Wylie's pen, the editor of *True* magazine explained that the red-blooded adventure pulps were so popular among men because they 'stimulate the masculine ego at a time when man wants to fight back against women's efforts to usurp his traditional role as head of family' (cited in Brenton, 1967: 30).[23] More widely, the blustering misogyny and homophobia of these 'macho pulps' (along with that of Wylie and Spillane) can also be equated with the amalgam of social, sexual and political fears that fuelled McCarthyite paranoia – the 'macho pulps'' vulgar machismo and abhorrence of 'effete' cosmopolitan culture mirroring the Wisconsin Senator's tirades against 'egg-sucking phony liberals', who, with their 'pitiful squealing . . . [hold] sacrosanct those Communists and queers' in the American government intent on betraying American interests (McCarthy, cited in Wittner, 1974: 95).

The fantasy, male-dominated world of sex and action offered in the 'macho pulps' might have attracted a minority of middle-class readers – exhibiting, perhaps, an 'underworld primitivism' similar to that White (1993: 7–10) identifies among the readers of *National Police Gazette* during the previous century. For the most part, however, the target audience of the post-war pulps were blue-collar workers and ex-servicemen – *Male* magazine sizing-up its typical reader as:

> a fellow somewhere between 20 and 45 . . . You probably have some Army time behind you – or at least most of your friends have seen active service . . . You follow a minimum of one sport avidly . . . You've tried your hand at fishing and hunting . . . You have a dash of the gambling instinct . . . You like your reading matter strong, highly spiced and laced with rugged, rough-and-tumble, jumping from the page pictures . . . To sum you up – you're a complete MALE. (*Male*, July 1950)

This 'rugged, rough-and-tumble' world of the 'complete MALE' certainly contested the ideal of the domesticated breadwinner. Yet it did so from a position of belligerent reaction. Through their tough-guy bravado and boisterous lechery, the 'macho pulps' (along with Wylie, Spillane and their ilk) fought a desperate battle to 'put women back in their place', stemming the tide of social change they saw as besieging American manhood. But while the 'complete MALE's' coarse braggadocio and disdain for 'soft' materialism may have struck a chord at the lower reaches of the social scale, it was a refrain largely alien to middle-class men. In making their own challenge to the ideal of family-oriented domesticity, middle-class men looked toward brands of masculine vigour that were more at ease with the interests and desires of consumerism.

THE LUST FOR LIFESTYLE: THE MASCULINE CONSUMER AND THE NEW MIDDLE CLASS

The breadwinner archetype was a powerful ideological force but, even in the iciest depths of the Cold War, it was never all embracing. According to May, the ideological power of 'containment culture' was only ruptured in the late 1960s, when a new '"uncontained" generation . . . rejected the rigid institutional boundaries of their elders' and 'substituted risk for security as they carried sex, consumerism, and political activism outside the established institutions' (May, 1999: xxvi). However, while the counter-culture and women's liberation movement of the 1960s may have posed new challenges to the political assumptions of the preceding era, the '"uncontained" generation' did not have a monopoly on sex and consumerism. As previous chapters have testified, since the beginning of the century there had existed articulations of masculinity grounded in an engagement with consumer culture and hedonistic desire – and during the postwar era they were newly invigorated.

Pivotal to the codification of the consuming male during the 1930s, *Esquire* magazine maintained its affinity with the masculine consumer after 1945. Throughout the 1940s and early 1950s *Esquire* continued to appeal to the man of taste and distinction, its regular features on fashion and good-living complemented by a series of guidebooks for the aspiring *bon viveur* – for example, *Esquire's Handbook for Hosts* (1949), *Esquire Etiquette* (1953) and the *Esquire Cook-Book* (1954). *Esquire's* interest in the predilections of masculine campus culture also continued, with regular attention to collegiate fashions and its autumnal 'Back to Campus' section regularly detailing the latest vagaries in student style.

Esquire's halcyon days, however, were over. Paradoxically, the 1946 Supreme Court ruling that had secured the magazine's distribution also paved the way for a flood of competitors once wartime paper rationing had ceased. Many of the new men's magazines of the late 1940s and early 1950s were down-market 'macho pulps' or 'pin-up' titles, but others began to pose a more direct challenge to *Esquire's* sales. Titles such as *Varsity* (launched in 1946) were specifically targeted at the leisure-minded undergraduate and ate into *Esquire's* college market, though it was *True* magazine that emerged as *Esquire's* chief competitor. While its imitators became increasingly lurid, the mid-1940s saw *True* gradually repitch itself as a working-class equivalent to *Esquire*, repackaging the formula of masculine consumerism for 'the hunting, beer and poker set' in an attempt to cash-in on more lucrative advertising revenue (Pendergast, 2000: 208).[24] Managing to poach some of *Esquire's* best contributors and illustrators (including Petty and Vargas), *True* began reconfiguring itself in terms of more consumerist and style-conscious ideals, with attractive, full-colour features on men's fashion and even, in 1949, the offer of a booklet of helpful style tips – *True's Guide to Good Appearance*. The move proved a commercial masterstroke. *True's* popularity soared and in 1948 it became the first men's magazine with a circulation in excess of a million. *Esquire,* in contrast, struggled to find a sense of direction, eventually being guided to a new niche as a quality features magazine after Alfred Gingrich returned as editor in 1952.

For Pendergast the success of *True*'s new incarnation testifies to a triumphant hegemony of the cultural logic of consumerism across the field of American masculinity. This assessment, however, is premature. Models of masculine consumerism were certainly conspicuous in *True*'s features and advertising during the late 1940s. But this does not mean that consumption-oriented values had taken firm root within working-class masculine cultures. As Pendergast himself concedes, *True* 'faced an up-hill battle in convincing its readers to orient their sense of self toward goods and leisure' and always had to provide sufficient features to satisfy the rugged outdoorsman and men who 'thought of themselves as tough, no-nonsense, hard-drinking guys' (Pendergast, 2000: 225; 232). Within the middle class, however, the ethos of the male consumer was undoubtedly proliferating, a consequence of the profound social and economic transformations that attended postwar affluence.

The middle class flourished during the postwar boom. Between 1947 and 1957 the number of salaried workers increased by 61 per cent as white collar career opportunities multiplied among the expanding business corporations. The provisions of the GI Bill, passed in 1944, also contributed to this growth by affording veterans unprecedented access to opportunities in education and training.[25] Between 1947 and 1953 the number of solidly middle class families (with an annual income of between $4,000 and $7,500) grew from 12.5 million to 18 million, with the percentage of those earning between $7,000 and $10,000 per year rising from 5 per cent to 20 per cent between 1947 and 1959 (US Bureau of Census, 1975: 289–90). Indeed, it was the scale of this growth that sustained the postwar 'ideologies of affluence' – dominant ideological discourse projecting the fortunes of the prosperous middle class as the defining experience of American society as a whole.[26]

Crucially, however, the American middle class not only got larger after 1945, it also changed in composition and cultural character. The American economy's growing dependence on the servicing of consumer demand brought with it a major expansion in the number of salaried managerial and technical workers and 'culture producers' of all kinds – administrators, academics, journalists, advertisers and other professions whose economic role centred around the production and dissemination of symbolic goods and services. Pierre Bourdieu (1984) identifies the emergence of a similar 'new petite bourgeoisie' in his analysis of post-war France – but, while Bourdieu's 'cultural intermediaries' did not come into their own until the late 1960s, the American 'new class' became recognizable as a social formation significantly earlier.

In the US a 'professional-managerial class' (as it is termed by many social theorists)[27] first began to take shape with the emergence of a consumption-oriented economy at the turn of the century. The interwar growth of the consumer industries and state agencies saw the professional-managerial cohort become better defined – even becoming a topic of popular debate with the publication of James Burnham's *The Managerial Revolution* in 1941. It was, though, the boom years of the 1950s that were decisive in the rise of the professional-managerial group – commentators such as C. Wright Mills (1951) chronicling the way this group's ranks were swelled through the growth of consumer industries, the service sector, the state and corporate bureaucracies, the mass media and the emerging military-industrial complex. Despite its occupational diversity, the Ehrenreichs (1979: 14; 1990: 12) argue that this professional-managerial group was bound together by common experiences, interests and worldview, coming to represent a distinct and recognizable middle-class formation that constituted roughly 20 per cent of the American population.[28]

Like Bourdieu's 'new petite bourgeoisie' of 1960s France, the ascending middle class of 1950s America established their status as a social formation through the consumption of distinctive cultural goods and signifiers. Their cultural priorities were exemplified by the new concept of 'lifestyle'. By the 1950s the term was already being deployed by market researchers to denote the distinctive consumption practices of different social groups. It was, though, the developing consumer tastes of the new middle class with which the notion of 'lifestyle' became most closely associated.[29] Among advertisers and marketeers, especially, the concept of 'lifestyle' was used to denote the mores of 'a new middle class of college-bred administrators, professionals and managers' who were oriented to a culture of 'play, fun and excitement' and who took 'endless delight in pursuing a lighthearted existence of interpersonal repartee and pleasure based on a moral code that bore no relationship to babbitry and its protestant morality' (Bensman and Vidich, 1995a: 249–52, originally published 1971).

And as this new, expressive and cosmopolitan middle-class culture gradually took shape, models of masculinity anchored on stylistic expression and conspicuous consumption began to come into their own. Auguste Comte Spectorsky's *The Exurb-anites* (1955) bore early testimony to the legitimacy of masculine consumer pleasures within the culture of this new middle class. Spectorsky's popular satire of affluent life in Rockland County chronicled the tastes and proclivities of the 'exurbanite' – Spectorsky's term for an emergent upper-middle class subspecies remarkably similar to Bourdieu's 'new petite bourgeoisie'. Like Bourdieu's 'cultural intermediary', Spectorsky's typical exurbanite was an 'idea man' or 'symbol-manipulator' – 'a singularly commercial merchant of dreams for the rest of the nation' who collectively represented 'our nation's movers and shakers for ideas and opinions, for what is fashionable and what is fun' (1955: 7–10). The exurbanite lived in the counties fringing New York, but he remained decidedly urban in character since 'His person-ality, his way of life, his habits – all were (and are) somewhat flamboyant, and the word "suburbs" conjured up . . . a picture of dull and demure domesticity utterly foreign to him' (1955: 6). Moreover, in contrast to the suburban breadwinner's moderation and self-denial, the exurbanite was a connoisseur in the arts of style and leisure – his lifestyle was formulated around the consumption of distinctive goods (exotic cocktails, foreign sports cars, elegant ornaments), while he was 'so busy relaxing . . . [and went] to such lengths in the diligent contriving of the casual, that the resultant appearance is quite convincing' (1955: 183). A satirical caricature, the exurbanite nonetheless related to genuine shifts taking place in American cultural life – this, perhaps, accounting for the popularity of Spectorsky's book. The figure of the exurbanite crystallized the rise of a masculine identity that broke away from traditional middle class values of thrift, restraint and 'fear of pleasure' and – like Bourdieu's 'new petite bourgeoisie' – elaborated in their place a culture rooted in consumption, stylistic expression and an 'ethic of fun' (Bourdieu, 1984: 367).

The traditional gendering of consumption as a feminine (and feminizing) cultural practice retained powerful influence – a degree of suspicion attending the hedonistic male throughout the postwar era. Within the culture of the new middle class, however, masculine identities posited on consumerist appetites became more acceptable and fully-formed. This was a version of middle-class masculinity tailored to the needs of the modern American economy. The middle class as a whole had embraced commodity consumption more fully after 1945, but the home-centred spending patterns of suburban family life remained governed by the traditional virtues of hard work and deferred gratification (Ehrenreich, 1990: 182; May, 1999: 148). This was a system of values increasingly at odds with an economy whose existence was coming to rely on ceaseless consumer spending. More appropriate to these economic demands were the cultural ethics and gender archetypes associated with the newly emerging middle-class faction. This group (again, like Bourdieu's 'new petite bourgeoisie') made a vocation of consumption, elaborating their distinctive cultural identity through a lifestyle oriented around the satisfaction of materialist and hedonistic desires.

*

Postwar American culture was rife with inconsistencies and competing voices. Dominant ideologies of family 'togetherness' promoted parenthood and home-making as the warp and weft of the American social fabric – but not everyone was 'homeward bound'. There continued to exist a diversity of (often contradictory) gender identities and, with the rise of a new middle-class formation, the breadwinner's commitment to family life and the home was increasingly challenged by a masculine ethos of conspicuous consumption and personal pleasure.

Revelling in a world of country clubs, golf tournaments and classy sports coupés, the exurbanite represented a form of masculinity very different to the breadwinner model of responsible domesticity. Yet the exurbanite was still a mature family man, devoted to the care and happiness of his children. A more thoroughgoing challenge to the breadwinner's button-down conformity came from the younger models of masculine consumption succinctly described by Joseph Bensman and Arthur Vidich in 1971. Reflecting on twenty years of change in middle-class patterns of life, the two authors discerned the rise of a lifestyle that was liberal, consumption-driven and epitomized by such youth-oriented archetypes as:

> the fun-lover [who] specializes in active social participation – sports, indoor and outdoor parties, dancing, discotheque, world travel, hunting safaris, flying and skiing. This group in its focus on 'fun' most obviously models itself on the jet set and is primarily concerned with movement, gaiety, and remaining eternally young. (Bensman and Vidich, 1995b: 269, originally published 1971)

More than the 'grey fox' of exurbia, it was these younger models of male consumerism that led the way in the emergent middle-class 'morality of pleasure as a duty'. And in emphasizing youthful excitement and an 'ethic of fun', the lifestyle culture of the new middle class was influenced and informed by the rise of a distinctly 'teenage' universe of recreation and narcissism.

NOTES

1 For anthologies which highlight the dimensions of uncertainty and conflict central to postwar American life see Foreman (ed.) (1997), May (ed.) (1989) and Meyerowitz (ed.) (1994).

2 The exceptional character of the postwar nuclear family is underlined by subsequent trends. By 1974 the median age for marriage for women had risen to nearly twenty-two, while 40 per cent of women aged between twenty and twenty-four were still single. By the early 1970s the divorce rate had climbed to 26 per 1,000 marriages, while the birth rate declined through the 1960s to reach 15 per 1,000 women by 1973 (Bremner, 1982: 28). For more consideration of the unique features of family demography during the 1950s see Coontz (1992: 25–9), Mintz and Kellogg (1988: 177–201), Skolnick (1991: 50–4), Scott Smith (1995) and Weiss (2000: 15–47).

3 For a more detailed account of the sexual fears and ferment of the postwar era see D'Emilio and Freedman (1997: 276–300) and Freedman (1987).

4 Despite their ponderous recitation of quantitative data, both Kinsey reports became best sellers. Kinsey's findings, meanwhile, were widely referenced and hotly debated throughout the media. Discussion of the popular impact of Kinsey's work can be found in D'Emilio (1983: 33-7) and D'Emilio and Freedman (1997: 285–8).

5 Kozol (1994) examines how *Life* magazine celebrated the postwar family as a bastion of American culture. Haraloich (1992), Spigel (1992), Taylor (1989) and Weisblat (1994) all provide detailed accounts of American television's veneration of suburban domesticity during the 1950s and early 1960s.

6 Accounts of postwar suburbanization are provided in Fishman (1987: 155–81), Gelfand (1982), Jackson (1985: 231–71) and Palen (1995: 56–67).

7 For further discussion of the ideological connotations to suburban, family life see Haralovich (1992) and Spigel (1992a; 1992b; 1997a; 1997b). Accounts of suburban 'ranch-house' architecture and its symbolic resonance can be found in Clark (1989), Ford (1994: 166–9) and Wright (1983: 248–55).

8 Stimulus was also provided by the greater availability and acceptability of consumer credit. The first credit card (Diner's Club) was launched in 1950, while the overall figure for instalment credit rose from $4 billion in 1954 to $43 billion six years later (Jezer, 1982: 126). The exponential growth of advertising also propelled consumer spending ever forward, the 1950s seeing gross advertising expenditure rise by 75 per cent – faster than the growth of Gross National Product, personal income or any other economic index.

9 In *The Myth of the Middle Class* (1982), Richard Parker contends that between 1945 and 1959 income distribution changed very little – with the wealthiest 10 per cent of the population earning around 29 per cent of the national income, while one per cent of income was divided up among the nation's poorest 10 per cent.

10 Rostow later became head of the State Department's Policy Planning Staff and was a close advisor to President Kennedy.

11 Alongside this feature on the prosperity of American family life was a profile of the latest US military hardware – a juxtaposition that neatly illustrates the way strategies of foreign and domestic containment complemented one another.

12 D'Emilio (1983: 40–56; 1989) provides an incisive analysis of how Cold War rhetoric fused fears of communism with anxieties about homosexuality and sexual identity. Savran (1992) and Sinfield (1994) make similar observations.

13 Pells (1985) offers a useful overview of postwar liberal, intellectual critiques of 'conformity' in American culture.

14 According to Huyssen (1986), there exists a long and connected tradition in which 'mass culture' has been pejoratively characterized as 'feminine' – passive, sentimental and repetitive – whereas 'meaningful' culture has been configured in terms of 'masculine' virility and creativity.

15 See, in particular, Wylie's contributions to *Playboy* magazine during the late 1950s and early 1960s – 'The Abdicating Male: And How the Gray Flannel Mind Exploits Him Through His Women' (*Playboy*, November 1956), 'The Womanization of America' (*Playboy*, September 1958) and 'The Career Woman' (*Playboy*, January 1963).

16 Whyte himself saw suburbia as 'the packaged villages that have become the dormitory of the new generation of organization men' (1956: 10), while Reisman (1958) followed suit with his own attack on 'The Suburban Sadness'. See Mumford and Gordon et al. (1962) for further contemporary critiques of suburban life.

Berrett (1997) highlights the way the diet of 'the organization man' also figured prominently in discourse around the 'debilitation' of the suburban male.

17 Breines (1985, 1986) explores the relationship between postwar perceptions of masculine 'decline' and contemporaneous fears of female strength.

18 Partly as a response to the developing sense of national torpor, in 1959 President Eisenhower appointed a Commission on National Goals to conceive a set of (ultimately ill-defined) long-range objectives to re-energize the national spirit.

19 Kennedy first foregrounded the theme of the 'New Frontier' in his speech accepting the Democratic Party nomination for the presidency in July 1960.

20 The more prurient aspects to Kennedy's presidency are chronicled in Hersh (1998: 222–46). Kennedy's hedonistic predilections are underscored (somewhat ironically) in the title for the projected second volume to Nigel Hamilton's biography of the President – *JFK: Playboy of the Western World*.

21 For an account of the survival of American feminism during the postwar decades see Rupp (1982). Meyerwitz's (1994) anthology underlines the plural constructions of femininity during the 1950s.

22 Mass circulation picture magazines were especially prominent in revering Hemingway as the personification of 'timeless' masculine virtues. As early as 1949 *Life* had contributed to the author's heroic aura with a laudatory profile entitled 'A Portrait of Mister Papa'. Three years later *Life* published a special Hemmingway cover issue that included the full text of *The Old Man and the Sea*, together with an editorial eulogizing the author as a steadfast rock of American vigour.

23 For an extended analysis of the postwar 'true adventure' pulps see Osgerby (2000).

24 A similar shift also took place in *Argosy*. Launched at the beginning of the century as a successful fiction magazine, a slump in circulation had seen *Argosy* rebrand itself as a 'true adventure' pulp during the Second World War. But during the late 1940s it tentatively followed *True*'s lead by including more features on style and consumption.

25 Officially known as the Serviceman's Readjustment Act, the 1944 GI Bill provided veterans with a range of financial benefits, including the guarantee of up to four years education or job training – a provision taken up by over eight million ex-servicemen (Adams, 1994: 152).

26 Lears (1989) draws on the ideas of Antonio Gramsci to explain this process, arguing that the 1950s saw the middle class emerge as a 'hegemonic historical bloc', successfully establishing (albeit temporarily) its values and interests as an authoritative worldview.

27 From a neo-Marxist perspective, the Ehrenreichs define the professional-managerial class as 'salaried mental workers who do not own the means of production and whose major function in the social division of labour may be

described broadly as the reproduction of capitalist culture and capitalist class relations' (1979: 12). A similar analysis is offered in Ehrenreich (1990: 12) and Lears (1989: 51). Conservative commentators have also identified an emergent social formation of middle-class professionals – although from this perspective the 'New Class' are reviled as the agents of permissive liberalism. Various permutations of this formulation are collected in Bruce-Briggs (1979).

28 Bruce-Briggs (1979: 217–25) provides comprehensive occupational and educational data to illustrate the ascendancy of the professional-managerial group during the 1960s.

29 See Lazar (1967, originally published 1963).

Chapter 5
'The Old Ways Will Not Do': Youth, Consumption and Postwar Leisure-Style

American consumers, especially younger consumers, in living out the [American] Dream exude optimism for the future. They feel sure that tomorrow will be better than today. American consumers believe that they can continue to expand their consumption and increase their relative amount of pleasure rather than merely limit desires. They feel sure they can continue increasing the area of purchasing power under their control. One result of this optimistic outlook is that American consumers see virtue not so much in curbing desires, but rather in realizing oneself by acquiring the necessary goods and symbols.

> William Lazar, 'Life Style Concepts and Marketing' in Eugene Kelly and William Lazar (eds) *Managerial Marketing: Perspectives and Viewpoints* (Illinois: Homeword, 1967: 8, originally published 1963).

'THE TORCH HAS BEEN PASSED TO A NEW GENERATION OF AMERICANS ... ': YOUTH AND SOCIAL CHANGE IN POSTWAR AMERICA

In 1955 Esteves Kefauver set about his task with grim determination. Four years earlier the Tennessee Senator had made his mark as head of the Senate investigation into organized crime, where he had been unswerving in his quest to expose national racketeering. Having tackled the Mob, Kefauver set his sights on another spectre that ostensibly menaced postwar America – juvenile delinquency. Appointed in 1953, the Senate Subcommittee to Investigate Juvenile Delinquency had already been underway for two years when Kefauver assumed its chairmanship, but under his direction the proceedings gained both energy and added *gravitas*. Lasting into the 1960s, the Subcommittee's investigation responded to (and gave greater credence to) popular perceptions of a postwar tide of juvenile crime.

There was nothing especially new about these fears. Wartime had already seen a heightening of anxieties related to delinquency. Yet, as James Gilbert (1986) meticulously shows, the 1950s saw public concern about juvenile crime climb to unprecedented levels. Between 1953 and 1958 fears were especially pronounced. A plethora of exposés in magazines, newspapers and newsreels depicted a form of delinquency that seemed frighteningly new in its extent and severity.[1] This portrayal, moreover, seemed borne out by empirical evidence, with a relentless rise in official statistics for youth crime. Closer examination, however, questions these perceptions. According to Gilbert, the 1950s rise in indices of juvenile crime was largely a statistical phenomenon, the outcome of new strategies of law enforcement and changes in procedures for the collation of crime data (Gilbert, 1986: 66–70). Rather than being rooted in a genuine explosion of adolescent vice, Gilbert sees the 1950s alarm around juvenile delinquency (or the 'J.D.' phenomenon, as it was dubbed) as articulating 'a vaguely formulated but gnawing sense of social disintegration' (1986: 77). Just as wartime fears of juvenile crime had acted as a symbolic focus for broader anxieties about the social impact of the war, so the J.D. 'moral panic' of the 1950s served as a vehicle for a broader sense of alarm in the face of rapid and disorienting change.

As the previous chapter demonstrated, despite outward appearances of confident optimism, a powerful undercurrent of unease ran through postwar America. Traditional values seemed to be assailed by the nature and pace of cultural change, a sense of uncertainty further intensified by the insecurities of the Cold War. Amid the wider climate of suspicion and apprehension, therefore, the issue of delinquency struck a deep resonance – particularly because developments in the world of youth seemed to crystallize those forces deemed most threatening to social stability. Perceptions of a more permissive sexual code among young people stoked fears of moral disarray, while the expansion of a commercially based and peer-oriented youth culture challenged dominant ideologies of family-centred 'togetherness'. Young people's affluence and the growth of a commercial youth market were perceived as weakening the family's cohesive power – adolescent taste seeming to be increasingly independent of parental influence. Moreover, the popularity of cultural forms such as rock 'n' roll prompted particular fear as white, middle-class youngsters appeared to fall under the spell of lower-class and black cultural values.[2]

The development of a youth culture based around the consumption of commercial goods and entertainments also fed into wider misgivings about the impact of 'mass culture'. The perception that American cultural life was being debased and corrupted through the tightening grip of commercialism was vigorously articulated in the controversies surrounding delinquency. The Kefauver Subcommittee, for example, considered a range of potential causes of juvenile crime – but they became preoccupied with the possible influence of the media. Throughout the mid-1950s the Senators heard testimony from a parade of experts and moral crusaders, many citing the media's proclivity for violence as having a woeful impact on the nation's youth.[3] Throughout the hearings, however, the Subcommittee's findings were inconclusive. Scrutinizing the comics industry, followed by television and Hollywood, the Kefauver hearings found little evidence of a clear link between the media and juvenile crime. Nevertheless, while the clamour for a tightening of federal censorship was resisted, the Subcommittee demanded that the media exercise stricter self-regulation – a call that was generally acceded to.

Though Kefauver left the Subcommittee in 1957, its hearings continued for several years. By the beginning of the 1960s, however, the intensity of the J.D. panic was dissipating. Criticisms of the media remained prominent and juvenile crime statistics continued to rise, but by the end of the 1950s a more positive set of youth stereotypes had come to the fore. Here, young people were portrayed, celebrated even, as an excitingly new and uplifting social force with the power to refresh and revitalize American 'national purpose'. This was an iconography powerfully mobilized by John F. Kennedy, in both his public persona and his vision of the 'New Frontier'. From the beginning of his political career, JFK had cultivated an association with youth – the slogan for his first campaign for Congress in 1946 announcing that 'The New Generation Offers a Leader'. And in 1960 it was a theme he played on to great effect as he ran for Presidential office. Rebutting Harry Truman's suggestion that he might lack the maturity or experience demanded by the Presidency (Kennedy was still only forty-three), JFK made a virtue of his youthful vigour, elaborating an imagery that evoked romantic notions of youth, modernity and progress:

> This is still a young country, founded by young men . . . and still young in heart . . . [yet] the world today is largely in the hands of men whose education was completed before the whole course of international events was altered by two world wars. But who is to say how successful they have been in improving the fate of the world? . . . The world is changing, the old ways will not do . . . It is time for a new generation of leadership to cope with the new problems and new opportunities. (*New York Times*, 5 July 1960)

In office the theme continued. Assuming the Presidency, Kennedy announced that 'the torch has been passed to a new generation of Americans', JFK aligning himself with youth as a force for positive change (cited in Hellman, 1997: 105). Through his dynamism and charisma, Kennedy himself seemed to personify a new era of bold confidence and his administration captivated the American imagination with its aura of youthful idealism and energy. The precise nature of JFK's 'New Frontier' remained hazy, but at the forefront were ideals of self-sacrifice and public duty – exemplified in Kennedy's famous exhortation to the American people to 'ask not what your country can do for you – ask what you can do for your country'. And the same sense of selfless altruism figured in the way Kennedy mobilized images of youth as an agent of progress, epitomized by his inauguration of the Peace Corps in 1961.[4] This deployment of the rising generation as an avatar of progress contributed to the 'rehabilitation' of images of youth at the end of the 1950s – the 'bold, young man' increasingly displacing the 'malevolent delinquent' as the dominant representation of America's young.

At the same time other, less public-spirited, forces also helped construct a positive iconography of youth. As James Gilbert argues, the rise of more positive social responses to young people during the late 1950s and early 1960s was 'derived

5.1 'Fulfilment of the nation's hopes depends heavily on its young people'. (*Saturday Evening Post*, Vol. 229, No. 34, 23 February 1957)

from a further extension of the market economy in American cultural life' (1986: 214). One of the most striking features of postwar social change was the galloping success of commercial leisure industries specifically geared to youth demand. These industries were serviced by a new army of advertisers and marketeers who worked both to gauge and to exploit the desires of what was perceived as a uniquely affluent breed of young consumer – the 'teenager'. Constructed as the embodiment of modern prosperity, the teenager became symbolic of wider changes in patterns of American life. In some quarters 'teenage' culture was treated with contempt, derided as the worst example of commercial massification. More widely, however, the late 1950s and early 1960s saw the teenager cast in radiant terms. Here, youth was taken as the epitome of an America in which the sheer pace of economic growth seemed set to engender a newly prosperous age of fun, freedom and social harmony. Taken as the quintessence of social transformation, 'teenagers' were perceived as being at the sharp end of the new consumer culture, distinguished not simply by their youth but by a particular style of conspicuous, leisure-oriented consumption.

And it was among the American middle class that this upbeat 're-branding' of youth registered greatest impact. In the rhetoric of marketeers and social scientists alike, the 'teenager' was presented as essentially classless – an image redolent of the wider Cold War mythologies of universal abundance. In reality, however, the modes of consumption that defined the 'teenage' lifestyle were relatively specific to the white middle class. The burgeoning commercial youth market of the late 1950s and early 1960s was largely a middle-class province, a product of the wider socio-economic changes taking place within this group. Moreover, the ethos of hedonism and hectic consumerism central to the 'teenage' experience came to set the pace for the new values and lifestyles evident among ascending sections of the middle class. With the rise of the new, middle-class 'ethic of fun', a more liberal set of social, sexual and cultural mores came into play – an ethos that was formed in tandem with (and drew inspiration from) the developing 'teenage' realm of leisure and material gratification.

'A CASTE, A CULTURE, A MARKET': YOUTH, CONSUMPTION AND COMMERCIAL LEISURE

The wartime economic revival re-energized the commercially based youth culture that had first arisen during the 1920s and 1930s. As before, young women represented an important consumer group, the epithet 'bobby-soxer' being coined in the 1940s to denote the new image of sweaters, full skirts and saddle shoes sported by adolescent girls as they jitterbugged to the sounds of big band swing or swooned over Mickey Rooney or Frank Sinatra. The 'Swoonatra' phenomenon attracted particular public attention. Though already in his mid-twenties, Sinatra was promoted as the boyish kid from Hoboken, the singer capturing thousands of young hearts in 1942 as he sold out a month-long engagement at New York's Paramount Theater – his return to the venue, two years later, bringing Manhattan to a standstill as thousands of amorous fans besieged Times Square.

Young women's significance as a consumer group was further confirmed by the runaway success of *Seventeen* magazine. Helen Valentine, *Seventeen's* first editor, had originally developed the idea of a magazine geared to the college girl market while working as promotions editor of *Mademoiselle*. In 1944 she perfected the concept with the launch of *Seventeen* – its premier edition of 400,000 copies selling out within two days and its circulation topping the million mark within sixteen months. Into the 1950s and 1960s young women remained a driving force within the youth market, *Harper's* magazine reporting in 1959 that:

> The junior miss leads the way in endorsing 'separates', 'man-tailored' shirts, ballet slippers, and skintight 'stem' skirts or ballooning layers of petticoats. She has built seamless leotard tights . . . into a multi-million-dollar industry [and] one manufacturer of girls' clothing who started out eighteen years ago with a $4,000 investment has, by concentrating on teen-age preferences, blossomed into a $30 million business with six factories around the country and a listing on the American Stock Exchange. (*Harper's*, November, 1959)

During the 1950s youth as a whole became more significant as a consumer market. This was indebted to a combination of factors. Demographic trends were obviously important in providing a foundation for growing youth demand. Wartime increases in the birth rate, followed by the postwar 'baby boom', ensured that the teen population spiralled from 10 to 15 million during the 1950s, eventually hitting a peak of 20 million by 1970. The 1960s, meanwhile, saw unprecedented growth in the eighteen to twenty-four age group, its numbers leaping from 16,128,000 to 24,687,000 – a staggering rise of 53 per cent across the decade (Jones, 1980: 81). The postwar expansion of education, meanwhile, further accentuated the profile of young people as a distinct social group. During the 1950s the high school system was expanded considerably, but it was in colleges and universities that the most dramatic growth took place. The provisions of the GI Bill partly accounted for the rise in higher education enrolments. But, additionally, many youngsters were also choosing to remain in education for a longer period of time. In 1950 about 41 per cent of high school graduates went on to college, but by 1960 this had risen to 53 per cent (Modell, 1989: 266), the trend giving a new lease of life to the campus peer culture that had first surfaced between the wars.

Above all, however, the vital stimulus behind the growth of the commercial youth market was the scale of young people's spending power. During the war, young people's economic muscle had been boosted by industry's demand for youth labour as a replacement for drafted workers. A peacetime drive to reverse the trend brought a rise in levels of school attendance, though youth spending was sustained by a combination of parental allowances and part-time work. In 1956, for example, 35 per cent of boys and 22 per cent of girls aged between thirteen and eighteen had permanent part-time jobs, while nearly 51 per cent of boys and 28 per cent of girls worked full-time during the summer – patterns of employment that, according to some estimates, gave young people a total income in excess of $9 billion (Gilbert, 1957: 21, Tables 1–6).

The rich-pickings offered by this spending power inevitably attracted the attention of marketeers. *Seventeen* magazine started the ball rolling, Helen Valentine hiring a professional research team – Benson and Benson from Princeton – to survey her readership's buying habits, thus furnishing merchandisers with valuable information on the tastes of a highly lucrative demographic market (Palladino, 1996: 103–4). Nor was Valentine alone in recognizing youth's economic potential. She was quickly followed by a new marketing army that delved into the whims and caprices of the youth market. A young entrepreneur from Chicago led the field. An enterprising nineteen year old in 1945, Eugene Gilbert was working as a shoe store clerk when he noticed that few youngsters shopped in the store, even though it was stocking the latest styles. After persuading the owner to advertise more directly to young buyers, Gilbert was struck by the sudden rise in sales and began to consider market research among his peers as a business proposition. By 1947 the young entrepreneur's research organization, Youth Marketing Co., was prospering. With plush offices in New York, the company employed a battalion of 300 market researchers and boasted accounts with such prestigious clients as Quaker Oats, Maybelline, Studebaker, and United Airlines. Gilbert himself became a figure of some celebrity. Profiled by national magazines like *Newsweek* and *Harper's*, he was hailed as a leading spokesman for, and interpreter of, commercial youth culture. Pronouncements in his two syndicated newspaper columns – 'Girls and Teen Merchandising' and 'The Boys' Outfitter' – charted the latest shifts in young people's tastes, while his book *Advertising and Marketing to Young People* (1957) became a manual for those hoping to court adolescent desires.

Gilbert evangelized youth as a commercial market of unprecedented import- ance. As he explained in an interview with *Advertising Age* in 1951, 'Our salient discovery is that within the past decade teenagers have become a separate and distinct group within our society, enjoying a degree of autonomy and independence unmatched by previous generations' (*Advertising Age*, 26 February 1951). News- papers, magazines and a legion of commentators shared the young ad-man's enthusiasm in relating the growing scale of youth spending. In 1959, for example, an awe-struck edition of *Life* announced 'A New $10-Billion Power: the US Teenage Consumer' – the magazine describing how American youth had 'emerged as a big-time consumer in the US economy . . . Counting only what is spent to satisfy their special teenage demands, the youngsters and their parents will shell out about

$10 billion this year, a billion more than the total sales of G.M [General Motors]' (*Life*, 31 August 1959). By the early 1960s media fascination with youth spending was reaching a crescendo. In 1964 *Newsweek* averred that 'the country's 28 million youngsters between the ages of 13 and 22 control a collective purchasing power that has long since ceased to be child's play, with US youngsters expected to spend more than $24.5 billion in 1964' (*Newsweek*, 30 November 1964). Two years later, meanwhile, the same magazine devoted a special edition to a survey of the young generation's tastes and lifestyles – *Newsweek* asserting that 'the high school set has graduated from the ice-cream, soda-fountain and bicycle circuit into the big leagues of US consumption' (*Newsweek*, 21 March 1966).

Elements of hyperbole undoubtedly crept into some of the more extreme claims made for the magnitude of youth's spending. Nevertheless, an array of manufacturers scrambled to cash in on what they regarded as a potential goldmine. The range of products geared to the young was literally boundless, consumer industries interacting with and reinforcing one another in their efforts to woo the youth market. Of the $10 billion in discretionary income wielded by the young consumer in 1959, *Life* estimated that 16 per cent (roughly $1.5 billion) went to the entertainment industries, the remainder being spent on an assortment of leisure commodities – from fashion and grooming products to cars and sporting goods (*Life*, 31 August 1959).

The growth of the youth market registered especially strongly in the field of popular music. The most dramatic index of change was the arrival of rock 'n' roll – a genre of popular music tied much more closely than its predecessors to mass marketing and youth demand. The roots of this new genre lay in black rhythm and blues (R 'n' B) where the phrase 'rock 'n' roll' had developed as a familiar euphemism for sex. During the 1940s patterns of African American migration spread the popularity of rhythm and blues to northern and western cities where a proliferation of black radio shows regularly featured R 'n' B records produced by Atlantic, Chess, Sun and a growing number of other independent labels. The music was geared to a black audience, but began to pick up a significant white market as young radio listeners tuned into the late night shows.[5] With its driving four-four beat, raw vocals and openly sexual lyrics, black rhythm and blues (like jazz in the 1920s and 1930s) appealed to white youngsters through its aura of daring excitement and sexual passion. Its crossover into a white market was also galvanized by entrepreneurs such as Alan 'Moondog' Freed. In 1951 Freed was a disc jockey in Cleveland and began to feature R 'n' B records in his playlist. Moving to a bigger station in New York in 1954, Freed continued to champion the original black R 'n' B performers, though in being pitched to a mainstream youth market, the music was steadily 'whitened'. Rebranded as 'rock 'n' roll', it retained its associations with rebellious exuberance, but its sexual explicitness was toned down as the major labels recruited white performers to produce 'acceptable' covers of black R 'n' B standards. Decca secured early successes with 'whitened-up' interpretations of R 'n' B – Bill Haley scoring hits with 'Shake, Rattle and Roll' in 1954 and 'Rock Around the Clock' in 1955. The biggest commercial coup, however, came in 1956 with RCA Victor's signing of Elvis Presley. The singer had enjoyed small-scale success on Sam Phillips' independent Sun records, but with the backing of a major label Presley became a cultural phenomenon. Within six months of signing to RCA Presley had sold over eight million records and before the year was out he represented a $20 million industry.

The speed with which Presley was contracted to a three-picture movie deal was indicative of the way the film industry was also realigning itself to the youth market. As Thomas Doherty (1988) shows, the decline of adult cinema audiences during the 1950s forced the American film industry to seek out new markets – and youth became the prime target. In 1956, for example, Columbia Pictures capitalized on the rock 'n' roll boom by backing Alan Freed and Bill Haley in *Rock Around the Clock*. *Shake Rattle and Rock!* (1956), *Don't Knock the Rock* (1957) and many others quickly followed. During the late 1950s the 'teenpic' industry came of age, producers such as Roger Corman and Sam Katzman specializing in a glut of quickly made, low-budget sci-fi, horror and romance features aimed at young audiences. Films such as *Hot Rod Gang* (1958) and *Ghost of Dragstrip Hollow* (1959) exploited adolescent crazes, while the success of *The Wild One* (1954), *Rebel Without a Cause* (1955) and *The Blackboard Jungle* (1955) laid the way for a slew of 'J.D. flicks' – films such as *Untamed Youth* (1957) and *High School Confidential* (1958) purporting to sermonize against the 'evils' of juvenile crime, but simultaneously revelling in the threatening postures and salacious exploits of their young anti-heroes.[6]

The developing medium of television also began to address the youth market more directly. In the early 1950s shows featuring pop music acts and their fans became a staple of local TV stations' afternoon and Saturday morning schedules. Beginning in 1952, Dick Clark's Philadelphia-based *American Bandstand* was the most famous, the show's success prompting a transfer to the ABC network in 1957 where its audience figures could touch 20 million. However, while the 'teenpics' were unabashed in their appeal to age-specific audiences, TV shows always had to allow for the domestic environment in which they were watched. Hence *American Bandstand* was carefully chaperoned by the avuncular and level-headed Clark. The centre of attention, however, was always the young, sassy audience who packed into the studio to frug to the latest sounds. And, in giving national visibility to youth styles and fashions, shows such as *American Bandstand* helped propagate the clothes, dances and gestures of the developing youth scene. Overall, the intercession of the media helped define and disseminate the styles and attitudes of the emerging youth culture – commercial industry promoting, popularizing and giving coherence to youth's stylistic expressions.

The expansion of the youth market during the 1950s and early 1960s also saw the young, male consumer move centre stage. More than ever before, young men were addressed as a market of narcissistic consumers. 'Joe College', especially, attracted eager commercial attention. Eugene Gilbert estimated that by the mid-1950s the college market had an annual buying power of over a billion dollars, the average student's disposable income being more than a third larger than that of the average American (Gilbert, 1957: 177). Sociologist Jessie Bernard also underlined the importance of young men as a consumer market, arguing that 'the later teen-age culture is predominantly a male phenomenon', youth consumption at the older end of the scale being a 'phenomenon in which young men outnumber young women by about half' (Bernard, 1961: 2–3). And, significantly, *Esquire*'s 1965 special edition on youth culture and commerce depicted the typical 'affluent teen' as a consuming male. 'In the time it takes you to read these lines', *Esquire* apprised its readers, 'the American teen-ager will have spent $2,378.22' – a glossy, double-page photo-spread showing a satisfied young man relaxing among the trophies of his conspicuous consumption (*Esquire*, July 1965).

This commercial youth market (as we saw in Chapters 2 and 3) already existed during the 1920s and 1930s. But its scale of expansion in the 1950s and early 1960s was unprecedented and gave much greater definition to young people as a cultural group associated with particular consumer tastes. These tastes, however, prompted concern among many commentators. In its 1957 special issue on youth, for example, *Cosmopolitan* magazine rhetorically asked 'Are Teenagers Taking Over?' – the inside copy only half jokingly conjuring with images of 'a vast, determined band of blue-jeaned storm troopers forcing us to do exactly as they dictate' (*Cosmopolitan*, November 1957). The mandarins of mass culture theory also cast a disapproving eye over the flourishing youth market. For example, in the same year that he lamented the 'other-directed' conformity of *The Lonely Crowd*, David Reisman also condemned a popular music industry that had the power 'to mold popular taste and to eliminate free choice by consumers' (Reisman, 1950b: 361). The most trenchant critique, however, came from Dwight Macdonald. In 'A Caste, A Culture, A Market', his two-part *New Yorker* profile of Eugene Gilbert, Macdonald described a generation of young consumers who, he claimed, represented 'a new American caste' with 'a style of life that was fast becoming *sui generis*'. For Macdonald, however, this was a generation that fell easy prey to the wiles of commerce. 'These days', he dolefully explained, 'merchants eye teenagers the way stockmen eye cattle' (*New Yorker*, 29 November 1958).

Concern also registered in the social sciences. During the 1920s and 1930s sociological studies of youth had tended to focus on the issue of working-class delinquency. During the 1950s this theme continued, but analysis also broadened. More attention, for example, was given to what many perceived as the new problem of 'middle-class juvenile delinquency'.[7] Moreover, rather than simply focusing on issues of delinquency, a greater amount of research considered the wider social and cultural dimensions to the 'youth experience' – this exemplified by the diversity

5.2 'The Affluent Teen – and it's all his.' (*Esquire*, Vol. LXIV, No. 1, 14 July 1965.)

of papers included by the American Academy of Political and Social Science in an edition of its journal specially dedicated to the phenomenon of *Teen-Age Culture* (1961).

In their discussion of adolescent life, social scientists often echoed the themes prevalent in critiques of conformity and massification. Paul Goodman's *Growing Up Absurd* (1960) articulated the concerns perfectly through its portrayal of a young generation whose efforts to develop an authentic sense of self were stifled by large and impersonal institutions. Other authors developed similar themes of a melancholy adolescent anomie. Edgar Friedenberg, for example, emerged as a leading critic of the modern education system, first with *The Vanishing Adolescent* (1959) and then with *Coming of Age in America* (1965). For Friedenberg, a combination of institutional constraints and peer pressure was asphyxiating youngsters' endeavours to develop autonomous and meaningful lives. The psychologist Kenneth Keniston, meanwhile, was even more sombre in his portrait of a 'new alienation' – a condition of 'estrangement, disaffection, anomie, withdrawal, disengagement, separation, non-involvement, apathy, indifference, and neutralism' which was all the more alarming for being seen 'especially clearly in American youth, poised hesitantly on the threshold of an adult world which elicits little deep commitment' (Keniston, 1967, 3, 4).

Social scientific opinion, however, was far from unanimous in denouncing trends in American adolescence. As early as 1942 Talcott Parsons had coined the term 'youth culture' to denote a distinct set of social structures inhabited by the young – a theme he pursued during the early 1950s in work that stressed the 'positive function' of this system in easing transition from the security of childhood to the responsibilities of adult life (Parsons, 1954: 101). Other researchers followed Parsons' lead. Erik Erikson's *Childhood and Society* (1950), for example, presented adolescence as a confusing – though not especially deviant – stage of identity formation. In *Generation to Generation* (1956), meanwhile, S.N. Eisenstadt emphasized the mediating role of adolescent peer culture and later went on to stress 'the more positive attempts of youth to forge its own identity . . . [thereby] connecting social and political values with personal development in a coherent and significant manner' (Eisenstadt, 1962: 41). The period's most widely known study of American adolescence also depicted youth culture as relatively benign. James S. Coleman's *The Adolescent Society* (1961) was nervous in its survey of Illinois high school cliques, depicting an adolescent culture increasingly divorced from the wider adult world in terms of its attitudes, symbols and values. Nevertheless, Coleman was ultimately optimistic in arguing that prudent adult intervention could guide the peer culture towards socially beneficial goals.

Postwar responses to the developing world of American youth were, therefore, never wholly pessimistic. Alongside postwar depictions of youth as the most deplorable index of cultural decline there were always voices that were more approving. And, by the beginning of the 1960s, it was these more positive accounts that came to the fore. A trend marked, above all, by the rise of the 'teenager' as a pre-eminent icon of leisure, pleasure and exhilarating consumption.

'FUN, FUN, FUN': THE TEENAGE AESTHETIC AND THE MORALITY OF PLEASURE

A word first coined during the 1940s, the 'teen-ager' was popularized by marketeers such as Eugene Gilbert who used the term to denote a particular demographic segment of the consumer market. Its early hyphenation suggests an initial novelty, but by the late 1950s the 'teenager' had become a familiar archetype as advertisers and social scientists (along with an avalanche of books, magazine and news features) revealed to the American public what appeared to be a new generational strata with its own language, culture and values.

The concept of the 'teenager', however, amounted to more than simply a descriptive term for a generational group. Written into notions of 'teenage' tastes and lifestyles was a specific ideological construction of social change. Intrinsic to Eugene Gilbert's 'Teenage Market' and James Coleman's 'Adolescent Society' was the assumption that the new fads, fashions and social experiences of the young were creating a uniquely homogeneous and integrated generational culture in which the 'old' boundaries of class and race were steadily disappearing. In these images of a uniquely prosperous and integrated 'teenage' generation, therefore, Cold War mythologies of classless affluence found one of their purest manifestations. Dominant ideologies of 'ubiquitous abundance' were powerfully articulated in the positive stereotyping of 'teenage' America – newly affluent 'gilded youth' being presented as the vanguard of a liberated, exciting and pre-eminently classless modern society. During the late 1950s and early 1960s, therefore, the image of the affluent and autonomous 'teenager' became a standard-bearer for the 'new' America – an America which (according to dominant ideological discourse) was moving into a new era of growth, prosperity and classless plurality.

Just as the wider mythologies of 'universal prosperity' distorted the character of postwar socio-economic change, ideas of 'teenage affluence' and a new 'culture of youth' misrepresented developments in the lives of American youngsters. Rather than being inscribed by a common set of values, beliefs and behaviours, the postwar youth experience was still pervaded by important social divisions – large sections of the youth population being excluded from the 'teenage' lifestyle. As Grace Palladino argues, for example, 'teenage' America was almost exclusively white. The increase in African American high school enrolment had brought black and white youth together as never before,[8] and the growth of rock 'n' roll testified to important processes of inter-ethnic cultural exchange, but embedded racism and economic inequality meant that during the 1950s and early 1960s 'black teenagers remained invisible as far as mainstream society was concerned' (Palladino, 1996: 175–6).

Boundaries of social class also remained pertinent in the world of youth. In *Elmstown's Youth* (1949), for example, August Hollingshead acknowledged the existence of generationally based cliques, but highlighted the ways in which social behaviour was shaped by family and community background. During the Cold War giving attention to economic disparities could be a risky move, but a steady stream of research continued to acknowledge social class as a significant force within American youth culture, Bernard observing in 1961 that 'teen-age culture' was 'essentially the culture of a leisure class':

> Youngsters of lower socioeconomic classes are in the teen-age culture only in their early teens. They are more likely than children of higher socioeconomic class to enter the labor force or the armed forces or to get married soon after high school and, thus, to disappear into the adult world. This exit from the teen-age world by youngsters of lower class background means that those who remain are disproportionately from the higher socioeconomic class background. (Bernard, 1961: 2)

The styles, fashions and music of youth were, of course, hardly the sole prerogative of the white middle class. Throughout the 1950s and early 1960s working-class (together with African American and Mexican American) youth generated their own, highly visible, subcultural expressions which fed into (indeed, were a crucial influence upon) the wider constellation of modern youth culture. The predominant images of conspicuous 'teenage' consumption, however, were chiefly related to developments in the white middle class. The array of 'teen-' products and advertisements geared to Eugene Gilbert's 'teenage consumer' were pitched to a relatively well-heeled and respectable market of middle-class, white youngsters. And, within middle-class life as a whole, the connotations of vibrance and energy associated with teenage culture registered a huge impact. For the new middle class, especially, the unbridled and leisure-oriented style of 'teenage' consumption was intoxicating and became symbolic of the affluent good life venerated in their emerging 'ethic of fun'.

During the mid-1960s, the iconography of liberated and youthful 'good times' gravitated around notions of 'Britishness'. In American eyes Britain had formerly been associated with traditionalism and staid decorum, but these perceptions were transformed as the arrival of Beatlemania, together with the dazzling art and styles of fashionable London, saw British cultural imports accrue connotations of ebullience and exciting 'difference' (Miller, 2000: 17, 33). *Time* magazine's 1966 cover story on 'London: The Swinging City' captured this sense of Britain as the hub of refreshing cultural change pioneered by a newly empowered young generation. 'Youth is the word and the deed in London', *Time* explained, 'seized by change, liberated by affluence . . . everything new, uninhibited and kinky is blooming at the top of London life' (*Time*, April 1966). Women's fashions imported from Britain – for example the miniskirt and Mary Quant's trendy designs – made a big contribution to the sense of youthful verve developing in American cultural life. But the styles of British *men* also made a big impression. In its survey of the London scene, for example, *Time* had been impressed by 'the new, way-out fashion in young men's clothes' – British men's fashion seen as expressing an excitingly heightened sense of individuality and flamboyance. Media excitement also surrounded the arrival of British 'Mod' attire on American shores. In autumn 1966 men's fashion ranges were a 'Mod' bonanza.[9] 'The Mod Shirts Are Here' proclaimed the advertising campaign for Jayson's *'authentic* Mod look from England', while the 'London Look that gets admiring glances every time' was the by-line for the new 'Carnaby Cut' trousers introduced by Key Man Slacks (manufactured, somewhat incongruously, in El Paso).

Before 'Swinging London's' ascension as a pre-eminent symbol of consumer hedonism, however, California had set the pace for America's 'new frontier' in leisure, pleasure and good living. Long before the post-1945 boom, the Golden State had taken its place in the American consciousness as a utopia of relaxed prosperity.[10] Rich in natural resources, California's early socio-economic growth was spurred by the nineteenth-century gold rush and the completion of the transcontinental railroad. The economic boom of the 1920s, meanwhile, consolidated California's reputation as a verdant 'promised land', the decade seeing two million newcomers pour into the state. Though hard hit by the 1930s Depression, California's economy was revived during the Second World War, the state's population growing by a further two million as the aircraft plants skirting Los Angeles and the shipyards of the San Francisco Bay (together with numerous other industries) expanded to meet wartime demand. Growth continued into peacetime as the aerospace and electronics industries flourished, California becoming the second most populous state in 1950 and taking the lead in 1962. California also pointed the way forward in the profound cultural changes of the 1950s and early 1960s – the state leading the nation in freeway construction and the development of new suburbs and shopping complexes. It was hardly surprising, then, that this period saw 'Californian Culture' promoted as a model of affluent, dynamic and exciting lifestyles – Gallup Poll results showing that Americans rated California as the 'best-state' and the 'ideal place to live', while Los Angeles scored first place among cities for 'best-looking women' and came a close second in terms of climate, beauty of setting and brilliance of night life (cited in Marchland, 1982: 167).

The Californian lifestyle was also characteristically youthful. During the 1960s, the number of young Americans grew exponentially, but in the Western states this increase was especially pronounced – the fifteen to twenty-four age group growing by 83 per cent in the cities and nearly 100 per cent in the suburbs (Jones, 1980: 81). It was this group that were most closely associated with the 'Californian' ethos of affluent fun and excitement – a cultural universe in which the automobile was pivotal. In the 1920s the car had already become a key component of young people's peer-culture. More than 40 per cent of a sample of Californian high-school boys had use of the family auto and almost a quarter owned their own, the car functioning as a 'mobile meeting place for the young' (Fass, 1978: 218). The amateur racing of 'speedsters' also emerged between the wars, the Southern Californian Timing Association being established in 1937 to administer the informal 'hot rod' comp-etitions held among the deserts and dry lake beds outside Los Angeles. During the 1940s and 1950s hot rodding continued to grow – the sport's evolution into a professional industry being attested to by the launch of Hot Rod magazine in 1948, the foundation of the National Hot Rod Association in 1951 and the proliferation of official 'drag strips'. The average hot rodder, however, tended to be a blue-collar member of the 'no-nonsense, practical, grease-under-the fingernails brigade' and the early 1960s saw a class-based schism between the rough-neck hot-rodders and the aficionados of the more cosmopolitan (and expensive) European sports car (Moorhouse, 1991: 171–3).

Hot rodding may have been a specifically working-class subculture, but the automobile was also a fundamental ingredient in middle-class youth's lifestyles. By 1958 nearly six million teenagers held driving licences, around one and a half million owning a car (Bernard, 1960: 3–4) and researchers described how – among the middle class especially – the automobile 'permeated every aspect of these youngsters' social life' (Myerhoff and Myerhoff, 1967: 121, originally published 1964). After school and at weekends, it was noted, affluent youngsters could be seen 'slowly cruising in their cars, up and down the neighbourhood streets, greeting acquaintances, chatting, taking friends for short rides, all with an air of easy sociability.' The car, therefore, represented more than a simple means of transport. It was a mainstay of middle-class youth's social lives and as such was revered as an object of prestige and desire:

> The majority of girls and boys owned their own cars and virtually all had access to a car, usually a late model American or foreign sports car. 'Custom jobs' were not rare and cars were often 'shaved', 'chopped', 'channelled', and 'pin-striped'. All were scrupulously clean and highly polished. The argot concerning the car was as elaborate and subtle as one might expect in view of its importance; such matters as 'dual quads', 'turning seven grand', 'slicks', '3:7 trans ratio' were frequently discussed with great intensity. (Myerhoff and Myerhoff, 1967: 121, originally published 1964)

Car culture became entrenched throughout 'teen' America, but California remained its spiritual home. With the inception of the interstate highway system in 1944 (and its subsequent development in the 1950s and 1960s), the state developed as a fulcrum in the nation's road system and highways such as Route 66 (linking Los Angeles with Chicago) and Route 101 (California's coastal artery) were enshrined in popular cultural myth. Cars, moreover, represented the lifeblood of West Coast 'teenage' culture. Tom Wolfe, in his account of Burbank's 1963 'Teen Fair' (which showcased the panoply of new products geared to the youth market) gave special attention to the 'Dionysian' auto designs of custom car gurus George Barris and Ed 'Big Daddy' Roth, Wolfe underlining the significance of four wheels within the Californian youth scene:

> I don't have to dwell on the point that cars mean more to these kids than architecture did in Europe's great formal century, say, 1750 to 1850. They are freedom, style, sex, power, motion, color – everything is right there. (Wolfe, 1969: 79)

Though important, cruising the strip in a Chevy Impala, Pontiac GTO or (Dad's) Oldsmobile was not the sole focus to the California-inspired youth culture of the late 1950s and early 1960s. The beach was also crucial. By the 1930s Southern Californian shores were already the haunt of cliques of youngsters – mostly lifeguards and their buddies – who, as well as socializing and taking things easy, began experimenting with the ancient Hawaiian sport of surfing. The rolling breakers at San Onofre, Malibu and Waimea Bay became home to small communities of young surfers who manhandled their hefty (as much as 100 lbs), wooden 'big-gun' boards into the water to ride the 'heavies' and 'shoot the curl'.[11] But the appeal of this nascent surfing scene was limited. Paul Johnson – a veteran of Californian surfing culture – recalled that before the 1960s the beach was the preserve of a small, pseudo-bohemian fraternity:

> The prevailing youth culture around the beaches was colored quite a bit by the local 'beat' scene. In the late fifties the beatniks emerged as the new avant-garde and there was a certain romantic appeal to their casual nonconformist attitude and their artsy-philosophical style. These characters usually had enclaves at the oldest and most established beach areas and thus they had strong influence on the surfers who were to arise and inherit the domain. (Johnson, 1984: 33)

By the late 1950s, however, a broader based and less esoteric beach-focused youth culture was taking shape. With the availability of lightweight, polyurethane boards, surfing quickly grew in popularity and developed into a major commercial industry. The advent of the transistor radio and portable record player, meanwhile, helped transform the beach into a key locus for Californian teen culture. The release of the Columbia Pictures' movie, *Gidget*, in 1959 was also an important catalyst. Based on the real-life adventures of Cathy Kohner (whose father, Frederick, had written the original novel on which the film was based), *Gidget* was a romantic comedy depicting a tomboyish (but still resolutely respectable) girl's infatuation with the offbeat world of the surfer. Popularizing the surfing scene as excitingly fun and laid back, the film's success lay in its portrayal of a lifestyle of liberated pleasure that was acceptable to middle-class eyes – or, as Johnson puts it, *Gidget* created 'just the sort of romantic world the teenage viewers would like to escape to; a sort of happy medium between their "normal" life and a flight into bohemian adventure' (Johnson, 1984: 36).

Shifts in the texture of youth culture are impossible to pinpoint with temporal precision, but by the beginning of the 1960s a recognizable surfing subculture existed among (mainly middle-class) Southern Californian youngsters. Up and down the Los Angeles and Orange County coastline an army of young surfers loaded their boards onto their woodies (wooden-panelled station wagons – the quintessential 'surfmobile') and set out to pit their skills against the 'swells' at a host of evocatively named surfing spots – Zuma Beach, Paradise Cove, The Wedge, Doheny, Mile Zero, Trestles and many more. The surfers' exploits, meanwhile were chronicled by a cottage industry of young filmmakers. The largely self-financed documentary features of Bob Evans (*Surfing the Southern Cross*, 1962), Don Brown (*Have Board, Will Travel*, 1963), Jim Freeman (*Let There Be Surf*, 1964) and, especially, Bruce Brown (*Slippery When Wet*, 1959; *Surf Crazy*, 1960; *Water Logged*, 1962; *Barefoot Adventure*, 1961; and the sumptuous travelogue *The Endless Summer*, 1966) focused on the wave-bound feats of their friends and fellow surfers and played to raucous audiences of young, West Coast surfing fanatics.

The 1960s surf subculture was, like all youth cultural formations, relatively amorphous. Rather than being formally demarcated and firmly bounded, youth cultures are always relatively fluid, young people's attachments often partial and transient as they wander across a range of identities and affiliations.[12] Nevertheless, the 1960s surf scene existed as a recognizable set of cultural orientations, marked out by particular rituals, argot ('Some gremmie's put a ding in my board!') and sartorial style. As Christopher Buckley recounts in his autobiography of an adolescence in 1960s Santa Barbara, the tanned and bleached-blonde (preferably by the sun, but peroxide would do) surf crowd developed a quite distinctive set of stylistic conventions:

> there was a dress code – white Levis, T-shirts, and wool Pendleton shirts. We all wore blue tennis shoes. If you were really cool you wore Sperrys, and if you weren't, the less popular Keds. But if you were a surfer, it was blue. (Buckley, 1994: 17)

Surf affiliates also defined themselves through their rivalry with other youth groups. Overlap always existed between the surf scene and the wider adolescent car culture, although a degree of mutual suspicion and animosity existed between the surfers and the 'ho-dads' – the more proletarian, leather-jacketed hot-rodders. As Paul Johnson recalls of his 1960s surfing days:

> Part of the thrill of involvement was an increasingly dangerous rivalry with the street-wise ho-dads. Incidents of conflict were not uncommon, and this served to toughen and radicalize the surfers somewhat, as a necessity for survival. (Johnson, 1984: 36)

Music, too, was a linchpin within Californian surf culture. Rooted in the rock 'n' roll guitar styles of Duane Eddy, the Ventures and Link Wray, surf music found its own figurehead in Dick Dale – 'The King of the Surf Guitar'. Himself a surfer, Dale perfected his distinctive playing style (a double-picked staccato, doused profusely with reverb) at the Rendezvous Ballroom in Balboa where, between 1959 and 1961, his shows attracted audiences of thousands. And between 1962 and 1964 innumerable instrumental surf bands followed in Dale's wake, groups such as The Chantays, The Surfaris and The Pyramids enjoying commercial success, while a myriad of other grass-roots surf combos found a niche playing at town auditoriums, local 'Battle of the Bands' competitions and campus parties.[13]

Instrumental surf music had a huge following in California, but made only moderate impact on the national market.[14] More than surf guitar instrumentals, it was the vocal harmonizing of clean-cut college boys Jan and Dean and the Beach Boys that took the sound of surf to its peak – 1963 seeing the Beach Boys hit number three with 'Surfin' USA', while Jan and Dean topped the charts with 'Surf City'. In their celebration of an idealized teenage lifestyle of cars, girls and sun-kissed beaches, the hits of Jan and Dean and the Beach Boys popularized surf culture well beyond its West Coast origins. By the early 1960s, the surf scene had become the defining aesthetic of American youth style as its mythology found resonance among a generation of middle-class youngsters who wanted to recognize themselves in the 'promised fantasy land of woodies and wetsuits, baggies and bikinis – of golden flesh and innocent sex' (Hoskyns, 1996: 57).

The media furore that surrounded Jack 'Murph the Surf' Murphy and his fellow jewel thieves in 1964, therefore, was indicative of the wider grip of 'surf fever' on the American consciousness. Christened the 'Beach Boy' gang and presented as easy-living sybarites with a flair for daring adventure, Murphy and his cohorts were configured as the embodiment of the youthful, affluent and avowedly hedonistic cultural tropes increasingly impacting upon American life. The reality, of course, was very different – Murphy's gang were thuggish, violent crooks – but their youthful charisma and beach culture associations ensured that their criminal escapade captured the early 1960s *zeitgeist* of youthful fun, exhilarating pleasure and abundant wealth.

Whether or not it was 'Murph the Surf' who (as he professed) first introduced surfing to America's East Coast is open to debate. But there is little doubt that by the mid-1960s surf culture had spread out from California to become a national obsession. Robert Santelli (1997), for example, documents how the surfing lifestyle had become an established facet of teen culture in New Jersey by 1964, while in 1965 *Time* magazine described how:

last week, from Maine to Miami, beaches with a rolling surf were bristling with the sleek Fiberglass slabs . . . Even landlocked youths strap their boards on top of their cars, take off on long surfing safaris and find just the right 'beach break'. (*Time*, 7 May 1965)

The impact of the 1960s surf scene on American youth culture was so significant that nationally successful, surf-oriented music acts sprang up in even the most unlikely locations. The Astronauts, for example, hailed from Colorado, The Rivieras from Michigan, The Trashmen from Minneapolis and Ronnie and the Daytonas from Nashville – locales hardly famous for their expanse of sandy coastline.

In the popularization of Californian youth style, the commercial media were decisive. Certainly, there were elements of surf culture that were self-evolved – for example the grass-roots musicianship of the umpteen instrumental 'surf' bands that sprung up across America.[15] 'Surf style', however, gained definition as a recognizable subculture only through the intervention of the media and the commercial youth market. The music industry, for example, was central to the dissemination of surf culture across America, major labels like Capitol and Atlantic eagerly seizing upon surf music as a way to generate new products and markets, while F.M. radio stations and local TV channels also played a big part in promoting the sound of surf. Hollywood was also vital. Columbia followed up the success of Gidget with two sequels (Gidget Goes Hawaiian, 1961 and Gidget Goes to Rome, 1963 – followed by a TV series in 1965), but even more important in establishing Californian surf culture in the American popular imagination was the American International Pictures (AIP) Beach Party series. Founded in 1954, AIP had made a reputation for cheap, teen-exploitation, schlock-horror and 'J.D.' movies. With its Beach Party films the company sought (and achieved) more mainstream commercial success. Beach Party (1963), the first of the series, set the tone for those that followed. Blending music and comedy, the film followed the romantic exploits of a vivacious bunch of Californian teens, led by Frankie Avalon and Annette Funicello. In Beach Party AIP hit upon a winning formula (filmed in two weeks for $500,000, the movie grossed $6 million) and the studio followed up with a torrent of eleven more beach spectaculars. The success of the AIP beach series prompted imitations from other studios and between 1959 and 1967 Hollywood released no less than thirty-one teen-beach musicals. Twentieth Century Fox, for example, dipped its toe in the water with Surf Party (1963) and The Horror of Party Beach (1963), Columbia waded in with Ride the Wild Surf (1964) and Paramount took the plunge with The Girls on the Beach (1965).[16]

Mediation by commercial industries, therefore, gave Californian surf culture both national exposure and stylistic coherence. Without this commercial intervention it is unlikely that the burgeoning surf scene would have existed as a recognizable cultural formation – instead remaining a vaguely defined, locally based leisure culture. Recognizing the commercial imperatives underpinning the 1960s surf phenomenon, however, should not diminish its cultural significance. Cultural commodities are never passively consumed. Individuals and groups always actively engage with commercial goods and texts, drawing on them as a resource through which to carve out their own identities and maps of cultural meaning – and the appeal of the 1960s surf aesthetic has to be understood in these terms, as an avenue through which middle-

5.3 *Beach Party* (AIP, 1963 – courtesy of MGM).

class youths made sense of, and responded to, the social, economic and cultural changes going on around them.

Many cultural critics, however, have been scornful of the 1960s surf scene. Doherty, for example, casts AIP's beach films as archetypal 'clean teenpics' – safely conventional in their presentation of 'well-behaved middle-class youngsters with few blemishes, facial or otherwise' (1988: 195). Gary Morris goes further. For Morris, the beach films were an exercise in reassuring conformism ('predictable', 'antiseptic' and 'virtually sexless'), while the wider 1960s surf culture was a 'sugar-coated' and 'reactionary' product of middle-class affluence – the pleasures of the beach representing 'a gift from parent to child as a reward for conformity' (1993: 7). And, indeed, the middle-class character of the sixties surf scene was unmistakable, *Time* magazine noting in 1965 that, where once the surfer had 'the manners of a hoodlum . . . drank excessively, smoked pot . . . and earnestly avoided all forms of work', modern surfers were 'clean-cut collegians whose hair is as short as their surfing history' (*Time*, 7 May 1965). But while the 1960s surfing explosion was undoubtedly a white, middle class phenomenon, to read it as a straightforward reproduction of established bourgeois values misunderstands the basis of its appeal.

A more astute analysis is offered by R.L. Rutsky (1999). Rather than interpreting the 1960s beach films as exemplars of a reactionary bourgeois conformity, Rutsky draws attention to these texts' elements of sexual, cultural and ideological difference – beach culture being represented as 'a place of freedom, where the responsibilities of work, school, and marriage are temporarily suspended in favour of the playful hedonism of parties, surfing, teenage sexuality, romantic flings' (Rutsky, 1999: 14). The eroticism of the 1960s beach movies, for example, may well have been sanitized in the coy romance of Avalon and Funicello, but a sexual charge was still clearly evident – Rutsky pointing to the heavily sexualized imagery of bikini-clad teens doing the watusi to pulsating rock 'n' roll at beachside shindigs (Rutsky, 1999: 17). The wider surfing culture, meanwhile, was notable for the way it eschewed conformity to the world of work and onerous commitments in favour of a less constrained universe of 'personal enjoyment, fun, and parties on the beach' (Rutsky, 1999: 16). Rutsky overstates the case, however, in presenting the sixties surf scene as 'explicitly *anti-bourgeois*' (my emphasis). In its hedonistic values and cultural orientations surf culture was *adaptive* rather than rebellious. Rather than confronting or resisting the dominant cultural order, the 1960s surf phenomenon (along with the wider cosmos of 'teen' consumerism of which it was a part) helped pioneer and popularize the new, expressive and indulgent lifestyles integral to white, middle-class America's move away from an ethos of inhibition and restraint into a world of pleasure and personal gratification.

PARADISE OF FORBIDDEN PLEASURES: POPULAR EXOTICA IN POSTWAR AMERICA

The bikini was one of the most striking symbols of the free-and-easy hedonism central to 1960s beach culture. Women's two-piece swimsuits had appeared during the 1930s, but the more suggestive, low-cut minimalism of the bikini was developed simultaneously by two French designers in the summer of 1946. Couturier Jacques Heim was first off the mark, launching a suit he called the *atome* (a reference to its diminutive proportions) in his Cannes fashion boutique. But it was his rival, Louis Réard, who stole the lead. A mechanical engineer by trade, Réard developed an even skimpier version of the swimsuit for his family's lingerie business – the designer naming his creation 'the bikini' just weeks after America's atom-bomb test blasts at Bikini Atoll in the South Pacific. The bikini, therefore, was brimming with powerful connotations, combining a sense of explosively new sexual candour with notions of exotic sensuality in a palm-laden idyll. And by the mid-1950s the bikini had been unleashed from Parisian fashion catwalks and the beaches of the Côte D'Azure to become a worldwide sensation – especially in America, where film starlets such as Jayne Mansfield, Marilyn Monroe and Brigitte Bardot helped popularize the new, daringly sexy, swimsuit style. As Rutsky (1999: 19) argues, the bikini was also a central motif in 1960s beach movies, where its omnipresence underscored the films' ambience of unfettered pleasure. The eroticism of the bikini, moreover, also corresponded with the wider surf scene's emphasis on 'exotic' nonconformity – Rutsky highlighting the way 1960s surf culture rifled through the sport's Pacific Island origins to 'appropriate elements of cultural, racial and sexual otherness for white, middle-class, and largely male consumption' (1999: 21). Nor were the bleached-blonde surf set alone in appropriating stereotypes of 'exotic otherness'. The late 1950s and early 1960s saw a popular vogue for exotica and primitivism in an imagined paradise of forbidden pleasures.

The romantic myth of the 'exotic primitive' has featured in Western culture since at least the eighteenth century – Polynesian images and references possessing an especially rich history in American popular culture after the US expanded its sphere of influence into the Pacific during the early twentieth century. By the 1920s it was already common for American films, popular music and literature to draw on the South Seas as a signifier of easy living and sensual pleasure. And, as the horizons of American commodity consumption widened, so too did the enthusiasm for pseudo-Polynesian exotica – the mythology of the island paradise coming to stand for consumerism's beguiling promise of indulgence and unabashed pleasure seeking in a land of plenty.

America's fascination with 'exotic primitivism' was exemplified in the craze for Polynesian-themed restaurants and bars.[17] The fad was pioneered during the 1930s by the unlikely figure of Ernest Beaumont-Gantt, a restaurateur originally hailing from New Orleans, whose small Hollywood bar evoked the delights of distant, tropical shores through its 'exotic' decor and potent cocktails. With a move to bigger premises in 1937, Beaumont-Gantt's South Seas fantasy was extended – the budding mixologist adopting the persona of a salty island trader, Don Beach, and christening his new restaurant Don the Beachcomber's. Kitted-out with tropical plants and palm trees, bamboo and rattan furniture, together with flickering torches, decorative puffer fish and fishnet floats, Don the Beachcomber's was the model for thousands of South Seas restaurants that followed in Don's sandy footsteps. The chief competition came from Victor Bergeron, an ambitious Oakland tavern-owner inspired by a visit to Don's thriving emporium in 1938. Returning home, Bergeron also recreated himself as a roistering island-hopper – Trader Vic – and re-vamped his bar as a South Pacific hideaway. Priding himself as a culinary innovator (among his triumphs, Bergeron claimed to have invented the mai-tai cocktail in 1944), Trader Vic recognized the tantalizing appeal the South Seas fantasy could weave for Americans hungry to taste the fruits of the good life – his 1946 *Book of Food and Drink* explaining how:

> those gentle natives, the Polynesians, know how to have fun in simple, unaffected ways. The beauty of their surroundings, the ease with which they acquire food and clothing are not for us who have built up a complicated, war-torn civilization which is a far cry from island ways. But some of those can be injected into our own lives, to help us relax and have fun. (Trader Vic, 1946: 17)

Rather than killing-off the dream-world of exotic leisure, the Second World War fuelled America's tropical fantasies. The Pacific campaign was a harrowing ordeal for many US servicemen, but some GIs also returned home with stories of sun-drenched seashores and beautiful women in island havens such as Bora Bora and Oahu. Such were the experiences chronicled by James Michener in *Tales of the South Pacific*, his Pulitzer Prize-winning novel of 1947 from which Rodgers and Hammerstein drew inspiration for their blockbuster musical, *South Pacific*. Following its success on Broadway *South Pacific* came to the big screen in 1958, Joshua Logan's film adaptation making full use of lush visuals, spectacular locations and (somewhat excessive) colour filters to heighten the sense of aroused desires in a tropical paradise. Nor was *South Pacific* alone in serving up a luscious cinematic cocktail of sultry passions. Esther Williams also starred in a series of romantic musicals that included *On an Island With You* (1948) and *Pagan Love Song* (1950), while the 1962 film version of *Mutiny on the Bounty* depicted a South Seas life that was abounding with irresistible pleasures.

Public imagination was also fired by Thor Heyerdahl's successful Kon Tiki voyage from Peru to Polynesia in 1947.[18] The entry of Hawaii to the Union as the fiftieth state in 1959 and the growth of holiday travel, meanwhile, also ensured America's continued fixation with exotic iconography. Hence Don the Beachcomber and Trader Vic both flourished during the 1950s – the former coming to boast a nationwide chain of sixteen restaurants, while the latter expanded into an international franchise of twenty-five Polynesian-style brasseries. Across America Don and Vic were also followed by thousands of imitators – the horde of recreational shrines including such temples as Trader Dick's and Harvey's in Nevada, the Tonga Room in San Francisco and Luau 400 in New York (billed as 'An Island Paradise on New York's East Side'). Other leisure enterprises also made extensive use of pseudo-Polynesian imagery. When Disneyland first opened in 1955, for example, its 'Adventureland' attraction included a South Seas gift shop called 'The Tiki Trader', while carved idols guarded the entrance to a jungle river ride. In 1962, meanwhile, Adventureland's 'Tahitian Terrace Restaurant' was opened and 1963 saw the unveiling of Disney's first 'Enchanted Tiki Room' – a themed environment using sophisticated tape machines and automation (squawking parrots and singing flowers) to create the sensations of a bewitched tropical kingdom.

The 1950s and early 1960s saw the tropical fantasy enshrined as one of the pre-eminent leisure styles of American culture. *Tiki*, a Polynesian god of fertility, gave his name to an aesthetic of 'ersatz exotica' as carved wooden and stone idols were planted in American gardens and affluent suburbanites spent their summer afternoons chatting around sizzling *luau* barbecues, their drink cabinets adorned with pineapple ice-buckets and figurines of swaying *hula* girls. *Tiki* themes also filtered into interior design and architectural style – Bamboo and rattan furniture gracing the living rooms of discerning sophisticates, while 'South Seas' motifs surfaced in the design of hotels such as the Kon Tiki in Arizona ('A Little Bit of Waikiki in the Heart of Phoenix') and Californian apartment complexes such as the Tahitian Village in the San Fernando Valley and the Polynesian Village in Playa Del Rey.[19]

Tiki style also found its soundtrack in the 'exotic sounds' of lounge musicians such as Martin Denny, Les Baxter and Arthur Lyman, whose easy-listening timbres crystallized notions of a tropical paradise in modern suburbia. Fusing traditional instruments with bird calls, jungle sounds and percussion, Martin Denny was indisputably the 'Big Kahuna' of the 'exotic sound' – Denny topping the album charts in 1957 with *Exotica*, while his single 'Quiet Village' climbed to the number two slot the same year. A plethora of Denny releases ensued, all with suitably arousing titles – *Exotica 2* and *3* being followed by *Forbidden Island*, *Primitiva*, *Hypnotique* and *Afro-desia*. Denny's album covers, too, were evocative, their seductive portraits of model Sandy Warner launching her career as the 'Exotica Girl'. Inspired by Denny's colossal success (before retiring he had clocked up thirty-seven album releases, with sales in excess of four million), his collaborators Les Baxter and Arthur Lyman also showcased their own brands of the 'exotic sound' – their albums *Taboo*, *Ritual of the Savage* and *Tamboo!* purveying the same images of 'exotic primitivism' and torrid sexuality.[20]

The postwar ardour for 'exotic' themes and imagery also registered in the sphere of men's fashion as the Hawaiian shirt became *de rigueur* for Americans at leisure. The distinctively colourful 'aloha' sports shirt first emerged in the early twentieth century as Hawaiian plantation labourers decorated their plain workshirts with striking tribal designs. The shirt's popularity grew during the 1920s and 1930s, American tourists and military personnel creating a thriving souvenir market. Shirt production took place on an increasingly large scale, pioneered by clothes manufacturer Ellery J. Chun (often credited as the creator of the original 'aloha' shirt), who mass-produced enormous numbers of the vibrantly coloured garments for his family's store in downtown Honolulu. The war further promoted the fortunes of the 'aloha' shirt. Demand in Hawaii was boosted by the arrival of thousands of servicemen, who also popularized casual, 'island' styles on their return to America. A 1946 fashion spread in *Esquire*, for example, announced the arrival of 'Tropics at Home' as 'many of the ex-military refuse to give up the cool, shall we say, "informality" of uniforms worn on island outposts during the war' (*Esquire*, August 1946). In 1951 the Hawaiian shirt even got a Presidential seal of approval, a grinning Harry Truman appearing on the cover of *Life* magazine sporting a particularly natty example (decorated with light blue sea-birds) and by 1955 *Look* magazine was reporting that the American clothes industry was gearing-up for a boom in 'the wildest men's sport shirts ever seen' (*Look*, 25 January 1955) as Hollywood stars such as Montgomery Cliff, Frank Sinatra, Tony Curtis and Elvis Presley all helped to popularize the 'aloha' shirt style.[21]

The postwar vogue for *tiki* decor, backyard *luaus* and the gamut of 'Polynesian' pop culture can be situated in a much longer history of western representations of the South Pacific and its peoples. Constructed in terms of an alien and exotic 'otherness', these have simultaneously served as a focus for both the fears and the desires of Western culture. Alongside stereotypes of the murderous savage there has always existed the romantic (and equally racist) myth of the 'exotic primitive' who is unconstrained by the mores and taboos of modern civilization. bell hooks interprets such stereotypes of exoticism and otherness as inherently exploitative in the way the Western imagination has configured them as a spectacle of eroticism and risqué indulgence – 'others" ethnicity becoming the 'seasoning that can liven up the dull dish that is mainstream white culture' (1992: 21). In this flirtation with otherness, however, hooks also recognizes a potential for the dislocation of the status quo, hooks arguing for an acknowledgement of the ways 'the desire for pleasure, and that includes erotic longings, informs our politics, our understanding of difference [so that] we may know better how desire disrupts, subverts and makes resistance possible' (hooks, 1992: 39). Subversion and resistance, however, are not qualities one would immediately associate with the 1950s fad for *Tiki* kitsch. Indeed, in *Tiki*'s stereotyping of 'South Seas' culture as alluringly exotic, there surfaced elements of racism and sexism of the crassest order. Rather than radical or transgressive, it is better to see the *Tiki* experience as a *transformative* encounter – offering postwar Americans a mythologized Polynesian fantasyland where they could throw off the work ethic and the inhibitions of prudish sobriety to luxuriate in an Eden of sensuality and personal pleasure.

Tiki exotica and the 1960s surf scene, then, were phenomena cut from the same cultural cloth. Though they were embraced by different generational groups, Tiki and 'surf' were closely allied cultural forms – both representing avenues through which white, middle class America began to experiment with the possibilities of a culture based on leisure-oriented consumption, recreation and more liberated forms of sexual expression. Indeed, the degree to which Tiki and 'surf' overlapped with (and mutually informed) one another as transformative experiences for the American middle class was neatly exemplified by the Beach Boys' first record release in 1961 – a single that coupled the songs Surfin' and Luau. Written by twenty-year-old Beach Boys Brian Wilson and Mike Love, Surfin' captured the essence of the exuberant Californian youth culture. Equally significant, however, was the single's (less well known) flip-side – Luau. Written by Bruce Morgan (son of the record's producer), the song celebrated the Hawaiian-style parties that were all the rage as the suburban middle class revelled in a kitsch paradise where the imagined freedoms of the South Seas had been magically transplanted to American backyards – or as the song itself enunciated (without a hint of irony):

> You don't need to live in the islands
> To have a lot of fun
> Just pretend your patio
> Is an island in the sun.[22]

'THE GOOD LIFE': YOUTH, CONSUMPTION AND THE 'NEW LEISURE'

Fantasies of 'exotic' pleasure blossomed in a society increasingly conscious of leisure as a potent socio-economic force. At the close of 1959 Life magazine's 'Special Double Issue on the Good Life' paid homage to America's growing levels of recreational time and disposable income. Life's account of 'our new found good life, growing out of our new-found leisure' was not devoid of misgivings – the magazine's editorial conceding that the cultural repercussions of Americans' pursuit of happiness were 'not altogether an edifying sight', while an article by Sloan ('Gray Flannel Suit') Wilson called for an end to the 'confusing eulogies of leisure which, without the most careful definition, seem to be calls for sloppy self-indulgence' (Life, 28 December 1959). Overall, though, Life was upbeat and celebratory in its survey of the 'Big and Busy US Playground'. In effusive tones, the magazine described 'a vast new economic force, the Leisure Business, which could not exist if everyone worked at "useful things" and which, by the buying power it releases and by the dreams it satisfies, has filled the whole economy with energy and ambition'. Estimating the postwar leisure boom represented a spending power of around $40 billion a year (or more than 8 per cent of America's GNP), *Life* emphasized the plurality of the 'new "leisure masses"'. Ultimately, however, the magazine conceded the relatively class-specific nature of 'the new leisure', observing that 'the leisure market is supported mainly by people who make from $4,000 up a year after taxes' (*Life*, 28 December 1959).

The expansion of commercial recreation during the 1950s and 1960s was heavily indebted to the new consumerist and leisure-oriented middle class and their 'morality of pleasure as a duty'. The youth market was also central to these changes, 'teen' demand nourishing the postwar growth of commercial leisure. More than this, though, patterns of young people's consumption also provided important reference points for a middle class feeling its way into the unfamiliar world of hedonistic materialism. Eugene Gilbert, for example, drew on Elihu Katz and Paul Lazarsfeld's (1955) study of 'opinion leaders' to highlight teenagers' tastes as not only an influence on their parents' household spending, but also as a source from which:

> almost all mass buying trends originate. The mass adult market may not feel all the trends in this storm center, but most of those that reach the adult market have their beginnings here. (Gilbert, 1957: 28)

Others, too, recognized the impact of teenage culture on adult lifestyles, although not all shared Gilbert's enthusiasm. In their denunciation of 'teen-age tyranny', for example, Grace and Fred Hechinger lamented the way Americans seemed to be 'growing down rather than growing up', the nation standing 'in such awe of its teen-age segment that it is in danger of becoming a teen-age society, with permanently teen-age standards of thought, culture and goals' (Hechinger and Hechinger, 1962: x). Singling out trends in middle-class culture, the Hechingers bemoaned the rise of what they termed the 'fun ethic' and called for a return to the traditional values of hard work and self-denial:

> First to go should be the idea that everything must be 'fun,' with fun interpreted as the effortless accomplishment of something pleasant. The 'fun ethic' itself is barefaced fraud, and the fact that it has been sold to adults as well as teen-agers only makes it worse. In reality, of course, the reverse is usually the truth: most pleasant things must be accomplished by varying amounts of effort which can be exciting, stimulating or, at times, downright difficult and troublesome. (Hechinger and Hechinger, 1962: 224)

The Hechingers were outspoken in their critique of the impact of teenage leisure, denouncing popular dance crazes such as the Twist as 'bump-and-grind exhibitionism' and a 'flagrant example of a teen-age fad dominating the adult world' (Hechinger and Hechinger, 1962: 112–13). More generally, however, the dynamic connotations surrounding youth consumption were enthusiastically embraced within American culture – not least by the admen of Madison Avenue. During the late 1950s American advertising had been beset by a sense of malaise, the industry perceiving itself as lacking innovative flair. The early 1960s, however, saw a 'creative revolution' in advertising strategy as a new generation of admen began to identify with the contemporary youth scene. Their aim was partly to appeal to the growing youth market but, as Thomas Frank (1997) cogently argues, the 'creative revolution' also traded on youth as an icon of rebellious autonomy. Advertisers deployed the concept of 'youthfulness' as a shorthand signifier for self-fulfilment and 'hip' nonconformity that could appeal to the new consumer value systems that aspired to break away from stodgy conformity and explore new horizons of individuality and excitement.

Though Frank's analysis dwells on products and advertising campaigns of the later 1960s, he acknowledges that within American consumer culture 'the move to this more hip style was fully established by 1965' (1997: 133). By the early 1960s advertisers and manufacturers were habitually identifying their products with the vitality and independence of youth. In 1963, for example, Pepsi let rip with the rallying cry 'Come Alive! You're in the Pepsi Generation', while the 'Dodge Rebellion' entreated customers to 'Break Away From the Everyday'. But the product that best encapsulated consumer industries' infatuation with youth was the Ford Mustang.

The sporty Mustang first rolled off assembly lines in April 1964. Originally a gleam in the eye of Ford designers in 1961, the car was a response to both the popularity of foreign sports cars and to what the company's researchers perceived as 'a renewed interest in driving just for the fun of driving'.[23] The car's responsive handling and high performance were set off by its sleek good looks – the long hood and short deck winning the Tiffany Award for Excellence in American Design and sparking a 1960s trend for 'pony cars'. The Mustang was a huge success. Ford's first-year sales estimate of 100,000 units was surpassed in just four months, with some 22,000 orders taken on the first day of availability and more than 417,000 Mustangs sold in twelve months – then a record for first-year car sales. The Mustang owed part of its success to its affordability (the car was relatively inexpensive at $2,368) and to Ford's advertising buildup – initiated long in advance of the car's launch. But the Mustang phenomenon was also indebted to Ford's deft marketing. Drawing on marketeers' concepts of 'lifestyle', Ford developed the Mustang as a car that could be 'individualized' to suit the tastes of a variety of consumer groups. As Ford's promotional copy explained, the Mustang was 'The Car Designed to be Designed by You', its basic chassis providing 'a highly versatile foundation on which the buyer can literally custom-tailor his [sic] own special kind of car'. Mustangs arrived in three basic models (convertible, hardtop or fastback), but from there the Mustang buyer could 'make of the car almost anything he desires', the dazzling array of options including three different V-8 engines, three versions of transmission, quick-ratio steering, special handling suspension, sports tyres and a virtually limitless range of other optional extras.

A pioneering step towards 'niche-marketing', the Mustang's extensive option package allowed Ford to adapt its product to suit a spectrum of 'lifestyle needs'. Above all, though, the Mustang was designed to be a 'youth' car. In the Mustang, Ford created a product that could exploit the increasingly profitable youth market, but which could also appeal to consumers who sought to identify with the 'youthful' themes of adventure and fun. And both strategies were a big success. As expected, the Mustang sold enormously well to the young, with more than half of the car's first-year buyers aged under thirty-four. But the car was also a hit with older age groups, 16 per cent of sales going to men in the forty-five to fifty-five age group – the 'young at heart' clambering aboard the bandwagon of 'youthful' and exciting consumerism. The success of the Mustang, then, is testimony to the way in which 'youth' had become a motif not just for progress and regeneration, but for the dreams, desires and ideals of the middle-class consumer.

*

During the late 1950s and early 1960s modern, American leisure style took its recognizable form. Based on the consumption of commercially produced goods and entertainments, this was an approach to leisure that emphasized hedonistic enjoyment and individual fulfilment. Ethically and aesthetically, this leisure style was tied to the emergence of a middle-class faction whose habitus was centred around freedom, pleasure and the fulfilment of consumer desires. The rise of this group's 'ethic of fun' did not go uncontested and often conflicted with older, more conservative bourgeois value systems – but during the late 1950s and early 1960s the new leisure ethos became a cultural force to be reckoned with.

Youth was pivotal in these developments. The rise of a huge commercial youth market was not only a major shot in the arm to the American economy. It also laid the basis for a new 'teenage' aesthetic that made a project of self-realization through the consumption of leisure-oriented signifiers. 'Teenage' consumers, themselves, were an important market for the growing array of leisure and 'lifestyle' industries. But, more than this, they also experimented with and pioneered the tastes and attitudes that informed the developing culture of the 'new petite bourgeoisie'. The 'teenage' fetish for fun and individuality paved the way for the ascendant 'morality of pleasure' and its prioritizing of personal desire.

This was, though, almost wholly a white cultural domain. The bleached-blonde hues of the 1960s surf phenomenon underscored the racial exclusivity of 'teen' consumption, while African Americans were invisible in advertising pitches for products like the Mustang. America's minority ethnic groups were largely excluded from the consumer-fest of the 1950s and 1960s through a combination of low incomes and entrenched white racism. Despite its racial exclusionism, however, the 'morality of pleasure' routinely appropriated and stylized symbols of ethnic 'otherness' as signifiers of unashamed pleasure seeking and 'exotic' difference.

Gender, too, was a crucial factor in the new leisure order. The 1920s and 1930s had already seen the rise of 'a new masculine logic that stressed personality, self-realization, sexuality, youthfulness, and leisure' (Pendergast, 2000: 261). But with the rise of the 'new petite bourgeoisie' during the 1950s and early 1960s, ideals of masculinity formed around hedonistic consumerism were further extended and intensified. In this milieu the playboy archetype came into his own – the new moral code of the middle class evidenced most obviously by the emergence of a masculine identity that prioritized youthful pleasure, conspicuous consumption and 'liberated' sexual desire.

NOTES

1   How far these fears were actually shared by the general public is debatable, although Gilbert cites Gallup poll surveys suggesting a peak of public concern in 1945 followed by a more sustained period of anxiety between 1953 and 1958 (Gilbert, 1986: 63).

2   For example, in his 1958 survey of suburban youth crime, Salisbury reported that 'much public concern over delinquency stems not from an increase in anti-social conduct but from the fact that patterns of conduct formerly exclusive to poor, working-class or lower-middle-class youngsters, have spread to the middle class as a whole and to upper-class youth, as well' (Salisbury, 1967: 191, originally published 1958).

3   The retinue of witnesses included, for example, Frederic Wertham whose 1953 study, *Seduction of the Innocent*, had presented comics as a font of juvenile depravity.

4   A detailed account of Kennedy's role in the establishment of the Peace Corps is provided in Wofford (1980: 243–84).

5   There exist innumerable accounts of the early history and development of rock 'n' roll, though Gillett (1983) represents one of the best.

6   McGee and Robertson (1982) elaborate a full account of the development of the 'J.D.' film genre.

7   See, for example, England (1960) and the various contributions collected in Vaz (ed.) (1967). The theme also gained wide exposure through its treatment in *Rebel Without a Cause* (1955) – a film that also touched on contemporary perceptions of a masculine 'crisis' through its depiction of a weak and ineffectual suburban father.

8   Between the early 1940s and the late 1950s the percentage of African American students who finished high school virtually doubled (Gilbert, 1983: 19).

9 Frank (1997: 190–1) notes the flurry of media attention that accompanied the arrival of the 'Mod' look in 1966.

10 Starr's monumental history of California (1973, 1985, 1990, 1997) elaborates a comprehensive account of the state's development and its place within the mythologies of the American Dream.

11 An evocative photographic record of the Californian beach culture of the late 1930s exists in James (1996), while Kampion and Brown (1998) provide a lively popular history of the American surfing subculture. Burt (1986) and White (1994) also offer valuable accounts of the rise of the Californian surfing scene in the early 1960s.

12 Muggleton (2000) highlights the qualities of transience and fluidity endemic to youth subcultural styles.

13 A concise history of the 'surf guitar' genre can be found in Otfinoski (1997: 121–45), but the definitive accounts exist in Blair (1995) and Blair and McParland (1990).

14 Though in 1961 Dick Dale's 'Let's Go Trippin' crept into the *Billboard* charts and 1963 saw The Pyramids reach number eighteen with 'Penetration', while the Chantays' 'Pipeline' climbed to number four and the Surfaris' took the premier slot with 'Wipe Out'.

15 Dalley (1996) provides an encyclopaedic review of the 'grass-roots' surf bands of the early 1960s.

16 The fullest narrative of the development of the 1960s beach musical is presented in McParland (1992).

17 A concise history of Polynesian-themed bars such as 'Don the Beachcomber's' and 'Trader Vic's' can be found in Lanza (1995a: 66–74).

18 Heyerdahl's Kon Tiki exploits were popularized through both the publication of his account of the voyage (*The Kon-Tiki Expedition*, first published in America in 1950) and the release, in 1951, of his Academy Award-winning film of the adventure. The publication, in 1955, of Heyerdahl's chronicle of his expedition to Easter Island (*Aku Aku: The Secret of Easter Island*, serialized three years later in the *Saturday Evening Post*) further fuelled America's fascination for all things 'exotic'.

19 The term '*Tiki* style' has been coined by contemporary critics to denote the postwar fad for 'South Seas' themes and images. During the 1950s and 1960s themselves the term '*Kon-Tiki* style' was more commonly used – denoting, especially, the vogue for Polynesian-inspired architecture. The most authoritative guide to the *Tiki* phenomenon exists in Kirsten (2000), while *Tiki* style past and present is assiduously excavated in Otto von Stroheim's journal of 'urban archaeology', *The Tiki News*. Congdon-Martin (1998), meanwhile, chronicles the impact of pseudo-Polynesian motifs on American popular culture – the volume being based on the California Heritage Museum's 1997 exhibition, 'Aloha Spirit – Hawaii's Influence on the California Lifestyle'.

20 Lanza (1995b: 119–28) provides a thoroughgoing survey of the rise of the 'exotic sound', Jones (1997) also offering some adroit observations. However, the most evocative odyssey through the soundscapes of American exotica is provided by Toop (1999).

21 Schiffer (1997) and Steele (1984) both provide engaging histories of the 'aloha' shirt.

22 *Surfin'* b/w *Luau* was originally released by Candix records in December 1961. Various versions of *Luau* can currently be found on the DCC compilation CD of early Beach Boys' material – *Lost and Found* (DCC, DZS-054, 1991).

23 Lee A. Iacocca, Ford Motor Company Vice President, Press Release, 13 April 1964.

Chapter 6
High-Living with the 'Upbeat Generation': the Cultural Currency of *Playboy*

The *Playboy*, illustrated by the monthly magazine of that name, does for the boys what Miss America does for the girls. Despite accusations to the contrary, the immense popularity of this magazine is not solely attributable to pin-up girls . . . *Playboy* appeals to a highly mobile, increasingly affluent group of young readers, mostly between eighteen and thirty, who want much more from their drugstore reading than bosoms and thighs. They need a total image of what it means to be a man. And Mr. Hefner's *Playboy* has no hesitation in telling them . . . For the insecure young man with newly acquired free time and money who still feels uncertain about his consumer skills, *Playboy* supplies a comprehensive and authoritative guidebook to this forbidding new world to which he now has access.

Harvey Cox, *The Secular City* (Bloomsbury: SCM, 1965: 199–200)

THE PRINCE OF PLEASURE: HUGH HEFNER, *PLAYBOY* AND THE ASCENDANCE OF THE MALE CONSUMER

Billing itself as 'entertainment for men', Hugh Hefner's *Playboy* magazine was one of the major success stories of postwar American publishing. By 1967 towering white letters spelling out 'PLAYBOY' crowned the Palm Olive Building (Chicago's most prestigious skyscraper) – patent confirmation of the meteoric rise of Hefner's commercial empire. Hefner – or 'Hef' as he self-consciously mythologized himself – had originally launched *Playboy* on a shoestring budget in November 1953, writing most of the copy himself and re-cycling classic short stories available in the public domain.[1] But, despite its humble beginnings, *Playboy* rapidly became a cultural phenomenon. Hefner had been uncertain of his magazine's potential – even asking printers to remove the date from the inaugural issue, fearing sales might be painfully slow – but *Playboy* was a virtually instantaneous hit. The magazine's first print run of 70,000 copies quickly sold out, its monthly sales skyrocketing to nearly a million a month by 1959 and soaring to in excess of 4.5 million over the next ten years. By the beginning of the 1960s it was already clear that Hefner had hit the jackpot. *Playboy*'s news-stand sales alone annually generated over $3 million, subscriptions garnering a further $1 million, while Hefner's merchandising enterprises were soon yielding well over $2 million from the sale of anything from tie-clips bearing his magazine's familiar 'Bunny' insignia, to 'Bunny Tails' tastefully mounted on decorative wall plaques.

As several critics have noted, the secret of *Playboy*'s success lay in the way it combined sex and status – winning a mainstream distribution and readership through its adept integration of pornography within the context of an upmarket lifestyle magazine.[2] For Gail Dines this strategy amounted to little more than a cunning subterfuge. According to Dines, *Playboy*'s fascination with consumption and high living was a smokescreen that functioned to 'cloak the magazine in an aura of respectability' – *Playboy*'s *bon vivant* pretensions providing a 'classy' veneer that served to legitimate its pornographic content (Dines, 1998: 46). In these terms, the attention that *Playboy* lavished on matters of style and leisure was relatively tangential to its real business of the subordination and sexual objectification of women. For Dines, therefore, *Playboy*'s catalogue of commodities was a means to an end, an avenue through which a reader might hope to attain the 'real prize: all the high quality women he wanted – just like the ones who populated the magazine' (Dines, 1995: 256).

Playboy's sexual content was undoubtedly fundamental to its success. From the outset Hefner could be candid about the central place of pornography in the marketing formula of his magazine. Six months before its launch, for example, the publisher's promotional material was assuring distributors that the venture was sure to be 'one of the best sellers you have ever handled . . . it will include male-pleasing figure studies, making it a sure hit from the very start' (cited in Miller, 1985: 39). Indeed, the runaway success of *Playboy*'s premier edition was largely indebted to its inclusion of a nude photospread featuring Marilyn Monroe. The star had posed for the photographs in 1949, before her fame, and Hefner could not believe his luck when he managed to pick up the publishing rights for a mere $500. With such sensational material, the selling power of *Playboy*'s first issue was guaranteed and Hefner promised distributors similar results with subsequent editions through the regular inclusion of 'a beautiful, full-page, male-pleasing nude study – in full natural colour!' (Miller, 1985: 39)

There is little doubt, then, that *Playboy*'s sexual content was intrinsic to the magazine's appeal and, able to exploit *Esquire*'s legal victories of the 1940s, *Playboy* further secured the acceptability of pornography within the mainstream of American culture. At the same time, however, *Playboy* amounted to more than simply a slickly packaged pornographic magazine. The maxim 'I buy *Playboy* for its articles' has, of course, become a standing joke, but during the 1950s and 1960s the magazine's features on fashion, leisure and lifestyle represented more than inconsequential filler. In its celebration of a masculine universe of consumption and narcissistic display, *Playboy* testified to the growing hegemony of a middle-class male identity for whom responsibility, domesticity and puritanical abstinence were anathema, while hedonistic fun and sensual indulgence were defining virtues.

6.1 'Entertainment For Men'. (*Playboy*, Vol. 8, No. 8, August 1961.)

The rise of Hefner's magazine during the 1950s and early 1960s marks, for Barbara Ehrenreich, a crucial moment in the displacement of a puritanical masculine 'breadwinner' ethos by a more hedonistic 'playboy' ideal. *Playboy*, Ehrenreich contends, was a 'visionary' bible for a new breed of consuming male. Against the grain of postwar ideologies of containment, she argues, *Playboy* 'encouraged a sense of membership in a fraternity of male rebels' (1983: 43). In the *Playboy* manifesto the ethic of the 'self-made man' remained alive and well, the magazine still espousing commitment to career advancement and the accumulation of wealth – with Hefner himself often presented as a model of 'self-made' success. But in the *Playboy* universe it was men themselves who harvested the fruits of their labour. Instead of the responsibilities of family life and the commitments of monogamous marriage, the magazine was replete with images of 'cozy concupiscence and extra-marital consumerism' (Ehrenreich, 1983: 43). As Ehrenreich notes (1983: 47), in one of *Playboy*'s earliest editions Burt Zollo, Hefner's friend and a regular contributor, exhorted readers to be 'out on the town with a different dish every night' and the magazine guided the aspirant swinger through all that the good life had to offer – from chic fashions and high-powered sports cars to exotic travel and gourmet food.

However, while Ehrenreich sees the 'playboy ethic' as something fairly unique to the postwar era, we have already seen how its origins existed much earlier. First appearing in embryonic form in the bachelor subcultures of America's flourishing cities of the late nineteenth century, the hedonistic male consumer took more recognizable shape during the prosperity of the Jazz Age. Indeed, this lineage was half acknowledged in Hefner's choice of title for his magazine. His initial preference, *Stag Party*, was vetoed by the publishers of *Stag* (a true adventure pulp), but Hefner was more than happy with the alternative of *Playboy*, feeling that it 'had a Scott Fitzgerald flavour . . . and conjured up just the image he wanted to project' (Miller, 1985: 54). Nevertheless, while the playboy brand of style-conscious masculinity stretched back to the turn of the century, Ehrenreich correctly highlights the 1950s and early 1960s as the moment when it came of age. With the rise of an emergent middle class whose trademark was a fervour for consumption and style, the playboy ethic was celebrated as a desirable masculine ideal. Combining the vivacious energy of youth with the footloose independence of the man-about-town, the figure of the 1950s playboy was the apotheosis of the 'ethic of fun' championed by the new bourgeoisie. Again, however, it is important to emphasize the 'mythic' qualities of the playboy creed. As an ideal of leisure-oriented masculine consumption, the playboy was a fantasy role-model that few men could actually attain. Instead, its significance lay in its capacity to function as an 'imagined identity' – a set of aspirational codes, attitudes and desires that offered men a meaningful way of constructing their identities in relation to the proliferating world of commodity consumerism. This 'imagined identity' took form across a constellation of cultural sites, though it gained its purest expression in the Playboy empire – Hefner's magazine positing itself as men's passport to the new frontiers of hedonistic consumption.

'ENTERTAINMENT FOR MEN'

Never one to underestimate his own achievements, Hefner has been happy to take credit for almost singlehandedly transforming the world of American men's magazines. In its twentieth anniversary issue, for example, *Playboy* maintained that before its arrival there 'had never been anything quite like it on the market' and in an extended interview Hefner argued that *Playboy*'s launch had been so successful because it was a unique product in a field dominated by 'outdoor-adventure books . . . [that] had a hairy-chested editorial emphasis' (*Playboy*, January 1974).[3] Yet Hefner's magazine was not quite the trailblazer it claimed to be.

In both its themes and format *Playboy* was clearly inspired by the formula originally developed by *Esquire* in the 1930s. Even the buck rabbit character that adorned *Playboy*'s early covers was a thinly veiled imitation of *Esquire*'s 'Esky' mascot. Indeed, Hefner had long been an avowed fan of the earlier 'Magazine For Men'. Since his school days Hefner had bought *Esquire* whenever he could afford it, later decorating his bedroom with Petty and Vargas pin-ups and regarding the magazine as 'the arbiter of taste and style, the very last word in male sophistication' (Miller, 1985: 42). And in 1951, after short stints as a copywriter with assorted publishing and advertising firms, Hefner had actually worked in *Esquire*'s subscriptions department. When, in the same year, *Esquire* relocated its Chicago operations to New York, Hefner elected to stay behind and began to formulate plans for the launch of his own magazine. From the outset he took his cues from his former employer, Hefner envisioning a periodical that used 'cheesecake' pin-ups to gain an initial toehold in the market, but which would go on to become 'an entertainment magazine for the city-bred guy – breezy, sophisticated . . . really making it an *Esquire*-type magazine' (Hefner, cited in Brady, 1974: 55). And, in his early sales pitches, Hefner underlined the pedigree of his venture, stressing to distributors that his new magazine was 'being put together by a group of people from *Esquire* who stayed here in Chicago when that magazine moved east – so you can imagine how good it's going to be' (cited in Miller, 1985: 39).

Nor was Hefner alone in aping the editorial strategies initiated by *Esquire*. As we saw in Chapter 4, during the mid-1940s *True* (a pulp adventure title) had already begun to reconfigure itself along the lines pioneered by *Esquire*, drawing back from the great outdoors and giving more attention to matters of fashion and consumption. And, while it is true that the fifties men's magazine market was still dominated by gritty 'outdoors' titles such as *Man's Life* and *Man to Man*, new titles were also beginning to follow *True* into the world of high-living consumerism. In 1951, for example, the Publisher's Development Corporation launched *Modern Man*. With features that were red-blooded, robust and resolutely 'manly' ('Hickok: Hell's Own Marshall', 'How to Run a Submarine'), *Modern Man* was a magazine whose appeal remained geared to the 'action man' rather than the 'leisure man', but it also showed a degree of affinity for up-scale consumption through its glossy presentation, regular 'shopping' coverage ('Gadget Corner') and features that addressed more elegant sensibilities ('The Ten All-Time Classic Cars', 'Modern Art For Men'). After leaving *Esquire*, Hefner had worked for a short time in sales promotion for *Modern Man*'s publisher and would have been aware of the magazine's format and its attempt (along with *True*) to assume *Esquire*'s mantle as the spokesman for the sybaritic bachelor – the original men's lifestyle magazine having taken a new direction as a general features title.

Originality and innovation, then, were not necessarily Hefner's forte. His gift was as an entrepreneur, anticipating cultural trends and exploiting gaps in the market. His expertise lay in adeptly retooling and updating *Esquire*'s original format for a new generation of male consumers. Interviewed by *Newsweek* in 1955, Hefner affirmed that he wanted his magazine to be 'a younger, more virile *Esquire*' (*Newsweek*, 7 November 1955) – and it was a goal that *Playboy* realized more successfully than any of its competitors. *True* and *Modern Man* all tentatively appealed to men's consumer desires, but their pitch was still largely geared to the upper end of the blue collar market, the 'hunting, beer and poker set'. *Playboy*, in contrast, deftly cultivated an image as the confidant of a new generation of affluent, young blades. Shunning both horny-handed machismo and the burdens of suburban domesticity, *Playboy* was tailored to the interests of men from America's new, expressive and cosmopolitan middle class. Their 'morality of pleasure as a duty' was matched perfectly by the way *Playboy* fetishized the suave and sophisticated world of the connoisseur. As Hefner announced to readers in his premier editorial, *Playboy* did not intend to spend its time 'thrashing through thorny thickets or splashing about in fast flowing streams':

> we don't mind telling you in advance – we plan spending most of our time inside. WE like our apartment . . . We enjoy mixing up cocktails and an hors d'oeuvre or two, putting a little mood music on the phonograph and inviting in a female acquaintance for a quiet discussion on Picasso, Nietzsche, jazz, sex. (*Playboy*, November 1953)

Three years later Hefner elaborated further on his notion of the ideal *Playboy* reader. Again, it was an image closely equated with the ideals and lifestyle orientations of America's 'new petite bourgeoisie' – especially their penchant for stylistic expression and conspicuous consumption. As Hefner explained, to be a Playboy a man had to have a certain kind of worldview:

What is a playboy? Is he simply a wastrel, a ne'er-do-well, a fashionable bum? Far from it. He can be a sharp minded young business executive, a worker in the arts, a university professor, an architect or an engineer. He can be many things, provided he possesses a certain kind of view. He must see life not as a vale of tears, but as a happy time, he must take joy in his work, without regarding it as the end to all living, he must be an alert man, a man of taste, a man sensitive to pleasure, a man who – without acquiring the stigma of the voluptuary or dilettante – can live life to the hilt. This is the sort of man we mean when we use the word playboy. (*Playboy*, April 1956)

Sex, of course, was also integral to the world of *Playboy*. In full, glossy colour, the 'Playmate of the Month' centrefolds ensured the title won a competitive position in the men's magazine market, although *Playboy* always sought to distance itself from its more bawdy 'pin-up' rivals. To maintain its up-market appeal, *Playboy* configured its pornographic content as a mark of *risqué* daring, part of its wider zest for uninhibited enjoyment – wolfish indulgence presented as just one element in the magazine's package of swinging fun. The centrefolds also helped stake out *Playboy* as an unmistakably heterosexual text. While the male hedonist was a more established figure than he had been in the 1930s, stylistic pleasure and commodity consumerism remained closely bound up with feminine associations. Moreover, the heightened emphasis on marriage and family life during the Cold War ensured that any rejection of homemaking 'togetherness' in favour of a cosmopolitan single life risked added suspicions of sexual 'deviance'. As with *Esquire* before it, therefore, *Playboy* used its 'cheesecake' material as a guarantor of its 'manly' credentials. As Ehrenreich puts it, 'the breasts and bottoms were necessary not just to sell the magazine, but to protect it' (1983: 51). *Playboy*'s centrefolds existed, at least partly, as a device that could neutralize any suggestion of effeminacy – thus affording readers 'safe' passage into the realm of narcissistic and self-conscious consumption.

Twenty years earlier, men's fashion had been the *raison d'être* of *Esquire* magazine, but it only emerged as a key component in *Playboy* once the magazine was firmly established. Sporadic features during the first year of publication had seen *Playboy* cautiously dip its toe into the waters of men's apparel, but by 1955 it was ready to immerse itself more wholeheartedly in the pleasures of shopping for clothes.[4] That year saw Jack Kessie, a graduate of Drake University in Des Moines, appointed as the magazine's first fashion editor (under the pen-name Blake Rutherford). Kessie had already contributed a few freelance pieces to the magazine, but was appointed to the staff because 'he had the kind of casual elegance which Hefner thought exemplified the *Playboy* style' (Miller, 1985: 67).

Kessie's first feature – 'The Well Dressed Playboy: *Playboy*'s Position on the Proper Male Attire' (January 1955) – set the tone for the magazine's early fashion coverage. Resolutely didactic, it counselled readers to be 'conservative in all departments' to avoid being 'caught up in a perplexing, phantasmagoria of color combinations, patterns, styles, designs and cuts'. This sense of conservative elegance was informed, above all, by the smart-but-casual traditions of Ivy League style. 'Few will argue', Kessie asserted, 'against the fact that it is to the Ivy Leaguers that we owe the current national acceptance of the trim, tapered look in men's clothing' (*Playboy*, October 1955), the fashion editor affirming that there was 'an authentic Ivy look in active sportswear, just as there is in town' and decreeing that readers steer clear of 'the kind of gruesome garbage . . . touted as the hottest news from Majorca, the Italian Riviera, Cap d' Antibes and Southern California: Old Testament sandals, ballet-dancer shirts that tie north of the navel, too-short swim trunks laced and latticed up the side, etc.' (*Playboy*, July 1957). Instead, Kessie prescribed a style that would allow men to dress 'casually and correctly . . . and still retain individuality' – for tennis, white shoes and shorts, worn with a red Lacoste knit shirt; for swimming, 'trim, fly-front cotton poplin trunks with side tabs for a waist-clinching fit'; and for golf, 'pleatless, poplin, olive green shorts', teamed with 'a good-looking glen, plaid, long sleeved shirt' and 'the best golf shoes you can afford' (*Playboy*, July 1957).

Playboy's sartorial preferences, then, were ideally suited to the tastes of the rising middle class. 'The Well Dressed Playboy' was a man of classic discernment, yet side-stepped banal conformity through a careful eye for detail and an aptitude for distinction and individuality. With the appointment of Robert L. Green as *Playboy's* fashion director in 1959, this flair for (tasteful) individuality became even further pronounced. Less conservative than Kessie, Green accepted bolder colours, together with innovations in style and fit. The fashion features also embraced fantasies of the exciting good life with increasing relish, Green prompting readers to imagine themselves selecting a 'Wardrobe for a Jet Weekend' to Europe or donning 'sports car fashion' for a 'speed week in Nassau' (*Playboy*, April 1959; May 1959).

Trends in *Playboy's* fashion features reflected the magazine's developing enthusiasm for spectacular consumption. By the beginning of the 1960s the pages of *Playboy* had become a wonderland stocked full with expensive consumer goods designed to appeal to the affluent man of leisure – from 'The Compleat Sports Car Stable' and 'Hip, Hip Flasks' to 'The Strides of Stereo' and 'Scuba Gear and Scuba Dear' (*Playboy*, April 1957; September 1958; January 1961; June 1962). Every November, meanwhile, the magazine ran a feature on Christmas gifts suitable for the aspirant playboy, with glossy photo-spreads of desirable goodies piled mouth-wateringly high.

This emphasis on dazzling consumerism was reinforced by *Playboy's* advertising. For the first year of its publication the magazine had included virtually no advertisements, Hefner explaining to readers that this was because the editors wanted 'to first create a truly new and distinctive men's magazine' before opening up its pages to advertisers (*Playboy*, December 1954). An explanation closer to the truth might have been that advertisers were wary of appearing in *Playboy*, uncertain of how the magazine might be received by the public. Even after *Playboy* had clearly established itself in the commercial market, advertising remained fairly limited – generally gadgets and assorted nik-naks geared to the discerning bachelor (record racks, cuff-links, dinner jackets, fur-covered ice-buckets) – and it was not until the early 1960s that higher calibre advertisers mustered the confidence to ply their wares in the magazine. Hefner, meanwhile, always claimed to be choosy in the kind of advertising he would accept. 'We could fill our pages with advertising if we were willing to take everything submitted', the editor boasted in an editorial of 1956, explaining that he turned down 'four ads for every one accepted' in order to ensure that *Playboy* was 'the smartest, freshest, most interesting men's magazine in America and the best possible editorial and advertising medium for anyone selling to the class male market' (*Playboy*, May 1956). Such a selective approach ensured a virtually seamless flow between advertising and editorial, the totality steering readers through a sumptuous array of home furnishings, luxury cars, stereo equipment, clothes and the full gamut of extravagant entertainment and recreation.

Like *Esquire* before it, therefore, a large part of *Playboy*'s rationale was to 'colonize' the traditionally 'feminine' spaces of commodity consumption on behalf of men. Indeed, shopping had been an important item on the magazine's agenda even in its very first issue, with the inclusion of a 'house' advertising section entitled 'The Men's Shop', which promoted an assortment of bachelor-oriented merchandise. By 1955 this had been formalized as a regular feature, 'Playboy's Bazaar', an addition that was followed two years later by the launch of the Playboy Reader Service – a promotions department that supplied readers with the addresses of retailers who sold the goods illustrated in the magazine.[5] Two other regular features also pointed to *Playboy*'s business of colonizing the feminine – its love of cooking and its attention to interior design.

Cookery, of course, had been a staple ingredient of *Esquire* twenty years before, and in *Playboy* the *Esquire* kitchen was revived and re-equipped for the modern male epicure. During the 1950s and early 1960s Hefner's own tastes in food and drink were legendarily pedestrian – the editor's diet largely consisting of platefuls of fried chicken and gallons of Pepsi cola – but in Thomas Mario *Playboy* found a gastronome without equal. As head waiter at a men's club on Long Island, Mario had contributed his first article, 'Oyster Stew for a Quartet of Playboys', early in 1954 and his panache was such that he soon found himself appointed as *Playboy*'s food and drink editor. Though Mario's prose was laden with painful puns and agonizing alliteration (his article 'Happy as a Clam' described 'a mischievous mollusc's piquant personality on the land, on the sea, on the table'), he retained his position as *Playboy*'s *maître d'* over the next twenty years.

Perhaps more than any of its departments, it was *Playboy*'s attention to culinary matters that ran the greatest risk of compromising its readers' masculine self-image. Under Mario's stewardship, however, cookery was configured as a complex art to which men could proudly lay claim. *Playboy* invested cooking with masculine attributes by presenting it as a challenging skill in which men were uniquely gifted. According to the magazine, a man could feel confident in presiding over 'a certain amount of entertaining at home in his bachelor quarters' because:

> It does not mean – when he has a few pals over for a buffet dinner before going out for the evening – that he'll ask them to perch on kitchen stools while he mashes the potatoes. That's woman's work. But just as surely as women generally outrank men in culinary experience, so men, traditionally, dominate gourmet cooking and gourmet dining. The great chefs and the great *bon vivants* are testimony to it. (*Playboy*, September 1957)

Mundane kitchen chores, therefore, remained 'woman's work', while men could confidently plunge into the specialized knowledge and sense of performance associated with the gourmet. In Thomas Mario's hands, for example, even something as rudimentary as an omelette was transformed into a poetic mystery 'as perfect and as priceless as a sonnet', while carving a joint of meat was an act of chivalry 'esteemed as one of the fundamental social graces appurtenant to cultivated manhood' (*Playboy*, February 1958; November 1961). Cooking was further cast as a manly enterprise by being presented as an undertaking that, like any other masculine pastime, demanded the possession and mastery of a battery of appropriate tools. As *Playboy* explained in its 1957 article on 'Gear and Gadgets for the Bachelor's Buffet', the aspiring gourmet required the right kind of 'manly' equipment:

> Not for him the embellished and decorated gear that floods the shops and warms the heart of the housewife. The gourmet uses handsomely wrought, masculine gadgetry, functional ware that's fine-lined and clean-limbed, that gleams with the colors of polished metal and oiled hardwoods, man-sized gear that fits his hand as feliticiously as it does his job. (*Playboy*, September 1957)

With a solidly 'masculine' range of implements at his disposal, there could be no doubting the manliness of the playboy chef. For carving meat *Playboy* suggested an armoury of no less than twenty-six assorted knives and accoutrements – a collection eclipsed only by the demands of the 'Basic Bar', which (in addition to its 'minimum basic booze supply' of three crowded shelves of liquor bottles) also necessitated an awesome stockpile of sterling bottle-toppers, chrome cocktail shakers and push-button olive grabbers (*Playboy*, January 1958). A combination of manful expertise and 'man-sized gear', therefore, guaranteed the virile attributes of the bachelor gourmet. In *Playboy*, moreover, culinary ability was also presented as an invaluable skill in the art of seduction – Hefner later reflecting that 'Our food and drink features were, in reality, a form of foreplay' (cited in Edgren, 1994: 56).

As with its cookery features, *Playboy's* attention to interior decor revived an interest formerly prominent in *Esquire*. The earlier magazine's urbane sophistication had frequently extended into the realms of design and architecture – most obviously with the periodic inclusion of artist-rendered designs for rooms and furniture suited to the tastes of the style-conscious male. Typical was the 'Office for Big Shots', a fantasy design for the ultimate office that envisaged the top executive surrounded by a host of gadgets and an expanse of plush leather and mahogany (*Esquire*, September 1939). During the mid-1940s *Esquire*'s attention to design was further foregrounded in its 'Mechanical Prophecies' – a feature series of sleek, modernist designs for desks, offices and studies, all fully equipped with the latest technical wizardry. From its earliest days, *Playboy* had followed suit, its premier issue including a double page feature on 'Desk Design for the Modern Executive'. In *Playboy*, however, design aesthetics were given even greater emphasis as the magazine celebrated the sparkling world of the swinging bachelor. It was no accident that, from the outset, Hefner made it clear that in *Playboy* 'we plan spending most of our time inside'. For *Playboy*, the modern male's natural habitat was neither the great outdoors, nor (perish the thought) the ranch-house idyll of the nuclear family. Instead, the *Playboy* reader was invited to step into a world of high-class penthouses and fashionable apartments.

The penthouse's connotations of *á la mode* luxury safely displaced the 'feminine' associations of the 'private' that had been pivotal to the doctrine of 'separate spheres'. Instead, as Steven Cohan argues, the 1950s saw the interior of the stylish apartment become a key setting for the playboy's consumption-fixated lifestyle:

> The bachelor pad operated as a site of consumerism; it marked the single man's marginal position in relation to domestic ideology of the period, while at the same time allowing for his recuperation as a consumer whose masculinity could be redeemed – even glamorized – by the things he bought to accessorize his virility. (Cohan, 1996: 28)

Hardly surprising, then, that throughout the 1950s and 1960s 'bachelor pads' – both real and imagined – made regular appearances in Hefner's magazine. One of *Playboy*'s earliest treatments of the theme came in 1956 with a two-part article featuring blueprints and designs for 'Playboy's Penthouse' – 'a high, handsome haven – pre-planned and furnished for the bachelor in town' (*Playboy*, September 1956). Taking a cue from *Esquire*'s earlier artist-rendered designer dreams, 'Playboy's Penthouse' featured both overall views and water-coloured vignettes of the ideal home for 'a man who enjoys good living, a sophisticated connoisseur of the lively arts, of food and drink, and congenial companions of both sexes' (ibid.). The open-plan layout of 'Playboy's Penthouse', with its stress on 'function areas' rather than 'cell-like rooms', was reminiscent of the suburban ranch-house's effacement of boundaries separating public and private spheres – but here the similarity ended. To all intents and purposes 'Playboy's Penthouse' was the antithesis of ranch-house suburbia. Cosmopolitan and urbane, it was set in the heart of the throbbing city.

Moreover, located on the top floor of a modern skyscraper, 'Playboy's Penthouse' dominated the visual space of the metropolis, its commanding height drawing on a rich architectural heritage in which height was symbolic of superior status, masculinity and power (Weisman, 1992: 14). Furthermore, rather than being tailored to the ideals of family togetherness, 'Playboy's Penthouse' was designed with more raffish pastimes in mind. The dining room, for example, could not only accommodate 'a full production gala dinner', but was also 'perfect for all-night poker games, stag or strip', while the unique headboard of the luxurious bed was equipped with a bank of 'silent mercury switches and a rheostat that control every light in the place and can subtly dim the bedroom lighting to just the right romantic level'. In sum, the penthouse was, *Playboy* averred, 'a bachelor haven of virile good looks, a place styled for a man of taste and sophistication. This is *his* place, to fit his moods, suit his needs, reflect his personality' (*Playboy*, October 1956).

In the years that followed, *Playboy* turned its attention to a range of other designs for the affluent bachelor's ideal abode. In 1959 there appeared 'Playboy's Weekend Hideaway' – 'a bachelor's haven far from the madding crowd', where the confirmed urbanite could enjoy the pleasures of the countryside 'in measured quantities' and unwind in 'a gracious hideaway with the simplicity of contemporary elegance and the luxuriousness which the city man prefers' (*Playboy*, April 1959). In 1962, meanwhile, the magazine returned to the city with 'The Playboy Town House' – a 'luxurious and masculine . . . ultra-urban island of individuality in a sea of look-alike multiple dwellings' (*Playboy*, May 1962). The Town House was clearly inspired by Hefner's own Playboy Mansion. The financial success of his publishing empire had allowed Hefner to pursue the lifestyle of spectacular hedonism proselytized in his magazine and in 1960 he had paid $400,000 (in cash) for an imposing four-storied brick mansion in one of Chicago's most fashionable quarters, Hefner going on to spend a further $3,000,000 turning the building into a palace among bachelor pads. And throughout the 1960s the Playboy Mansion was regularly deployed as a backdrop to the magazine's articles on high-living – for example, as the setting for a 'Playmate Holiday House Party' (December 1961) or as the centrepiece for a sumptuous, thirteen-page 'pictorial essay' on 'Hef's hutch' (January, 1966).[6]

The 1960s also saw *Playboy's* regular inclusion of other photo-spreads featuring actual buildings and apartments that epitomized its ethos of luxurious pleasure. In May 1964 the spotlight was turned on an 'Airy Eyrie' on Malibu Beach, while the following year an apartment in a trendy Manhattan tower block was the focus (August 1965). Subsequent features lovingly scrutinized 'A Baronial Bi-level for a Busy Bachelor' (October 1965), 'A Palm Springs Oasis' (April 1966), 'A Texas Retreat' (October 1966), 'Exotica in Exurbia' (March 1967) and a 'New Haven Haven' (October 1969). In 1970, meanwhile, *Playboy* reprised its original theme with blue-prints for a 'Duplex Penthouse' – a 'coolly elegant urban haven that combines the intimate privacy of a roman atrium with architectonic spaciousness [*sic*]' (*Playboy*,

January 1970). Moreover, taking this as an opportunity to review its coverage of architecture and design, *Playboy* asserted that all its featured apartments shared a common engagement with masculine identities oriented to the good life:

> they have all had the same basic design purpose: to appeal to the urban bachelor who believes a man's home is not only his castle but also an outward reflection of his inner self; a place where he can live, love and be merry, entertain his friends with parties big and small, play poker with his cronies from the office or relax alone with a fond companion. (*Playboy*, January 1970)

Nor did the success of *Playboy*'s 'bachelor pad' features go unnoticed in the publishing industry. Many of the magazine's rivals developed their own imitations. In February 1957, for example, the inaugural issue of *Satan* magazine included a lavish photospread of the ideal 'Bachelor's Den' where 'comfort, convenience and contentment are the main ingredients', while in August 1960 *Rogue* magazine featured 'The Bachelor Apartment of Tomorrow', with 'bachelor blueprintery for 24-hour living – from bed to booze and back again'. Four years later, meanwhile, *Escapade* commissioned a young industrial designer to create a 'Bachelor's Beach Retreat' – 'the kind of bachelor's pad that could be built on the kind of money a rising executive or professional man might reasonably expect to have handy for such a project' (*Escapade*, August 1964). Others took a more tongue-in-cheek approach, *Adam* magazine proffering a 'Bedside Hideaway' that was fully equipped with roulette room and submarine dock (*The Adam Bedside Reader*, No. 3, 1960). None of these imitations, however, came close to the consummate skill with which *Playboy* mapped out the modern bachelor's design for living. Indeed, the swinging 'bachelor pad' became a central trope within Hefner's commercial ventures. Characteristic was his first television show, launched in 1959 on Chicago's WBKB channel. A weekly variety series hosted by Hefner himself, *Playboy's Penthouse* was presented as a sophisticated *soirée* in the company of a throng of genial celebrities and beautiful women – the whole affair staged in a studio constructed to resemble a plush penthouse, complete with wood-burning fire-place, tropical aquarium and a revolving bookcase that turned into a bar.[7]

The revolving bookcase in *Playboy's Penthouse* was indicative of wider motifs. Gadgets and hi-tech gimmickry were always staple features of the archetypal bachelor pad. Exemplary was not only *Playboy*'s regular features on the latest in hi-fi hardware, but also the magazine's visions of fantasy items such as the 'Electronic Entertainment Wall'. Combining the latest in television and hi-fi technology, this was 'a luxurious audio-visual unit for the ultimate in at-home enjoyment' (*Playboy*, October 1964). The obsession with push-button gadgetry might be seen, at least in part, as a desire for phallic accessories that could shore up a sense of masculine power. Yet, as Buxton (1990: 90) notes, the early 1960s craze for hi-tech gizmos also related to changing conceptualizations of technology. Breaking with traditional notions of machinery as bulky and cumbersome, the 1960s concept of the 'gadget' conceived technology as a miniaturized and individualized consumer product – precise, functional and emblematic of stylish cool. And in the world of *Playboy* the aesthetic of the 'gadget' reached its zenith in the 'Playboy Bed'. Originally an imagined design featured in the November 1959 issue, and then again as a centrepiece in the blueprints for 'The Playboy Townhouse' in 1962, the 'Playboy Bed' was turned into reality by Hefner in the early 1960s and was even treated to its own glossy photo-feature in his magazine (*Playboy*, April 1965). An immense eight feet in diameter, the circular 'Playboy Bed' was an exercise in luxurious hedonism. Not only was it motorized (able to both vibrate and rotate at the flick of a switch), but it was equipped with a profusion of push-button gadgets – telephone, radio, TV, stereo and even a mini-bar and refrigerator. More than a piece of furniture, the 'Playboy Bed' was a magnificent temple to the ethos of leisure-oriented consumption.

Another prominent feature in designs for the swinging bachelor was the recurring use of modernist themes. The classic bachelor pad was distinguished by its clean lines, sleek surfaces, imaginative use of wood and glass partitions and its obligatory pieces of stylish designer furniture made of steel, leather and wood – an Eames lounge chair, a Florence Knoll desk, a Noguchi coffee table and so on. This reflected Hefner's own enthusiasm for modernism, the editor recounting how, from his college days, his tastes:

> were very contemporary and that kind of held in terms of my own apartment. It was Mies and Wright kind of architecture and the Knoll-Herman Miller style of furnishings that most appealed to me. And you will find those tastes reflected in most of our early design pieces. (cited in Weyr, 1978: 63)

Modernist motifs were also conspicuous in the Playboy Mansion itself – its walls hung with abstract paintings by the likes of Jackson Pollock and Willem de Kooning, while Picasso's classic *Nude Reclining* hung regally over the central fire place. This use of modernist design underlined the playboy ethic's penchant for 'hip nonconformity', modernism's bold lines and slick minimalism starkly contrasting with the 'homely' cosiness of suburbia. At the same time, however, the interior decor of the Playboy Mansion was an eclectic mix of the traditional and the contemporary. Mixed in with the modernist designs were more archaic signifiers of the baronial and the baroque – dark wood panelling, suits of antique armour and gleaming white marble, all creating a sense of illustrious tradition. This emphasis on courtly splendour obviously carried connotations of power and affluence, though it also served to counter the nonconformist excesses of the modernist *élan*. By itself, the modernist aesthetics would have been a little too unorthodox – perhaps even hinting at a kind of overly highbrow, even effete, intellectualism. The addition of ersatz traditionalism functioned to anchor the aesthetic ensemble around a form of masculine identity that was hip and forward looking, yet was also rooted in securely masculine and bourgeois values.

THE PLAYBOY PHILOSOPHY

Playboy also paid its dues to the bourgeois values of free enterprise through its attention to the virtues of the 'self-made man' and the business of money making. Pre-eminently, this took the form of a regular column furnished by *Playboy's* 'Contributing Editor for Business and Finance' – none other than the oil and aircraft billionaire J. Paul Getty. Throughout the 1960s Getty's column proffered advice to the aspiring executive on how, through industriousness and determination, he too might succeed in the world of business – Getty's articles including 'You Can Make a Million Today' and 'How I Made My First Billion' (*Playboy*, June 1961, October 1961). The industrialist also lent his name to *How to Be Rich*, an inspiring guide to business advancement published by Playboy Press in 1965. Yet, even here, *Playboy* refused to toe the line of conservative masculine archetypes. Material achievement was a coveted goal, but the traditional routes to 'self-made' success – playing by the rules and putting one's nose to the grindstone – were eschewed in favour of independent thinking and autonomy. With a reputation as an iconoclast, Getty's very first article for *Playboy* launched a swingeing attack on the lack of imagination in contemporary business. Along with critics such as David Reisman and William Whyte, Getty perceived a 'crisis of conformity' in American culture, arguing that the 'organization man' had become the scourge of American commerce, Getty advising the career-minded executive:

> You'll go much further if you stop trying to look and act and think like everyone else on Madison Avenue or Wacker Drive or Wilshire Boulevard. Try being a nonconformist for a change. Be an individualist – and an individual. You'll be amazed at how much faster you'll get ahead. (*Playboy*, February 1961)

It was a theme to which Getty frequently returned. In 1962, for example, he announced that 'in the restless voice of dissent lies the key to a nation's vitality and greatness', the billionaire berating his countrymen for their tendency 'to automatically equate dissension with disloyalty' and to 'view any criticism of our existing social, economic and political forms as sedition and subversion' (*Playboy*, March 1962). Two years later, meanwhile, Getty lamented the rise of the 'Homogenized Man' and made 'a plea for the preservation of the individual in our increasingly pigeonholed society' (*Playboy*, August 1964).

A sense of left-field independence also surfaced in *Playboy's* literary pretensions. From the outset the magazine had included a literary element (usually material drawn from the public domain) as a way of securing its upmarket cachet. At first either Hefner himself or one of his sub-editors would select the stories, but it was soon clear that someone of greater experience was needed to administer literary matters. Hefner's choice was Auguste Spectorsky. As author of *The Exurbanites* – his 1955 satire on the new middle class – Spectorsky seemed an ideal choice, while his experience working with such magazines as *Park East* and *New Yorker* promised to add a further touch of class to the *Playboy* recipe. Tempted away from his job as a top television editor with NBC, Spectorsky joined *Playboy* in 1956 as editorial director and effectively took over the day-to-day running of the magazine. Spectorsky put particular effort into developing *Playboy's* literary content. Under his auspices the magazine announced the launch of a $1,000 fiction award in 1957 (with novelist Herman Gold as the first recipient) and, willing to pay handsomely for contributions, *Playboy* was soon attracting pieces from some of the most respected names in American literature, including such luminaries as Vladimir Nabokov, James Baldwin, John Steinbeck, Kenneth Tynan and Ray Bradbury.

Spectorsky and Hefner, however, did not always see eye-to-eye. The erudite Spectorsky could feel uncomfortable with *Playboy's* sexual content, avoided the Playboy Mansion whenever possible and was even 'openly contemptuous of much about Hefner's lifestyle, his friends, his parties' (Miller, 1985: 123). Initially, Spectorsky had even wanted *Playboy* renamed *Smart Set* and would have preferred to push the magazine towards being a more sober publication, more worthy of the intellectual community's attention. But Dines probably overstates the case in arguing that the tensions between Spectorsky and Hefner erupted into a full-blown split among the *Playboy* staff – between 'Hefner's "pro-sex camp" and Spectorsky's "pro-literature camp"' (Dines, 1998: 47). In his editorial policy, for example, Spectorsky's choice of copy was broadly congruent with Hefner's vision of a magazine that was *risqué* and independently-minded. Under Spectorsky, *Playboy* accepted stories with a rawness that other magazines would have balked at, including a Nelson Algren short-story concerning a drug-addicted prostitute's stormy relationship with her pimp. Moreover, if need be, Spectorsky was perfectly happy to leap to the defence of Hefner's interest in matters of the flesh. In 1962, for example, Spectorsky squared up to a savage critique of *Playboy* elaborated by Professor Benjamin De Mott in the journal *Commentary*. Responding to De Mott's denunciation of *Playboy* as a morally reprehensible publication that offered 'a vision of the whole man reduced to his private parts', Spectorsky averred:

> We feature girls because they're attractive, stories because they are entertaining, jokes because they are funny. Our vision is not that of a man reduced to his private parts, but of man enlarged through his capacity to interpret and enjoy life, one aspect of which – but by no means the only one – is the healthy enjoyment of sex. (cited in Weyr, 1978: 101)

Hefner, meanwhile, was as keen as Spectorsky for *Playboy* to stake a claim to 'serious' journalism. With this in mind, 'The Playboy Panel' was introduced in 1961, a discussion of 'Narcotics and the Jazz Musician' launching 'a series of provocative conversations about subjects of interest on the contemporary scene'. Hence the next decade saw a variety of commentators join round-table debates on topics ranging from 'Sex Censorship in Literature and the Arts' to 'Business Ethics and Morality' and 'A Crisis in Law Enforcement?'

Above all, however, it was the 'Playboy Interview' through which the magazine sought to establish a reputation for punchy social relevance. Beginning in 1962, the interview's probing question-and-answer format gave an insight into the minds of leading creative and political figures of the day – the 1960s seeing *Playboy* grill (among others) Ingmar Bergman, Federico Fellini, Michelangelo Antonioni, Salvador Dali, Stanley Kubrick, Norman Mailer, Henry Miller, John Kenneth Galbraith, Jean Paul Sartre, Marshall McLuhan and Fidel Castro. Perhaps most dramatically, the Playboy Interview delved into the ideas and motivations of key figures in the developing maelstrom of civil rights activism and racial conflict, its roster of interviewees including Martin Luther King, Malcolm X, Eldridge Cleaver, George Wallace, Robert Shelton (Grand Wizard of the KKK) and George Lincoln Rockwell (chief of the American Nazi Party).

By the early 1960s, then, *Playboy* had developed far beyond its original 'entertainment for men' formula. But, while the Playboy Interview and the Playboy Panel lent the magazine a sense of cultural import, its feet were still firmly planted in the 'ethic of fun'. Like *Esquire* before it (again), *Playboy* developed a reputation for ribald and irreverent humour. An aspiring cartoonist himself, Hefner recruited talents such as Jack Cole, Erich Sokol and Gardner Rea to provide the magazine's suggestive cartoons – their salaciousness given a 'tasteful' gloss through their colourful, full-page presentation. The late 1950s also saw the free-wheeling satirical cartoonist Shel Silverstein become a *Playboy* regular, while in 1957 Alberto Vargas contributed his first pictorial, 'Vargas Girls' appearing virtually every month in the magazine from 1960 through to 1978. The artist LeRoy Neiman was also a regular contributor. A long-standing friend of Hefner's, Neiman began his work for *Playboy* with illustrations for fashion features and the joke page (for which he developed the Femlin – an elf-like nude that became a *Playboy* mascot), though it was his 'Man At His Leisure' series that most fully captured the magazine's ethos. First appearing in the late 1950s, Neiman's series of impressionistic, oil-painted tableaux chronicled the spectrum of high-class masculine entertainments, from the classic ('The gala and sumptuous fun of a transatlantic crossing', 'Maxim's of Paris – the *bon vivant*'s paradise in the city of light') to the daringly modern ('Yugoslavia's nude beaches', 'New York's discotheque scene').

Overall, *Playboy* liked to see life as one big party. In its photo-spreads the magazine created male fantasies of uninhibited revelry – 'Playboy's Yacht Party' was a 'prescription for fine fun afloat . . . [with] the good ship Gallant and a carefree crew of beauties' (July 1957); 'Playboy's House Party' saw 'five frolicsome lasses warm a Miami mansion' (May 1959); while 'a dozen of the magazine's most dazzling pin-up beauties' were invited to the 'Playmate Holiday House Party', to be 'guests of honor for a weekend frolic' (December 1961). *Playboy* also loved to chronicle others' roguish escapades – with pictorials of bacchanalian antics at New York's 'Photographers and Models Ball' (July 1960) – as well as tips on how readers, too, could organize a lively shindig. In December 1961, for example, the magazine offered an assortment of hints on 'throwing the perfect playboy party', while in January 1969 it suggested a wild and futuristic New Year's bash, with ideas for 'a galaxy of avant-garde food, drink, costumes and decor for hosting a way-out wingding'. And when partying until the small hours did not appeal, *Playboy* could offer plenty of other options. In November 1955 the magazine introduced a regular 'Playboy After Hours' department, devoted both to reviewing books, records and films suitable for the discerning male and to the promotion of restaurants and bars where readers might find an atmosphere conducive to luxurious entertaining.

Foreign climes were also presented as a playground for masculine hedonism. *Playboy*'s matrix of affluent consumption and sexual pleasure was especially clear in the 'tourist gaze' of its regular 'travelogues' dealing with the world's fashionable resorts and enticing night-spots. *Playboy*'s obsession with 'exotic' locations and 'exotic' women was especially pronounced, with frequent nude pictorials of 'The Girls of Hawaii', 'The Girls of Tahiti' and so on (*Playboy*, August 1961; December 1966). By 1961 the magazine was even marketing 'Playboy Tours' of Europe and the Caribbean, inviting readers to join 'a group of cosmopolitan young men and women who share your interests and zest for enjoying a care-free, fun-filled holiday' (*Playboy*, March 1961). In this respect, *Playboy* shared the wider propensity for American popular culture to configure an exotic 'other' as the incarnation of sensuous desires. Just like the vogue for *tiki* bars and Polynesian kitsch, *Playboy*'s travelogues constructed the 'exotic' as an eroticized spectacle that promised release from suffocating western taboos (both social and sexual) – on one occasion, *Playboy* even advising enterprising hosts on the best way to hold their own 'urban luau', using 'exotic' decor, cocktails and Polynesian recipes to re-create a 'lush tropical atmosphere' in the comfort of their own 'sky-high apartment' (June 1966).[8]

A taste for 'difference' also surfaced in *Playboy*'s musical preferences. Just like *Esquire*, jazz (Hefner's own passion) was a *Playboy* staple. Its associations with spicy night-life and underground creativity made jazz an idiom that fitted perfectly with the image of intellectual hedonism cultivated by *Playboy*. Throughout the 1950s and 1960s the magazine ran regular reviews of new jazz albums, together with innumerable features and photospreads related to the world of jazz and jazz musicians. 1955, meanwhile, saw the launch of an annual *Playboy* Jazz Poll – 'the biggest, most successful popularity poll ever conducted in the field of jazz music'

(*Playboy*, February 1957) – another idea that first appeared in *Esquire* during the 1930s. By 1957 the *Playboy* version of the poll had generated *The Playboy Jazz All-Stars* album, featuring many of the finest jazz artists of the day,[9] followed in 1959 by *Playboy's* sponsorship of its own Jazz Festival. By deliberately cultivating these associations, *Playboy* linked both itself and its readership to the stylish and intellectual connotations that surrounded the world of modern jazz. Rock 'n' roll, in contrast, was kept at arm's length. The lower class and commercial associations of rock 'n' roll did not fit in with *Playboy's* vision of laid-back sophistication. As Leonard Feather explained in 1957:

> Rock 'n' roll may have the same roots as jazz, but it is, for the most part, a bastardized, commercialized, debased version of it. Its main appeal is to adolescent rebellion and insecurity. Rock 'n' roll shares a common beginning with jazz but it has evolved no further than a primitive, gibbering ape. (*Playboy*, June 1957)

And throughout the 1960s the magazine continued to favour jazz over both rock 'n' roll and pop. Indeed, though the Beatles were featured in the Playboy Interview in February 1965, it was only in 1968 (after they had developed into a 'serious' rock band) that the Fab Four were added to the magazine's All-Star roster of musicians – rock music's pretensions to creative authenticity being better suited to *Playboy's* 'intellectual' inclinations. Even in the late 1960s, however, *Playboy* maintained its preference for jazz. Jazz ideally suited the magazine's aspirations to being laid-back and *avant garde*, while at the same time allowing for a sense of refinement that clearly set it apart from the more subversive elements of contemporary youth culture.

Playboy may have snubbed the rawness and commercialism of rock 'n' roll, together with the rougher-edges of teen rebellion, but the magazine was in the forefront of the era's infatuation with youth. In distancing itself from the stuffy conservatism of the breadwinner archetype, *Playboy* drew on images and concepts of youth as a model for a new, dynamic and leisure-oriented brand of American male. Just as Madison Avenue employed the iconography of 'youth' as a metaphor for a new consumer value-system with an accent on pleasure and individuality, *Playboy* constructed itself as the spokesman for a new generation of young, male consumers – affluent, upwardly mobile and unencumbered by their elders' out-dated attitudes and moral code.

'Youthfulness', then, was central to *Playboy's* construction of a masculinity secure in its consumerism. As an early survey of *Playboy's* success observed, the magazine appealed to men in their early twenties by 'exhibiting the brashness of youth' (Ryan, 1957: 13), Hefner going to great lengths to cultivate a young readership – both as a means to attract lucrative advertising revenue and as a strategy in maintaining

Playboy's aura as a 'hip' and 'with it' magazine of the moment. From the outset, therefore, *Playboy* sought to develop a cachet with America's growing student body by projecting an image that combined *savoir faire* and disdain for convention with a sense of Ivy League élan. It was an astute tactic. In September 1955, citing survey data collected by the market researchers Gould, Leis and Benn, *Playboy* announced that 'over 70%' of its readers had attended college and 'over half of the "college" group are students at the present time and a good percentage may be expected to join the "College degree" group later' – the magazine proudly concluding that:

> The great majority of *Playboy*'s readers are business and professional men and the young men in college who will be in business and the professions in two or three years. *Playboy* has a greater percentage of college men in its audience than any other national magazine (24.6%). (*Playboy*, September 1955)

Hefner, though, was anxious to consolidate and extend this success and looked for a man who could further augment *Playboy*'s appeal to a readership of affluent, young consumers. It was a job tailor-made for Victor Lownes III. Two years younger than Hefner, Lownes was twenty-five when the two first met at a party in 1954. As a rakish, debonair and independently wealthy socialite, Lownes was virtually a walking-talking embodiment of the playboy mythology. He and Hefner were soon firm friends – Lownes becoming something of a role model for the publisher as the two men became a fixture on Chicago's circuit of ritzy night spots. At the time Lownes was at a loose end. Bored with the world of business, he had quit his grandfather's firm to dabble in promotional work. As another sideline he also began to contribute small pieces to Hefner's magazine. Hefner was convinced that Lownes would be a boon to *Playboy*'s operations and in mid-1955 appointed him as the magazine's editor in charge of promotion and advertising. It was a propitious decision, Lownes emerging as a power-house in *Playboy*'s corporate development.

Significantly, Lownes' priority was to throw his shoulder behind building up *Playboy*'s college market. As a student at the University of Chicago, Lownes had worked as a representative promoting Chesterfield cigarettes and he reasoned that a similar scheme could further establish *Playboy*'s campus appeal, helping to secure subscriptions and push products. With this in view, Lownes set up the Playboy College Bureau, using a list of Chesterfield representatives to recruit an army of young collegians to promote the magazine. The plan was inspired. *Playboy* soon had a presence on 300 university and college campuses throughout America, representatives selling subscriptions and organizing marketing events such as 'The Man on the Campus' – a 1956 fashion promotion run in conjunction with over a hundred clothes stores. The magazine also gave copious attention to matters of campus style, appealing to young consumers who wanted to look fashionably 'hip', yet still feel securely anchored within the affluent middle class. As *Playboy*'s 1958 survey of

'The Well-Clad Undergrad' explained, although 'there is almost a belligerently casual casualness of garb on campuses' (with a profusion of tee-shirts, jeans and sneakers), Ivy League style still carried the day:

> Ivy is the arbiter and criterion, [though] group individuality does exist – which is not surprising since young men are innovators and are jealous of their right to be different, but still enjoy membership (and the sartorial badges of membership) in their own groupings. Note, however, that the eminence of Ivy seems undisputed, despite its ebb and flow from campus to campus. (*Playboy*, September 1958)

In the years that followed, *Playboy* further cemented its links with Joe College through its coverage of the vagaries of student fashion. Every autumn the magazine ran 'College Check-List' and 'Back to Campus' features, with sartorial tips for the fashion-conscious undergraduate. Indeed, *Playboy*'s success with students was such that by 1958 it was claiming to be 'Big Magazine on the Campus', with nearly a quarter of its readership drawn from the ranks of undergraduate college students (*Playboy*, April 1958). This appeal continued into the sixties, so that by 1966 the magazine could crow that it was 'first choice for reading among better than half of the more than 3,000,000 males on campus today' (*Playboy*, September 1966).

An affinity for youth and the college market was (as chapter three demonstrated) a path already well trodden by *Esquire* in the 1930s. Indeed, the host of similarities between the earlier magazine and *Playboy* underscore the elements of continuity that existed between the male consumer codified between the wars and the 'new' playboy ethic of the postwar era. Amid the unparalleled affluence of the late 1950s and early 1960s, however, the archetype of the young, hedonistic male won a cultural purchase that far surpassed that of its predecessor.

During the late 1950s and early 1960s 'youth' became emblematic of a new era of dynamic modernity and 'liberated' consumerism. For men, the imagery of youthful consumption held special significance, influencing and informing the emergence of a model of masculine consumerism with an emphasis on leisure-oriented individualism. It was *Playboy*'s ability to present itself as a figurehead of this alliance between youth, masculinity and consumption that ensured its phenomenal success. Indeed, by the mid-1960s the magazine was increasingly whole-hearted in the way it threw itself into the spectacle of youth consumption – marked, perhaps most poignantly, by the way it bought into the mythology of the Californian surf set.

Features on beachwear were already a regular in *Playboy* in the late 1950s, but during the early sixties these developed into more spectacular fantasies of carefree surf-side leisure.[10] In July 1964 a special 'Summer Fun Issue' also included an extensive 'Beach Ball' feature that exhorted readers to 'set up a swinging summer beachhead', *Playboy* explaining how 'modern mores and technology have turned the waterside wingding into a combination of unfettered bash, casual banquet and mecca for the sports-minded (and especially the surfing set, the rapidly burgeoning legion of hardy sea-farers who dig the kicks to be found on the crest of a breaker)'. In December 1965, meanwhile, scuba gear and a surf board were conspicuous additions to Playboy's 'Xmas Gift Guide', while the following April's 'Playmate' was a 'Malibu Beachnik' who 'starts the day by limbering up on a skate board before heading for the Malibu surf'. By 1967 the West coast surf scene had been fully incorporated within Playboy's universe of male hedonism – July's 'Man at His Leisure' montage seeing Leroy Neiman pay homage to 'the dizzy marine manoeuvrings and beachside heroics of southern California's stoked-up surfers' (Playboy, July 1967).

It was, though, Hefner's own contributions which most explicitly delineated Playboy's dedication to autonomous and uninhibited pleasure. Promoting himself as the nemesis of the ascetic breadwinner, Hefner made great play of his disdain for self-denial and conformity – his commitment to a credo of freedom given full exposition in 'The Playboy Philosophy'. An attempt by Hefner to spell out, 'for friends and critics alike', the guiding values of his magazine, 'The Playboy Philosophy' was originally intended as a one-off article in Playboy's December 1962 edition. The idea, however, grew into a (somewhat laborious) twenty-five part series in which Hefner pontificated on matters of individual rights. Sex was a recurring theme – Hefner regularly lambasting puritanical morality, the obscenity laws and the Church as the enemies of both personal liberty and the freedom of speech. In contrast, the publisher presented himself as not only an agent of healthy sexual expression, but also a guardian of the principles of democracy originally established by America's founding fathers. These were qualities he sought to underline with the launch of the Playboy Foundation. Established in 1965, the Foundation's mission was 'to pursue, perpetuate and protect the principles of freedom and democracy' through administering grants to causes advocated by Hefner's 'Philosophy' – funds being given to campaigns for the legalization of abortion and sex education in schools and to William Masters and Virginia Johnson to support their research into human sexuality.

Significantly, Hefner's 'Philosophy' also celebrated the new affluence of the post-war consumer boom and 'the creature comforts and good life that are available to a majority in our middle-class economy' (Playboy, December 1964). Moreover, in this 'good life', youth was – once again – configured as a prime-mover. Enthusing over what he perceived as a revival of the 'optimistic viewpoint' and 'zest for living' that had originally made America great, the second instalment of Hefner's 'Philosophy' spotlighted the contribution of a new 'Upbeat Generation'. Here, Hefner presented his own potted history of American masculinity. In the early twentieth century, he argued, America's 'self-made' heroes had 'proved the importance of pluck, perseverance, honor and playing the game', while the 'Roaring Twenties' had been 'a yeasty time of innovation and adventure, when new notions and ideas were accepted almost as quickly as they were born' (Playboy, January 1963). But amid the travails of the 1930s depression, Hefner contended, men had lost their way –

Americans retreating into 'a concern for security, the safe and the sure, the certain and the known' (*Playboy*, January 1963). Revival, however, had come with postwar prosperity, Hefner arguing that the late 1940s had seen the emergence of 'a new generation' that 'seemed unwilling to accept the current shibboleths, chains, traditions and taboos' (*Playboy*, January 1963). The growth of a bohemian counter-culture, Hefner acknowledged, had been a factor in this break with the 'fetters of conformity', though more important were another, larger, group of men who were 'less colorful on the surface . . . but equally ready to throw off the shackles of sameness and security' (*Playboy*, January 1963). For Hefner this new 'Upbeat Generation' was a refreshing breath of fresh air in the way it 'refused to accept the old ideas and ideals passed along by the previous conformity-ridden generation' (*Playboy*, January 1963). In this 'Upbeat Generation' he saw a return to America's glory days of the 1920s, Hefner explaining that the 'Upbeats' were a group who combined the gumption of the 'self-made man' with the *joie de vivre* of the Jazz Age buck:

> The Upbeat generation clearly feels a strong kinship with the Roaring Twenties and the two periods share much in common in both spirit and point of view. The Upbeats can enjoy kicking their heels, participating in the same sort of fun and frivolity for which the Twenties are most famous, but they are equally capable of knuckling down to a particular job and getting it done. (*Playboy*, January 1963)

Tedious and rambling, Hefner's 'Playboy Philosophy' ultimately stretched to a mind-numbing 250,000 words. Yet the column proved to be one of *Playboy*'s most popular features, generating so much mail that Hefner quickly created 'The Playboy Forum' – a regular feature in which readers contributed comments on issues raised in his 'Philosophy'. Again, notions of a new era of hedonistic pleasure were a regular topic.[11] Elsewhere in the magazine, meanwhile, the same themes were a perennial. In 1965, for example, the Playboy Panel explored the 'Uses and Abuses of the New Leisure' – panellists discussing the pros and cons of the rise of the 'leisure-loaded American' (*Playboy*, March 1965).

What Hefner's pop history of American manhood (perhaps all too conveniently) omitted, however, was the significance of *Esquire* magazine in the story of the consuming male. In seeing the 1930s as a wasteland of sterile 'concern for security, the safe and the sure', Hefner was wide of the mark. The period (as Chapter 3 demonstrated) had actually represented a key moment in the codification of a consumption-oriented masculine identity. Indeed, in 1933 *Esquire* itself had announced the discovery of a 'New Leisure' in its first edition, the magazine coming to stand as the quintessence of affluent style for those men lucky enough to avoid the ravages of the Depression. Where Hefner was more accurate was in seeing the 1950s as marking a resurgence in masculine consumption. Above all, it was the emergence of the new middle class that underpinned this renaissance, the interests and aspirations of the 'new petite bourgeoisie' providing the bedrock for the ethos of hedonistic, masculine consumerism that *Playboy* magazine both courted and lovingly catalogued.

In fact, Hugh Hefner, himself, can be seen as emblematic of the rise of the new professional-managerial middle-class and their 'morality of pleasure as a duty'. Growing up in Chicago's comfortable suburbs, Hefner came from a straight-laced and conservative family (originally from the farmlands of Nebraska) whose devout Methodist principles emphasized a traditional, middle-class code of industry and temperance. Graduating from high school in 1944, Hefner volunteered for two years' unsatisfying army service, subsequently returning to Chicago to marry his girlfriend (they were legally separated by 1957) and study at the University of Illinois. Majoring in psychology, Hefner began to formulate vague ideas for a career in journalism, but on leaving university his ambitions brought little immediate success. By 1950 he had returned to academia, enrolling in Graduate School at Great Northwestern University to study sociology. Within six months, however, he had abandoned his studies in favour of a succession of copywriting jobs (including his post at *Esquire*) and a series of his own publishing ventures. The latter culminated in 1953 – when he was still only twenty-seven – with the runaway success of *Playboy*. Hefner's career history, therefore, stands as virtually a textbook example of the rise of the 'cultural intermediary' in 1950s America. Hefner's success in advertising and publishing exemplify Pierre Bourdieu's (1984) notion of a rising middle class who carve out a niche in new occupations based on the production and dissemination of symbolic goods and services. Moreover, the development of Hefner's own moral code can also be seen as personifying the rise of expressive and liberated 'new model lifestyles' typical of Bourdieu's cultural intermediaries. At university Hefner had become fascinated by the first Kinsey report (published in 1948) and increasingly questioned the values and restraints he had grown up with – the only term paper he produced at Graduate School being an essay on America's obscenity laws in which Hefner argued for a drastic revision of outmoded attitudes to sexual behaviour.[12]

In other respects, too, Hefner stands as an epitome of the 'cultural intermediary'. According to Bourdieu's analysis of the emergent middle classes in 1960s France, the new cultural intermediaries promoted their own 'social flair' and 'model lifestyles' in the cultural texts they produced – advertising, magazines and so on. This was achieved, at least partly, through the promotion of an 'individual' symbolic authority established through 'selling the vendors themselves as models and as guarantors of the value of their products' (Bourdieu, 1984: 365). In this respect 'Hef' was a consumate cultural intermediary. In *Playboy* he was regularly promoted as the embodiment of the daring-yet-tasteful lifestyle the magazine championed. In June 1957, for example, *Playboy* introduced its editor to its readers – celebrating Hefner as 'the man responsible for the pulse, the personality and the very existence of the magazine'. In a lengthy (self-penned) editorial, 'Hef' described himself as exemplifying 'the young urban man who appreciates the pleasures of an apartment, the sounds of a hi-fi, the taste of a dry Martini' and over the following decade the magazine lauded the publisher's taste through regular features on his house (the Playboy Mansion), his private jet-plane (the 'Big Bunny') and even his furniture (the omnipresent Playboy Bed).

*

The new 'morality of fun' epitomized in Hefner's 'Playboy Philosophy' was rich with the rhetoric of freedom. Yet it was hardly a blueprint for progressive social transformation. During the 1950s and early 1960s Playboy's politics were always fairly hazy. Victor Lownes has recalled that the magazine's inner-circle 'considered McCarthy an asshole', though Ray Russell – a long-standing executive editor – has insisted that the politics of Playboy's editorial team were, at best, ill defined:

> According to one school of thought, Playboy was a crusading journal . . . waging war against censorship and leading the vanguard of the sexual revolution. Sure, all of us who held top posts during the formative years would like to think we were bold iconoclasts and shapers of public opinion – but it simply isn't true . . . Our leanings were more left than right, but only in a vague, general way . . . Nobody was an active, card-carrying liberal. (cited in Weyr, 1978: 42–3)

Hefner's magazine, along with the other cultural texts and practices of the new male consumer, undoubtedly challenged both the traditional 'breadwinner' archetype and the Cold War ideologies of 'domestic containment'. But this was a challenge that took place from *within* the parameters of dominant ideological discourse. The success of the Playboy empire in the late 1950s and early 1960s marked what was effectively an *adaptive* shift in dominant articulations of masculinity. Rather than marking any kind of radical restructuring in social power relations, there evolved in the figure of the 'swinging bachelor' a form of masculine identity more appropriate to the demands of a society grounded on consumption and more at ease with the expanding vistas of commercial leisure and entertainment. Indeed, in its obsession with 'the individual pursuit of happiness' and 'the importance of the individual and his [sic] rights as a member of a free society' (Playboy, December 1962), Hefner's 'Playboy Philosophy' can be interpreted as amounting to little more than a wearisome, middle-brow update of classical liberalism and the principles of free-market capitalism.

Within this developing world of male consumer pleasures, moreover, gender relationships remained structured in terms of masculine, heterosexual dominance. For example, while Hefner styled himself as a champion of sexual liberation, Playboy was a pantheon to the sexual exploitation of women. It is a truism to say that Playboy's centrefolds were, from the outset, structured in terms of an objectifying male gaze – but, in the development of the 'Playmate of the Month' centrefold, the magazine significantly extended and naturalized the sexual objectification of women. The first Playmates had been selected from a job lot of 'pin-up' calendar photographs Hefner had bought at the same time he acquired the Marilyn Monroe pictures. When the supply had been exhausted, professional models were employed to pose for the feature. By present-day standards the pictures were unexplicit, though they were intended to generate what Hefner described as 'seduction-is-imminent' connotations (Miller, 1985: 69). An important change, however, took place in 1955. In an attempt to make the centrefolds 'more real' for the readers, Hefner persuaded Charlaine Karalus, *Playboy*'s subscription manager, to pose for a photo-shoot. Appearing as 'Janet Pilgrim' in the July edition, Karalus's appearance heralded a new approach in the centrefold. The 'seduction-is-imminent' genre was abandoned and replaced by the concept of the Playmate as 'the-girl-next-door' – women being photographed in the everyday settings in which *Playboy* had 'discovered' them, the images accompanied by short biographies and accounts of their likes and ambitions. A trademark feature of the *Playboy* centrefold throughout the late 1950s and 1960s, the 'girl-next-door' approach extended – by implication – the processes of sexual objectification to women in general, the magazine encouraging its readers to think of *all* women as likely pin-up fodder:

> We suppose it's natural to think of the pulchritudinous Playmates as existing in a world apart. Actually potential Playmates are all around you: the new secretary at your office, the doe-eyed beauty who sat opposite you at lunch yesterday, the girl who sells you shirts and ties at your favorite store. (*Playboy*, July 1955)

In keeping with his posture as a champion of liberal ideals, Hefner voiced sympathy for women's causes and, during the 1960s, made financial contributions to women's groups such as the National Organization for Women (NOW) and the National Institute for Working Women. Behind closed doors, however, the editor voiced withering antipathy toward the developing women's movement. In 1970 a leaked memo revealed Hefner's insistence that an investigative article on contemporary feminism be pulled in favour of a more strident hatchet-job. 'What I want', Hefner asserted, 'is a devastating piece that takes militants apart':

> What I'm interested in is the highly irrational, emotional, kookie trend that feminism has taken. These chicks are our natural enemy. It is time to do battle with them and I think we can do it in a devastating way . . . It is up to us to do a really expert, personal demolition job on the subject. (cited in Miller, 1985: 218)[13]

Rather than being addressed as equal and active participants in the fantasy of lavish high living, then, women were constructed as the objects of male consumption. There is, therefore, an important measure of truth to Sheila Jeffreys' (1990) arguments that the 'sexual revolution' was heavily mediated by patriarchal discourse. Despite her trenchant polemics, Jeffreys rightly points to the ways in which the libertine ethos of 'the swinger', rather than opening up new horizons of sexual freedom and equality, in some respects actually extended and intensified the sexual exploitation of women.[14]

NOTES

1   Full histories of the rise of the *Playboy* empire can be found in Brady (1975), Weyr (1978) and Miller (1985). Alternatively, the 'official' illustrated history of the magazine is provided in Edgren (1994).
2   See Dines (1995: 255; 1998: 45) and McNair (1996: 112).
3   A somewhat partisan historical account, Hefner's version of events has nevertheless been unquestioningly reiterated not only by biographers such as Weyr (1977: 2), but also by journalists such as Barber (1999) and academic critics such as Dines (1995: 257).
4   Conekin (2000) provides an excellent analysis of *Playboy*'s fashion coverage during the 1950s.
5   In 1967 the introduction of REACTS – the Reader Action Service – saw the service become computerized, *Playboy* proudly boasting that this was 'the first time a computer has been used for a "Where to Buy It" function' (*Playboy*, September 1967).
6   The Playboy Mansion retains its iconic status in *Playboy* folklore, 1998 seeing longstanding *Playboy* staffer Gretchen Edgren produce *Inside the Playboy Mansion* – a glossy, coffee-table tome dedicated to a celebration of Hefner's sixties residence.
7   Hefner was so taken with the format of the programme that in 1969 he recycled it with the launch of his first networked television series, *Playboy After Dark* – a show in which the magazine publisher hosted 'an hour-long party in the spectacular surroundings of his sky-high penthouse' (*Playboy*, April 1969).
8   An episode of *Playboy After Dark* also saw Hefner host his own 'penthouse luau'.
9   The 1957 Playboy Jazz All-Stars included such virtuosos as Louis Armstrong, Chet Baker, Dizzy Gillespie, Benny Goodman and Dave Brubeck.
10 Identical iconography appeared in the increasing amount of advertising the magazine attracted from swim- and leisure-wear manufacturers such as Catalina and Jantzen.
11 See, for example, contributions to the 'Forum' in *Playboy*'s editions for October 1963 and January 1964.
12 Hefner's biographer quotes the publisher as claiming to have doubted his parents' value system and 'the bullshit they accepted' from an early age:

> I was raised by parents who typified a generation that had passed. They really got that Horatio Alger kind of thing there, you know, and the Puritanism. I was

given an intellectual awareness by my folks, but at the same time a certain tradition that my intellectual awareness told me didn't make sense. So I began asking questions very early and developed a kind of a – not a negative rebel attitude . . . but an upbeat kind of rebel thing. I just couldn't buy a lot of the old answers and I pulled away from my traditional religious training rather early and started looking for other answers. (cited in Brady, 1975: 32)

13 The article that ultimately appeared, 'Up Against the Wall, Male Chauvinist Pig!' by Morton Hunt, was not quite a 'demolition job', but was unequivocal in its denunciation of 'militant man-haters [who] do their level worst to distort the distinctions between male and female and to discredit the legitimate grievance of American women' (*Playboy*, May 1970).

14 Clear and concise surveys of the various feminist perspectives related to pornography can be found in both Segal and McIntosh (1992) and Williams (1998).

Chapter 7
Bachelors in Paradise: Masculine Hedonism Comes of Age

In both his magazine and its allied enterprises, Hugh Hefner is a prophet of pop hedonism. He instinctively realized what sociologists had been saying for years – that the puritan ethic was dying, so that pleasure and leisure were becoming positive and universally adored values in American society. As Psychiatrist Rollo May has pointed out, a new puritanism has developed, a feeling that enjoyment is imperative, that to live life to the full, uninhibited life (in sex and in other areas) is everyone's duty.

Time, 'The Pursuit of Hedonism', 3 March 1967: 76–7.

TAKE-OFF TIME FOR THE 'JET-SET CASANOVAS'

Playboy magazine was both loved and loathed during the 1950s and 1960s. Capitalizing upon – and constituent in – the ascent of a model of masculinity anchored around style and consumerism, the magazine furnished an ideal for living that corresponded with the cultural orientations of the new, consumption-driven middle class that was emerging amid the prosperity of postwar America. From this group's vantage point *Playboy* could be celebrated as the herald of a new age of uplifting modernity – young, uninhibited and stylishly forward looking. During the 1950s, however, the new middle class was still taking shape, its development largely confined to the East, California and cosmopolitan enclaves in-between (places, in fact, that correlated with the concentration of *Playboy's* circulation).[1] More widely, however, the 'new bourgeoisie' was less well established, its ethos of hedonistic materialism still viewed with suspicion. As a consequence, *Playboy* sometimes faced an uphill task in securing its cultural legitimacy.

During the early years of its existence, *Playboy* faced opposition on a number of fronts. Foremost were forces that perceived the magazine as an affront to acceptable morality. Generally, the mid-twentieth century saw the US develop into a 'sexualized society', with not only a greater acceptance of sexual pleasure as a primary source of personal happiness (for both men and women) but also a shift of commercially produced erotic material from the cultural margins to the mainstream (D'Emilio and Freedman, 1997: 326–43). Nevertheless, sexuality remained a contested field. The 1950s were (as Chapter 4 demonstrated) a period of intense conflict around issues of sexual identity and representation – with family-oriented gender roles representing a cornerstone of the dominant ideological discourses of the Cold War. In this context, *Playboy*'s libertine outlook became a natural target for the opprobrium of moral crusaders.

Since the early twentieth century 'purity' pressure groups had challenged popular sexual representations of women, believing them to be exploitative and morally degenerative. By the 1950s, however, a more 'permissive' moral code was gaining ground. Indicative was the decision, in 1946, by the Supreme Court to veto the Post Office's powers of censorship, thus securing the survival of *Esquire* magazine and opening the door to a glut of new 'pin-up' publications – the 1950s economic boom sustaining an upsurge in both the supply of, and demand for, mass marketed 'cheesecake' literature. Heated public debate, however, was soon focusing on the social impact of what, by the mid-1950s, was already being spoken of as 'The American Sex Revolution' (Sorokin: 1956). Amid the wider Cold War climate of cultural anxiety, a revitalized anti-obscenity campaign began to take shape. The well-publicized sessions of a Select Committee on Current Pornographic Materials, appointed by the House of Representatives in late 1952, anticipated the Kefauver delinquency hearings of 1955 in their emphasis on the supposedly corrupting influence of the mass media – especially their perceived negative impact on young people. Middle-class women's groups were also voluble in their denunciation of the media's role in the transformation of American morality. A key force in the earlier 'purity' crusades, organizations such as the General Federation of Women's Clubs once again joined the fray, throwing their weight behind a campaign against the new wave of pornographic magazines (including *Playboy*), pressurizing retailers and lobbying for restrictive legislation.[2] Nor were they a voice in the wilderness. Key figures in the establishment also scrambled to man the moral barricades.

Though still smarting from losing its case against *Esquire*, the Post Office was soon targeting *Playboy* in its sights. As early as October 1954 Hefner had applied for reduced mailing rates for *Playboy*'s subscriptions and was confident of securing the all-important discount. But *Playboy*'s editor reckoned without Arthur Summerfield – a Postmaster General whose traditional moral convictions were as unyielding as those of Frank Walker, his predecessor who had earlier locked horns with *Esquire*. Summerfield at first stalled Hefner's request, then refused it outright, disputing *Playboy*'s status as a 'regular' publication (the staff's heavy workload had forced them to skip the March 1955 edition). Hefner appealed, but again his request was turned down, this time on the more forthright grounds that *Playboy* was deemed offensive. Moreover, in some parts of the country – especially the southern Bible Belt – the magazine had not been reaching subscribers (possibly through local postmasters acting as moral vigilantes), while even incoming mail to *Playboy*'s Chicago offices was being delayed. Slugging out the case in court, Hefner was finally vindicated and in November 1955 *Playboy* was awarded both its mailing privileges and compensation. Yet the struggle testifies to the wider sense of conflict that still existed between the traditional bourgeois morality of puritanism and self-discipline and the new code of hedonism and material desire.

Opposition to the ethos of playboy consumerism did not only come from middle class moral guardians. Hostility also existed in more proletarian quarters. Although magazines like *True* were beginning to address their working-class readerships as consumers, for the most part a model of masculinity rooted in narcissistic style and sensual pleasure remained anathema to blue-collar masculine ideals. Indeed, some men's magazines geared to working-class readerships were not only rigorous in their affirmation of traditional machismo but were also strident in their antipathy towards what they perceived as the encroaching values of 'unmanly' hedonism. In 1961, for example, the inaugural editorial of *Lucky* magazine called for a return to a more 'virile', 'straight-talking' and 'hairy-chested' form of masculinity and – in a barely disguised broadside against *Playboy* – argued that other men's magazines had 'now become so self-conscious with success that they have taken to filling their pages with a limp-wristed, pseudo-sophisticated literature' which addressed the American male as though he were 'a giggling, braceleted, dilletantish [*sic*], foppish, devious jerk who hides his effeminacy behind a glorification of bachelorhood' (*Lucky*, March 1961). In a similar vein, the readers of *Wildcat* were assured that the 'Jet-Set Casa-novas' were really 'Passion-Poopers', the magazine relating 'the peculiar paradox of the rich playboys who spend fortunes to make themselves appear to be virile sex-symbols, yet who are really anxiety-ridden, sexually inadequate caricatures of men!' (*Wildcat*, November 1963).

The venom of such attacks, however, betrayed a sense of desperation. By the beginning of the 1960s, the rough-hewn brand of rugged machismo espoused by down-market pulp magazines like *Lucky* and *Wildcat* was increasingly out of step with the cultural tempo. Increasingly it was the hedonistic male consumer – the young, middle-class 'swinging bachelor' – who carried the day. At the beginning of the 1950s the single man had still been predominantly conceived as an awkward and morally dubious figure, existing beyond the regulating embrace of the nuclear family. By the end of the decade, however, the 'swinging bachelor' had come into vogue. The antithesis of the organization man's button-down conformity and the breadwinner's family centred conservatism, the 'swinging bachelor' emerged as the purest expression of the new middle class 'morality of pleasure as a duty'. And in the late 1950s and early 1960s he spread his wings, becoming enshrined as an icon of dynamic and prosperous modernity.

THE 'INNEST IN-GROUP IN THE WORLD': THE POPULAR ICONOGRAPHY OF MASCULINE HEDONISM

As the success of *Playboy* testified, the emergent models of masculine consumerism registered conspicuous presence in the sphere of magazine publishing. A glossy eulogy to the world of narcissism and recreation, *Playboy*'s sales and profits had soared by the early 1960s, features in *Time* and *Newsweek* regularly charting Hefner's achievements as the Playboy empire developed into a national institution.

Within three years of its launch, *Playboy*'s circulation was quickly closing on that of *Esquire*.[3] By 1959 *Playboy*'s sales had actually eclipsed those of the original 'magazine for men', giving further impetus to *Esquire*'s attempts to recast itself as a forum for quality journalism. *Esquire*'s publishers, however, were not blind to the developing market of style-conscious males and, in 1957, replaced their trade journal, *Apparel Arts*, with a revamped version of *Gentlemen's Quarterly* – the magazine that had been *Esquire*'s immediate precursor in the 1930s, but which was relaunched as a new, upmarket fashion magazine for the 1950s man of style. Other publishers also sought to capitalize on the growing prominence of narcissistic masculine consumerism. By July 1957 *Playboy* was already bragging that it was 'The Most Imitated Magazine in America', the late 1950s and early 1960s seeing the appearance of a host of titles that pitched themselves as *Playboy*-esque connoisseurs of stylish cool and *risqué* pleasure. The roster of *Playboy*'s coattail-riders ran into dozens, including such titles as *Gent* ('An Approach to Relaxation', launched in 1956), *Gay Blade* ('For Men With a Zest for Living', also 1956), *The Dude* ('The Magazine Devoted to Pleasure', 1956), *Escapade* ('Pleasure for Everyman', 1956), *Nugget* ('Entertainment in a Lighter Mood', 1956), *Rogue* ('Designed For Men', 1956), *Satan* ('Devilish Entertainment for Men', 1957), *Hi Life* ('The Live-It-Up Magazine for Gentlemen', 1958), *Bachelor* ('The Magazine for the Young at Heart', 1959) and *Millionaire* ('You Don't Need to be a Millionaire – Just *Think* Like One', 1964). These titles had a slick and colourful presentation and a higher quota of sexual content than *Playboy* – although their production values were poorer overall. Geared to a less affluent market, they were only pretenders to the throne of swinging bachelordom and they measured their circulations in hundreds of thousands rather than *Playboy*'s millions.

Further down-market, many blue-collar men's magazines also began to pay homage to the mythology of the 'swinging bachelor' – the archetype's growth as a cultural force reflected in the way a number of former 'macho pulp' titles reconfigured themselves to mimic *Playboy*. The early 1960s, for example, saw former 'true adventure' magazines like *Cavalcade* and *Cavalier* rebrand themselves as chronicles of a more 'sophisticated' lifestyle of fine food and drink, foreign travel and 'tasteful' erotica. Well into the 1970s surviving 'macho pulp' titles maintained their commitment to 'blood 'n' guts' action in the great outdoors, but they were increasingly an anachronism. Indeed, when interviewed, these magazine's editors openly acknowledged the lumpen and outdated quality of their products – *Male*'s editorial director conceding that 'A majority of our readers own a home – but a home in some place like Arkansas. Our readers lag behind the trends.' The editor of *Men* and *Stag*, meanwhile, was more succinct – 'We try to reach the guys who want to read sophisticated magazines like *Playboy* . . . but can't understand them' (*Esquire*, November 1976).

Nor was 'sophisticated' masculine style confined to the realm of men's magazines. At the same time as *Playboy* and its ilk were celebrating the upmarket verve of the 'swinging bachelor', seductive soundscapes of an intoxicating good life could be found in the bewitching harmonies of easy-listening mood music. High-fidelity (hi-fi) sound technology was initially marketed to the young professional – no stylishly appointed bachelor pad was complete without a state-of-the-art turntable nestling alongside the drinks bar and lava lamp – and throughout the 1950s and early 1960s a host of album releases catered to the roguish tastes of the martini man. Several arrangers and composers stood out as mood music virtuosos. While Martin Denny's 'exotic sounds' served up luscious slices of Polynesian promise, Herb Alpert and the Tijuana Brass conjured with the enticing vibrance of life south of the border. Film scores by John Barry and Henry Mancini, meanwhile, combined the essence of nonchalant cool with the flourish of fast-paced thrills. Perhaps above all, however, it was Burt Bacharach who stood out as the maestro of moodsong. As easy-listening aficionado Dylan Jones explains, Bacharach and his sleek melodies captured the spirit of the times – especially the 'swinging' panache of the playboy archetype:

> it was Bacharach who had the jet-set cool: the looks, the urbane sophistication, the cars and the girls. He personified the sixties bachelor . . . Bacharach was the ruler of the open-plan hi-fi, a man who pushed fifties mood music into tomorrow. If Kennedy was your president, then Bacharach was your composer. (Jones, 1997: 15)

The 1950s and early 1960s were also the hey-day of the dinner-jacketed crooner. Tony Bennett, Vic Damone and Matt Monro all had hits and were regulars on the cabaret circuit, though it was another trio of stars whose performance most fully encapsulated the flavour of 'swinging bachelorhood' – Sammy Davis Jr., Dean Martin and Frank Sinatra.

Possibly the foremost black entertainer of the 1950s and 1960s, Sammy Davis had started early in show business. As a child during the 1930s he had featured with his father in a vaudeville revue, Davis returning to the act after his wartime service. Struggling against segregation and racist exclusion was not easy, but during the 1950s Davis broke into the big time – singing, dancing and wisecracking his way to being one of America's quickest rising nightclub and recording artists. Dean Martin's star was also in the ascendant. 'Dino' enjoyed a string of hits in the mid-1950s, the singer bringing a languid sensuality to the crooning style popularized earlier by the likes of Bing Crosby and Perry Como. Martin also starred alongside comedian Jerry Lewis in a series of film comedies (Martin playing the suave straight

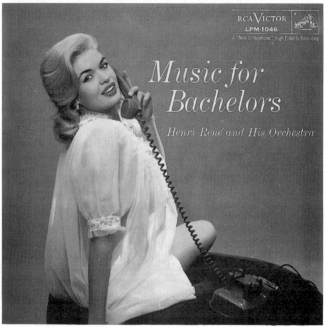

7.1 'Music For Bachelors.' (Top: Cy Coleman, *Playboy's Penthouse*, Everest, 1960; Bottom: Henri René, *Music for Bachelors*, RCA Victor, 1956.)

man to Lewis's goofy clown), although critics doubted the singers' career would survive following the duo's acrimonious split in 1956. Within a year, however, Martin had bounced back with a series of high-profile screen roles and further chart hits.

In their show business personae, Sammy Davis and Dean Martin were both 'men of the moment' – Davis (the quick-fire joker) and Martin (the *louche* lounge lizard) personifying the rise of a masculine identity predicated on debonair style and a thirst for the good life. More than either Davis or Martin, however, it was Frank Sinatra who ruled as the sultan of swinging manhood. Sinatra's days as a darling of the bobby-soxers had worn thin by the late 1940s. His record sales were declining and his films were less bankable. When MGM terminated his movie contract in 1950, it looked as though Sinatra's stardom was well and truly ebbing. The slide, however, was reversed by an Oscar-winning performance in Columbia Pictures' wartime epic, *From Here to Eternity* (1953). With the film's success Sinatra was back at the top. Musically, he also took a new direction. A contract with Capitol Records and an alliance with arranger Nelson Riddle brought an end to the boyish warbling. Instead, albums such as *Songs for Swingin' Lovers!* (1956), *A Swingin' Affair!* (1957) and *Come Fly With Me* (1958) saw a new Sinatra – richer, deeper and more dynamic. The singer also developed a loose, conversational rhythm and a finger-snapping spontaneity that made him a natural icon of insouciant masculinity.[4] Sinatra's well-publicized carousing, womanizing and tempestuous affairs, meanwhile, ensured him a devil-may-care charisma that struck a chord with the emerging moral code of autonomous pleasure. Hardly surprising, then, that Sinatra was Hugh Hefner's favourite singer.

The 'swinging bachelor' also made his presence felt in Hollywood. From the early 1950s to the mid-1960s, a number of screen stars emerged whose films and public image embodied the ascendance of the independent, male hedonist.[5] Rock Hudson, in particular, stood out as 'the quintessential but fabricated heterosexual bachelor' (Cohan, 1997: xxi). Hudson's series of romantic comedies with Doris Day were pivotal in the projection of the actor as an icon of footloose masculinity. Exemplary was *Pillow Talk*, the film that launched Hudson and Day's screen partnership in 1959. As bachelor songwriter Brad Allen, Hudson stars as an archetype of the playboy rascal. The chic decor, designer furniture and abstract paintings of Allen's apartment mark out his upwardly mobile and cosmopolitan lifestyle, while its hi-tech gadgetry serve to confirm his heterosexuality – at the flick of a switch the door is latched, the lights are dimmed and a hi-fi fills the room with seductive mood music; a second switch activates the readily prepared sofa bed. The Hudson/Day comedies, however, were charged with contradictions. Alongside the representations of hedonistic bachelorhood, more conservative ideologies of 'togetherness' and 'domestic containment' also surfaced, with the swinging lifestyle of Hudson's characters ultimately held in check by romance and marriage. Moreover, as Richard Meyer argues, Hudson's star persona presented a sexuality that was relatively unassertive and benign, always tempered by 'a measure of safety, of "gentle giant" reassurance' (Meyer, 1991: 260).

Other actors furnished a more thoroughgoing articulation of the playboy ethic. Bob Hope, for example, had already crafted his screen image as a wise-cracking Lothario during the 1940s with Paramount's *Road to . . .* film series, and during the 1950s and early 1960s he maintained his affable wolfishness in numerous movies and television shows. *Bachelor in Paradise* (1961) was typical. A tale of romantic trysts in suburbia, the film is perfect testimony both to the contemporary caricature of the suburbs as the epitome of stultifying conformity and to the growing prominence of the playboy archetype. Hope is cast as a hard-up author whose mounting tax bill forces him to undertake research on love-life in a typical Californian suburb, in the process antagonizing virtually every married man in the neighbourhood through his wayward advice to their frustrated wives. The roguish bachelor, then, was a part Bob Hope made his own and the 1950s and early 1960s saw him reprise the role in an array of films and TV specials, including *Bachelor School*, a 1964 comedy show that featured Hope alongside his own troupe of beautiful dancers – the Bachelorettes. Tony Curtis was also a contender as the silver screen's high-priest of bachelorhood. Young and athletic, Curtis had established his career as a swash-buckling matinee idol in the early 1950s, but by the end of the decade – especially after his role as a millionaire impostor in *Some Like It Hot* (1959) – he was increasingly associated with *Playboy*-esque roles. A close friend of Hugh Hefner and a regular visitor to the Playboy Mansion, in 1962 Curtis was lined-up to play the *Playboy* editor in a projected bio-pic. Screenplay problems meant the film never materialized, though Curtis still carved out a niche as a carefree playboy in comedies such as *The Great Race* (1965) and *Boeing-Boeing* (1965) – the latter casting the star as an international jet-setter who, by successfully juggling flight schedules, maintains simultaneous relationships with three different air stewardesses.

Again, however, it was the trinity of Sammy Davis, Dean Martin and Frank Sinatra whose screen roles and public image presented the most conspicuous para-digm of the playboy swinger, especially when – together with comedian Joey Bishop and actor Peter Lawford – they combined in the boisterous clique known as the 'Rat Pack'. Most of the group had been associated with the original Rat Pack of the mid-1950s – an informal troupe of Hollywood celebrities formed around Humphrey Bogart and famed for their late-night drinking sessions. Following Bogart's death in 1957 the original circle had dissolved, but by the end of the decade the press were talking of 'the Clan' – Sinatra and his show business cronies who were regularly seen socializing and partying together. Sammy Davis, however, objected to the epithet 'Clan' (for obvious reasons) and so the Rat Pack was re-born – this time with Sinatra as 'Chairman of the Board'. And throughout the early 1960s the Rat Pack were renowned for carousing around the plush nightspots of New York, Los Angeles and (especially) Las Vegas, carving out a reputation for rowdy drinking marathons and licentious horseplay.[6] It was a notoriety in which they revelled, 'the boys' even concocting their own 'hip' argot to enhance their aura as a fraternity of laid-back swingers – 'The Big Casino' was death; 'A Little Hey-Hey' was a good time (either socially or sexually); and anything boring or tiresome was 'Dullsville, Ohio'. The Rat Pack's taste for fast living and alcohol-fuelled hi-jinx hit a special high point when they convened for a month-long 'Summit' meeting in 1960. With the idea of producing an all-star film, Sinatra and his drinking buddies assembled in Las Vegas where, by day, they filmed the crime-caper movie *Oceans 11* and, by night, performed to packed houses at The Sands casino – and then had 'A Little Hey-Hey', swilling booze and partying with showgirls into the small hours.

Although most were married and had children, the Rat Pack's antics were a far cry from the dutiful domesticity of the breadwinner ideal. And the acres of admiring column space they were accorded in the press was indicative of the loosening grip of the breadwinner ethic as a hegemonic system of masculine values. Instead, the popularity of Sinatra and his cohort is suggestive of the growing cultural purchase of the playboy code of masculine hedonism. Indeed, in the Rat Pack *Playboy* magazine recognized a kindred spirit. *Playboy* documented the 1960 'Summit' in a loving, six-page photo-feature, the magazine extolling the Rat Pack's 'talent, charm, romance and devil-may-care nonconformity' and applauding the 'wild iconoclasm that millions envy secretly or even unconsciously – which makes them, in the public eye, the innest in-group in the world' (*Playboy*, June 1960). The Rat Pack also had admirers in high places. Even before he saw Sinatra and his colleagues perform at The Sands, Jack Kennedy had been fascinated by the entertainers. JFK, after all, embraced a similar masculine ethos – with his ceaseless philandering and passion for indulgent good times. With much in common, the playboy President and Sinatra became good friends, the two sharing their 'recreational interests' at a series of parties and get-togethers and Sinatra throwing his weight behind JFK's 1960 presidential campaign. Re-christened the 'Jack Pack', the Chairman *et al.* turned out in force at July's Democratic National Convention, Sinatra later presiding over a gala tribute to Kennedy the night before his inauguration.[7]

An affinity also existed between Kennedy and another icon of masculine hedonism – James Bond. A big fan of Ian Fleming's British spy hero, the President had listed Fleming's *From Russia With Love* among his ten favourite books in an interview with *Life* magazine in 1961 – and it was rumoured that the CIA had been forced to rustle up a martini-drinking super-spy after JFK had insisted on meeting the American counterpart to agent 007 (Wofford, 1980: 362). While Bond would have appealed to Kennedy's taste for adventure, it is likely that 007's amorous escapades and fast-paced lifestyle – like that of the Rat Pack – would also have struck a chord with the President. The 007 of Fleming's original novels, however, was still a relatively conservative figure – fairly reserved in his outlook and tastes. It was only with the release of the first Bond movie, *Dr No*, in 1962 (it opened in America in 1963) that

7.2 The Rat Pack, 1960. Left to Right: Frank Sinatra, Dean Martin, Sammy Davis Jr., Peter Lawford and Joey Bishop. (Pictorial Press)

the character of 007 was configured more fully as an agent of the swinging jet set.[8] As Tony Bennett and Janet Woollacott observe of Bond's 1960s incarnation:

> His attitudes towards sex, gambling and pleasure in general are distinctly liberal and his tastes and lifestyle have a decidedly international and cosmopolitan flavour. In a word, Bond is not old fashioned . . . Bond belongs not to the Breed but to a new elite – international rather than parochially English in its orientation – committed to new values (professionalism) and lifestyles (martini). (Bennett and Woollacott, 1987: 111)

Film historian James Chapman insists that, despite being financed by American capital, the Bond movies were essentially *British* texts – largely produced using British studios and film crews, generically originating in British fiction and embodying British notions of national identity (Chapman, 1999: 14). While this is true, in their glossy materialism and stylish brand of 'modernized' masculinity the 1960s Bond films owed a heavy debt to developments in American culture. Indeed, to a large part they were produced with the American market in mind. For example, whereas Fleming would have preferred the gentlemanly David Niven to play Bond, this was overruled by American film producers Albert Broccoli and Harry Saltzman who considered Sean Connery an actor whose relative lack of class signifiers would give him greater appeal to stateside audiences (Bennett and Woollacott, 1987: 55–6). Moreover, in being remodelled as a trans-Atlantic playboy, Bond was tailor made to the cultural shifts taking place in the US. In the early 1960s America was ready for Bond. The ascendance of a narcissistic masculine consumerism provided fertile ground for 007's stylishness and (hetero-)sexual freedom. Indeed, even before the release of *Dr No*, *Playboy* magazine had embraced 007 as one of its own. In an editorial of 1960, for example, *Playboy* proudly recounted a visit by Fleming to its offices, the magazine relating how the author had speculated that 'James Bond, if he were an actual person, would be a registered reader of *Playboy*' (*Playboy*, March 1960). And, as Bond-mania set in, *Playboy* enlisted 007 in its crusade for materialistic and libertine masculine ideals – the magazine lavishing attention on each new film and featuring numerous pin-up photospreads of the 'Bond girls', as well as serializing many of Fleming's stories and honouring the author with his own 'Playboy Interview' in December 1964. Not to be out-done, *Esquire* followed suit, with a special Bond-themed issue published in conjunction with the release of *Thunderball* in 1965 – a film that proved to be Bond's most profitable triumph at the American box office.

On television, too, the playboy adventurer became a stock character. He was especially conspicuous in a wave of action series imported from Britain – for example, *Secret Agent* (screened in CBS's 1965/6 season) and *The Saint* (syndicated in the early 1960s and then networked on NBC in 1967). These series, together with the Bond films, gained particular cachet through their traits of 'Britishness'. Just like the

Beatles, the mini-skirt and the mod fashions of 'swinging London', the 'Britishness' of action heroes like Bond and The Saint afforded them a sense of exciting 'difference'. Indeed, writing in *Vogue* in 1965, American sociologist Herbert Gans identified a marked change in American perceptions of Britain, with images of Britishness – especially British *men* – increasingly incorporated in domestic fantasies of sexual freedom and socially liberated lifestyles. Citing the American popularity of Richard Burton, Bond and the Beatles, Gans conjectured that an older image of the 'British gentleman' ('well-bred, sophisticated, reserved, public spirited') had been displaced by images of British men as 'potent sexual idols, armed with unusual energy and vitality, and given to public declarations of skepticism and satire' (Gans, 1965: 108). Their attributes of 'Britishness', then, gave characters like Bond and The Saint a special appeal – their qualities of 'difference' accentuating their connotations of thrilling modernity.

British playboy-adventurers may have been especially attractive to American audiences, but a proliferation of home-grown equivalents also proved popular. James Coburn, for instance, starred as secret agent and jet-set swinger Derek Flint in the action spoofs *Our Man Flint* (1965) and *In Like Flint* (1967), while Dean Martin delivered an equally sybaritic (not to say self-reflexive) performance as Matt Helm in the tongue-in-cheek spy quartet *The Silencers* (1966), *Murderer's Row* (1966), *The Ambushers* (1967) and *The Wrecking Crew* (1968). The late 1950s and early 1960s also brought a new wave of cool and stylish heroes to American television. The arrival of *Peter Gunn* (NBC/ABC, 1958-61), for example, showcased a new brand of hip private eye who was equally at home in bohemian jazz clubs and plush, uptown restaurants. A more unlikely working of the playboy-adventurer formula, however, came in *Burke's Law* (ABC, 1963–6) in which Los Angeles Chief of Detectives, Amos Burke, was also a millionaire *bon vivant* – arriving at crime-scenes in a chauffeur-driven Rolls-Royce.

Like many of the icons of masculine hedonism during the early 1960s, however, Peter Gunn (played by Craig Stevens) and Amos Burke (Gene Barry) were relatively mature. Indeed, by the early 1960s the Rat Pack were in their forties and fifties and even Sean Connery was fast approaching middle age. These icons certainly elaborated an identity that broke away from more conservative and traditional forms of masculinity through an onus on style and consumer desire. Yet it was an identity that found a more 'natural' home with younger, fresher role models. Indeed, in the realm of TV action shows, a younger generation of playboy-adventurers steadily came to the fore. Beginning with *77 Sunset Strip* (1958-64), Warner Brothers developed for the ABC network a slew of adventure series featuring young and glamourously debonair male heroes. *77 Sunset Strip* featured a pair of up-market and Ivy-League-educated private eyes, Stu Bailey (Efrem Zimbalist Jr.) and Jeff Spencer (Roger Smith). Fully equipped with modish wardrobe and slick hairstyles, the duo cracked cases in the world's ritziest glamour spots (helped out by their beatnik car lot attendant, Kookie). With the success of *77 Sunset Strip*, Warner followed with several spins on the formula – *Hawaiian Eye* (1959–63), *Bourbon Street Beat* (1959-60) and *Surfside Six* (1960–2) – all featuring young, trendy and sharply charismatic detectives who worked in exciting locations.[9] In a similar vein, *The Man From U.N.C.L.E* (NBC, 1964–7) also deployed images of 'young men of action and acquisition' – with a masculine style that was youthful, style conscious and avowedly cosmopolitan, though this time situated within a tongue-in-cheek spy narrative.

The playboy adventurers of the early 1960s were constructed as living in a liberated world of breathless consumption and pleasure, yet it is important to acknowledge the dimensions of sexism and racism that underpinned this 'liberation'. Figures such as Bond, Matt Helm and the *Sunset Strip* team can be read as 'global flâneurs'. Touring the world's fashionable resorts and night-spots in search of excitement and spectacle, they subject the world to their sovereign gaze, turning it into their own domain, their playground. This practice exemplifies what Michael Denning (1987) describes as James Bond's 'licence to look'. In his daring international missions 007, Denning argues, casts an imperialist and racist 'tourist gaze' in which unfamiliar and 'exotic' locations are represented as the object of Western, metropolitan scrutiny (Denning, 1987: 103–7). Indeed, this synthesis of tourism, consumption and sexual pleasure was identical to the processes of objectification elaborated in *Playboy*'s 'travelogue' features of the 1950s and 1960s. And, just like *Playboy*, Bond and his associates' 'licence to look' also extended to women. Just as their 'tourist gaze' constructed peripheral societies as objects of spectacle, so their 'male gaze' constructed women as the objects of a voyeuristic look – cars, clothes, 'exotic' locations and women all being configured as items for the playboy adventurer's consumption.

At the same time, however, it would be misleading to interpret the 1960s iconography of the hedonistic male as ideologically monolithic. Popular texts are always complex and ambiguous, permeated by contradictions and inconsistencies. Indeed, the rise of a masculinity predicated on consumer pleasure may not only have challenged more conservative models of manhood rooted in production and self-denial. The male consumer's emphasis on exhibition and performance may also have had more far-reaching implications, calling into question the sense of stability and unity traditionally equated with masculinity. The hedonistic male did not simply consume. Through his emphasis on conspicuous display he also became the object of others' consumption. By the 1930s, and possibly before, masculinity was (as Chapter 3 suggested) already being constructed as a spectacle in fashion advertising and popular texts such as *Esquire*. But during the 1950s and 1960s – as self-conscious, male consumption became more prevalent – masculinity was increasingly subjected to a spectatorial 'look'. In *Playboy*'s sumptuous fashion features, the super-spy's obsession with image and the Rat Pack's fastidious attention to the visual codes of style – always sharp-suited, yet meticulously 'casual' in front of the camera –

masculinity was increasingly positioned as the object of a scrutinizing gaze. And, as masculinity was steadily opened up to spectatorship, traditional representational systems were (to a degree) problematized and ruptured – perhaps making space for a plurality of more provisional gender identities.[10]

'A LIFE STYLE LIKE NOTHING YOU HAVE EVER EXPERIENCED BEFORE': THE FANTASY MADE REAL

The libertine and consumption-oriented 'swinging bachelor', therefore, became a prevalent image across American popular culture during the 1950s and early 1960s. The iconography of masculine hedonism constructed in men's magazines, easy-listening records and James Bond films was a mythologized fantasy, a lifestyle that very few men actually enjoyed. As an 'imagined identity', however, this fantasy made significant connections with the material world, offering representations of masculinity through which men could make sense of their place within a profoundly shifting cultural landscape. In a world increasingly dominated by the imperatives of commodity consumption, the fantasy of the 'swinging bachelor' furnished men – especially those within a rapidly transforming middle class – with an intelligible code of values that was reconciled with the expectations and demands of modern consumerism. As Jay McInerney reflects in his autobiographical account of the Bond films' appeal in sixties America, 007's lifestyle may have been a fantasy but it had a tangible cultural impact in its presentation of a beguilingly stylish and consumption-literate (yet still unmistakably 'manly') masculine archetype:

> At the time James Bond slipped suavely into America, I was looking for a new role model . . . . Bond was urbanely cool: aside from being great-looking, as incarnated by Sean Connery, he was also witty and well dressed and unflappable, the only movie hero we had ever seen whose first impulse, after killing a man, was to straighten his tie . . . Connery's Bond provided a kind of role model that hadn't existed in the US before then – a cultured man who knew how to navigate a wine list, how to field-strip a Beretta, and how to seduce women. (McInerney, 1996: 13–36)

McInerney's additional claim that Bond 'helped to usher in the sexual revolution' (McInerney, 1996: 32), however, needs to be placed within a more complex historical narrative. Indeed, the 'sexual revolution' is something of a misnomer. The changes in America's sexual codes during the 1960s were undoubtedly profound. Rather than representing a sudden, revolutionary challenge to prevailing norms, however, the 1960s shift in sexual morality is better seen as the culmination of longer processes of transformative *evolution*. Indeed, the era of most spectacular change in American sexual mores was probably the 1920s – a period in which sexuality first became significantly detached from associations with reproduction and instead became incorporated in the developing field of commercial pleasure (D'Emilio and Freedman, 1997: 241). Important change also came with World War Two, social upheaval being accompanied by unprecedented pre- and extra-marital experience. And, although the Cold War was a time of official moral retrenchment and conformity, the nation's sexual habits were (as Chapter 4 demonstrated) actually more liberal and varied than those sanctioned within the marital sex ethic. The publication of the Kinsey Reports, moreover, fed into a proliferation of public discourse around sexual behaviour. Though pressure from McCarthyite red baiters forced the Rockefeller Foundation to terminate his funding, Kinsey's revelations helped stir a bubbling cauldron of popular sexual fascination throughout the 1950s. Furthermore, as the legal judgements in favour of *Esquire* and then *Playboy* testified, the barriers of censorship were coming down and, though litigation and zealous anti-pornography campaigns still punctuated the 1950s, the mores of the middle class had shifted decisively and the purity crusaders increasingly found themselves outside the cultural mainstream (D'Emilio and Freedman, 1997: 284).

James Bond's brand of recreational sexual pleasure, then, exists in a longer history of sexual liberalization. Yet the early 1960s remain a period of special significance. They marked a moment at which what was once regarded as daring nonconformity became established features of middle class life. The rise of a new, consumption-oriented middle class brought with it 'a new accommodation with the erotic' (D'Emilio and Freedman, 1997: 300). With the emergence of a new, urban and consumerist middle-class culture, the affirmation of sexual pleasure took its place within the gamut of markers of a glamorous and distinctively modern lifestyle. And, as this new sexual liberalism took root, commerce came to play a bigger role within sexualized leisure. The success of *Playboy* and the pervasiveness of the sexual sell in advertising testify to consumer capitalism's growing presence in the sexual realm. A reinvigorated urban nightlife of bars and nightclubs, meanwhile, held out the promise of hedonistic pleasure and sexual adventure as the recreational sex ethic became more established. More widely, there also took shape new 'liminal' zones – geographic spaces where regulating cultural disciplines were relaxed and the fantasies of the playboy's 'ethic of fun' took on material existence.[11]

Since the beginning of the century, the beach had become territorialized as a site for leisure. As a space where the norms of everyday behaviour, dress and activity were suspended, the beach developed intimate associations with discourses of freedom, pleasure and sensuality. These reached their apex in the late 1950s and early 1960s with the rise of the Californian Dream of sun, sand and rolling surf. Southern Californian youth style was (as Chapter 5 argued) in the vanguard of the march into the new era of commodified and narcissistic leisure and, more generally, the Golden State was configured as America's liberal and laid-back summertime playground. And, alongside surfing, water-skiing and big game fishing, other exotic pastimes were added to the itinerary of the affluent man of leisure. Scuba diving became a particular craze. Following wartime developments in diving technology, recreational scuba equipment and instruction courses became widely available in the late 1950s, scuba diving becoming a totem of new, affluent and exciting lifestyles. On the east coast, meanwhile, Miami Beach was also developing a reputation for indulgent liminality. Already booming during the interwar decades, the resort combined Art Deco luxury with an ambience of permissive broadmindedness. Yet it was during the 1950s and early 1960s that Miami Beach hit its high-rolling years, with illustrious new hotel and entertainment developments and a booming nightlife that was a regular haunt for glitterati swingers – Frank Sinatra, Sammy Davis and company all putting in regular appearances.

For the real mecca of postwar hedonism, however, nothing could eclipse Las Vegas. The city's modern growth was triggered by the construction of the Hoover Dam in 1931, the same year that Nevada legalized quick divorces and gambling. Lenient gaming laws laid the way for the development of the legendary 'Strip' – a stretch of ritzy casinos extending south of downtown Vegas. The first, El Rancho, opened with a gala celebration in 1941, followed during the 1940s by The Frontier, The Thunderbird and The Flamingo (the latter bankrolled by New York mobster 'Lucky' Luciano and minded by his former hit-man, 'Bugsy' Segal). Postwar prosperity brought more dramatic growth, the 1950s seeing a wave of bigger and more glamorous temples to the good life, with the opening of The Desert Inn, The Sahara, The Sands, The Riviera, The Tropicana, The Showboat and The Stardust – the last, with its 1,000 rooms, then representing the world's largest hotel. A place where conventional moral codes were forsaken in favour of excitement and personal gratification, the exponential rise of Las Vegas belies any sense of the 1950s as a desert of abstinence and conformity. Instead, the spectacular popularity of Vegas suggests a growing enthusiasm (from some social groups, at least) for the pleasures of high living and licentious excess.

On a smaller scale, a vogue for 'key clubs' also instituted oases of liminal hedonism across America. The operating principle of these private clubs had existed since the 1930s, individual membership keys being issued to patrons of up-market bars and restaurants. In the early 1950s, however, the idea underwent a renaissance. In the forefront was Chicago's Gaslight Club. Launched in 1953 by Burton Browne, a local advertising executive, the Gaslight styled itself as an exclusive haven for lusty big spenders. Evoking a sense of opulent ribaldry, the Club's atmosphere combined the illicit thrills of the Prohibition era speakeasy with the elegant grandeur of the 1890s music hall. Thick carpeting, gilt ceiling friezes and gas-styled chandeliers were set off by rich oil paintings and marble statues, while the huge, ornately carved centrepiece bar announced the Club's sybaritic priorities with the engraved motto 'Work is the Curse of the Drinking Classes'. This, moreover, was an emporium dedicated to specifically *masculine* indulgence. Membership of the Gaslight was restricted to men (although women were permitted as guests), while the waitresses' uniforms were a suggestive interpretation of the 1890s bustle – the low-cut corset and abbreviated skirt being teamed with black mesh stockings and stiletto-heeled shoes. The Gaslight, meanwhile, cultivated connotations of clannishness and status through its membership policies, $25 keyholder fee and high prices ($2 for a shot of scotch). Despite the expense, however, there was more than enough custom to keep the club in business. Within three years of opening, the Gaslight boasted 3,800 keyholders and by the early 1960s Browne had opened additional clubs in New York, Washington and Paris.

Such success inevitably spawned imitators. In 1962 *Life* magazine reported on 'the lure of the key clubs', the Gaslight being followed by the Roaring 20s and the Gay 90s in Los Angeles, clubs which were 'gladdening the eyes of hungry, well-heeled *bon vivants*' (*Life*, 21 September 1962). It was, though, Hugh Hefner (always the shrewd entrepreneur) who most adeptly exploited the formula. In 1959 *Playboy* magazine had run a feature on the Gaslight phenomenon that drew over 3,000 readers' letters enquiring how to join the club. Recognizing the market potential, Victor Lownes pitched the idea of a Playboy Club to a responsive Hefner and plans were drawn up for the kind of masculine sanctuary that would bring into being the lifestyle evoked in the magazine. A failed club in downtown Chicago was stripped of its fusty decor and in its place appeared sleek leather and teak furnishings as the building was converted into a palatial 'bachelor pad', complete with Playboy Penthouse, Playboy Library and Playmate Bar (equipped, of course, with the latest in TV and hi-fi gadgetry). Impressed by the Gaslight's waitress costumes, the *Playboy* team decided their own staff's outfits should also boost their club's association with spicy excitement. Hefner's original idea was to have waitresses dressed in short, frilly nighties – though the impracticality of this as work garb was quickly realized. Yet the preferred alternative was only slightly more serviceable. Inspired by the magazine's rabbit logo, the famous Playboy 'Bunny' costume was born – a satin bodice (cut daringly high at the hip) accessorized with sheer black tights, oversized satin 'rabbit' ears and fluffy cotton tail (cuffs, collar and bow-tie were added later).

Opening in February 1960, the Chicago Playboy Club was an instant success. In its first month of business it was visited by 16,800 keyholders and their guests, and by 1961 the club's 106,000 keyholders (who paid $50 for the privilege) were ensuring that it was selling more food and drink than any other restaurant or club in town. Anxious to pre-empt possible competition, Lownes immediately pushed forward with plans for Playboy Clubs across America. By the end of 1960 franchises had already been sold for clubs in New Orleans and Miami and negotiations were underway for clubs in Phoenix, Arizona and St Louis. By the mid-1960s a chain of fifteen Playboy Clubs stretched from Boston to Los Angeles, accounting for nearly 40 per cent of the Playboy empire's revenues of $47.8 million. Meanwhile, 1966 saw Hefner's first overseas venture. With the opening of a $4 million Playboy Club in London's exclusive Park Lane, the Playboy organization was confirmed as a multinational conglomerate, with a network of clubs (boasting a membership of half a million keyholders), a Caribbean Playboy Hotel in Jamaica and a sprawling resort complex near Lake Geneva in Wisconsin.

Playboy liked to promote its enterprises as appealing to the highest caste of American consumer. For example, announcing the launch of the first Playboy Club, *Playboy* magazine described how 'its members hold the key to sophisticated pleasure':

> The Playboy Key – with the familiar rabbit emblem stamped upon it – has become a new and meaningful status symbol amongst men of means. No one who is really IN wants to be without it . . . The Playboy Club is a meeting place for the most important, most aware, most affluent men of the country. (*Playboy*, August 1960)

In reality, however, the world of Playboy was populated not by a 'most affluent' social elite, but by the new, style-conscious and aspirant middle class. As *Business Week* explained in 1966, the Playboy Clubs were essentially 'a middle class phenomenon' whose combination of chic display and affordability allowed a keyholder to 'buy dinner and an evening's entertainment in plush surroundings for himself and a date for less than $20' (*Business Week*, 25 June 1966). Indeed, Hugh Hefner's genius lay in recognizing and pandering to this class's desires and aspirations. Long before Pierre Bourdieu identified the French petite bourgeoisie's obsessive pursuit of expressive and liberated lifestyles, in America Hefner was capitalizing on prosperous middle-class men's quest to elaborate a discrete habitus through the consumption of distinctive cultural goods and practices. Hefner, for example, quickly realized the connotative power of the distinctive *Playboy* insignia and the way it could be used to market an array of products to a consumer group keen to associate itself with the magazine's universe of fashionable hedonism. From the beginning, therefore, merchandising was a cornerstone to Hefner's commercial empire as readers snapped up ties, cigarette lighters and golf clubs – all emblazoned with the familiar 'Bunny' logo. Throughout the 1960s potential for sharing in the *Playboy* ideal widened even further, with advertisements for Hefner's clubs and resorts promising 'A life style like nothing you have ever experienced before' (*Playboy*, April 1973). By 1972, in fact, it did not seem unreasonable for the Executive Vice-President of the Playboy empire to envision a lifestyle that took place within a total 'Playboy environment':

> A man gets up in his Playboy town house . . . calls a Playboy limousine to take him to the airport where he gets in a Playboy chartered plane, flies to New York, takes a Playboy limousine to a Playboy hotel in midtown Manhattan, changes into his Playboy suit, takes a Playboy ferry to a Playboy convention center on Randall's Island for his business meeting, that night goes to a Playboy

restaurant and then to a Playboy theater where he sees a Playboy movie . . . And while we don't have all of those things yet, we have many of them and we're exploring the rest. (cited in Weyr, 1978: 70)

'YOU'VE COME A LONG WAY, BABY': SEX, SINGLE GIRLS AND 'COMMODITY FEMINISM'

By the mid-1960s, therefore, a new 'lifestyle' sensibility denoted by stylistic self-consciousness, sexual autonomy and leisure-oriented consumption was an established facet of American culture. It was, though, a fairly class-specific phenomenon – characteristic of a growing middle-class faction who made a project of their purchase and display of consumer goods as they struggled to legitimate their constellation of tastes, dispositions and values. And, while the ideologies and imperatives of this group certainly placed an accent on individual freedom and sexual liberalism, there were always firm boundaries to this broadmindedness. The discourse of 'swinging' enjoyment, for example, largely spoke to heterosexual pleasures. Keen to appear the sexual liberal, Hugh Hefner admitted to experimenting with one homosexual experience, although he did not feel inclined to repeat it (Brady, 1975: 21). Some fairly progressive sentiments, meanwhile, surfaced in the Playboy Forum on Homo-sexuality in April 1971, but among the new middle class homosexuality remained largely beyond the pale until the 1970s – and even then was still regarded with unease.

Other disparities were also pronounced. While norms of acceptable sexual behaviour were becoming more liberal for both men and women, a gendered double standard persisted in the meaning of sexual experience. Meanwhile, in the new world of glamorous, hedonistic consumption, gender inequalities also remained pervasive. For example, not only were women sexually objectified in Playboy's centrefolds, they were also subordinated in Hefner's clubs – the obliging Bunny-girls existing as alluring decoration to the masculine world of lascivious fun. Life as a Bunny was governed by a set of stringent rules that underlined their status as subordinate subjects within the Playboy kingdom. Codified in the forty-four page Bunny Manual, the system of regulations defied irony. 'Always remember', the booklet soberly intoned, 'your proudest possession is your Bunny Tail. You must make sure it is white and fluffy.'[12] Sitting down was forbidden. Instead, Bunnies had to 'perch' expectantly. Dating customers was also strictly prohibited – though exception was made in the case of No. 1 Keyholders (celebrities, the Playboy editorial staff and their friends). The edicts of the Manual were inscribed in a system of merits and penalties levied by a Bunny Mother who was 'presented to new Bunnies as a friend, adviser and counsellor, but whose actual function more closely resembled that of a drill sergeant' (Miller, 1985: 103). Failing this, surveillance by private detectives could always pick up on Bunnies whose behaviour or appearance was not coming up to scratch. It was this, darker, view of the Playboy clubs that surfaced in 1963 when Gloria Steinem, then a twenty-eight year-old fledgling journalist, produced a two-part 'undercover' exposé for *Show* magazine. Infiltrating the New York Playboy Club, Steinem worked for four weeks as 'Bunny Marie' and her report painted a picture of exploitation and cynicism – dejected waitresses in excruciatingly uncomfortable costumes being leered at by drunken keyholders, while relentlessly cheerful *Playboy* propaganda told them what a glamorous job they had.

At the same time, however, the playboy milieu was not uniformly and over-whelmingly patriarchal. In the world of the 'swinging-bachelor' there were, admittedly, not many areas where women were able to win a degree of 'cultural space'. But there were a few. Kathryn Leigh Scott's (1998) oral history of women who worked as Playboy Bunnies offers a somewhat rose-tinted view of life at the 1960s Playboy clubs. Yet Scott's interviews with more than 250 former Bunnies still suggest that many women gained a genuine sense of independence (in both personal and financial terms) through working in what, at the time, were regarded as bold and exciting environments. In a period when conventional femininity and marriage were still promoted as the only acceptable routes for women, working in the glitzy world of the Playboy clubs may have appeared, to some at least, as 'deliciously empowering' (Scott, 1998: 6) – an enticing and relatively well paid alternative to a life of suburban domesticity and conservative respectability.

Overall, the realm of glamorous sexuality was a contradictory cultural terrain for women during the 1950s and early 1960s. In their studies of movie and fan magazines of the period, both Marjorie Rosen (1973) and Jane Gaines (1985) show how these texts' ambiguous representations of female film stars created spaces for multiple interpretations among their female readers. The ostensibly damning revelations about the 'scandalous' exploits of stars such as Marilyn Monroe or Jane Russell simultaneously offered women compelling images of an independent sexuality that broke away from dominant ideals of marriage and family. As Wini Breines contends, female passivity and agency co-existed side-by-side in the universe of postwar glamour, Breines echoing Kathy Peiss's observation that 'women's embrace of style, fashion, romance and mixed-sex fun could be a source of autonomy and pleasure as well as a cause of their continuing oppression' (Breines, 1992: 109–10). Therefore, while there is no doubting the sexually exploitative character of the playboy ethic, women were not always its passive victims. Instead, within the glamour of the 'swinging bachelor' mythology there existed spaces (albeit limited ones) in which women could win a degree of cultural autonomy that resisted dominant ideals of domestic-oriented femininity. For example, Bennett and Woollacott argue that, while women were certainly objectified and subordinated within the Bond-*esque* spy texts of the 1960s, these texts also broke with traditional constructions of passive femininity in their representation of active and (relatively) independent female protagonists (Bennett and Woollacott, 1987: 123). Indeed, on television, British spy shows such as *The Avengers* (screened on ABC in 1966–9) and American action series such as *Honey West* (ABC, 1965–6) and *The Girl From U.N.C.L.E.* (NBC, 1966) can be seen as offering images of women that were both independent and sexually confident.[13]

Alongside the figure of the 'swinging bachelor' it is even possible to trace the rise of a female equivalent – the cosmopolitan, single girl. The popular success of Helen Gurley Brown's *Sex and the Single Girl* in 1962 proclaimed the arrival of a new, independent and ambitious brand of femininity. 'Far from being a creature to be pitied and patronized', Brown announced in her buoyant and breezy advice manual, '[the single woman] is emerging as the newest glamour girl of our times':

> She has more time and often more money to spend on herself . . . A single woman never has to drudge. She can get her housework over within one good hour Saturday morning plus one other good hour to iron blouses and white collars. She need never break her fingernails or her spirit waxing a playroom or clearing out the garage. She has more money for clothes and for trips than any but a wealthy married few. (Brown, 1962: 3–4)

Unrepentantly forthright, Brown argued that the new single girl should relish not only her financial, but also her sexual independence. Outspoken about her premarital sexual experience, Brown encouraged women to follow her example. Admittedly, her message was hardly radical, Brown tutoring women in moulding their appearance and behaviour in ways that would appeal to men. But *Sex and the Single Girl* was undoubtedly groundbreaking, both in its candid affirmation of women's sexual desire and its enthusiasm for the pleasures of personal consumption. Insisting that her book was 'not a study on how to get married but how to stay single – in superlative style' (Brown, 1962: 8), Brown encouraged young women to explore 'the rich, full life' of modern consumerism – with a host of tips on choosing apartment furnishings, hi-fi equipment and fashionable clothes.

A focus of popular fascination and controversy, *Sex and the Single Girl* quickly became a bestseller. In the first year of publication alone, the book sold 150,000 hardcover copies. Brown, meanwhile, sold the movie rights for $200,000 – a film loosely based on the book appearing in 1964, starring Natalie Wood as the author and Tony Curtis as a wily investigative reporter-come-playboy. The same year also saw Brown publish another handbook, *Sex in the Office* (1964), this time showing career women 'how their office life can be rewarding, sexy and exciting'. Established as a guru of modern femininity, in 1965 Brown was appointed editor of *Cosmopolitan*, a magazine whose publishers were desperate to reverse its declining sales. Formerly a fairly staid general interest magazine for women, *Cosmopolitan* was repitching itself towards a younger, unmarried and relatively affluent readership even before Brown arrived. Under her editorship, however, *Cosmopolitan* became

7.3 Tony Curtis and Natalie Wood in *Sex and the Single Girl* (Warner, 1964).

the self-proclaimed bible of the single girl. The magazine promoted an image of femininity in which the chains of sexual repression had been thrown off and personal fulfilment was achievable through a prosperous and independent lifestyle. Moreover, as in *Playboy*, 'liberation' for the *'Cosmopolitan* Girl' was conceived in explicitly consumerist terms – the power of the single woman presented as lying not simply in her sexual confidence but, more broadly, in her expertise in image making and manipulation of consumer products. This proved a winning formula. Within months of Gurley Brown becoming editor, *Cosmopolitan*'s readership had increased 15 per cent and its advertising revenues had soared by half.

Nor was the new 'single girl' a phenomenon confined to media representations. Greater access to contraception – especially with the introduction of the Pill in 1960 – helped undermine ideologies in which women's sexuality had been subordinated to reproduction within the context of stable monogamy (Brunt, 1982: 152). The increased availability of the Pill to unmarried women during the 1960s was not a response to women's claims to sexual freedom, but a consequence of federal concerns about population growth and demands on social welfare. Regardless of the grounds on which they were made available, however, improved systems of contraception had a radical impact on gender relations by giving women greater control over their bodies and sex lives. An increased legitimation of female sexual pleasure was accompanied, moreover, by a trend towards the postponement of marriage as more women entered further education and gave greater priority to their careers as employment opportunities – especially within the expanding retail and service sectors – steadily opened up (D'Emilio and Freedman 1997: 309). For many women during the 1960s, therefore, marriage and motherhood were no longer seen as the only possible routes to a successful life. Moreover, although marked disparities continued to exist between men's and women's earnings (despite the passage of the Equal Pay Act in 1963), many young, single women were enjoying an enhanced disposable income. As a consequence, they attracted increasing attention from consumer industries, with a new wave of products and advertising campaigns geared to the affluent and independent 'single girl'. In the mid-1960s, for example, advertising for the Ford Mustang was partly pitched towards the 'single girl' market, while in 1968 a new cigarette brand, Virginia Slims, was targeted at the same group. Featuring images of fashionable and confident young women, the advertisements for Virginia Slims proclaimed the triumph of a newly empowered female consumer – 'You've Come A Long Way, Baby'.

According to Robert Goldman and his associates, advertising representations of strong and independent women do not necessarily articulate an emancipated feminine identity. In their analysis of advertising in women's magazines during the 1980s, Goldman et al. argue that the commercial market reroutes (and thus depoliticizes) feminist discourse into the logic of commodity relations. In these terms, advertisers 'connect the value and meaning of women's emancipation to corporate products', thus producing a kind of 'commodity feminism' in which feminist discourse is co-opted into the market and feminism is reduced to a simple 'attitude' or lifestyle that can be purchased in a perfume, a designer outfit or sleek sports car (Goldman et al., 1991: 335). The same argument could also be applied to the captivating world of the 1960s 'single girl' – while money and a career afforded her independence, this was compromised by being achieved only through engagement with the dominant forces of the market and its ideals of gender and sexuality. Such an interpretation, however, might be unduly pessimistic. Rather than duping women with images of a depoliticized feminism, the discourse of the glamorous and cosmopolitan 'single girl' might have offered a space in which women could engage meaningfully with the cultural shifts taking place around them, rejecting the dominant feminine ideals of passive, family-centred domesticity in favour of a sexually confident feminine identity that embraced the pleasures of modern leisure and personal consumption.

Indeed, the unlikeliest of texts might have been constituent in this elaboration of a more autonomous brand of feminine hedonism. By the late 1960s *Playboy* was read by over four million women every month (*Business Week*, 28 June 1969) and throughout the late 1950s and 1960s the magazine regularly featured correspondence from female readers. While some women attacked the magazine for its sexism, others voiced their appreciation of *Playboy*'s racy take on life which, as one reader put it, made 'a refreshing change from the whipped-cream pap of the so-called women's magazines' (cited in Meyerowitz, 1996: 22). Rather than evidence of a lamentable 'false consciousness', such sentiments might better be seen as indicating a process of appropriation in which the masculine ethic of indulgent hedonism was mobilized to defy traditional codes of femininity. The 'playboy philosophy', therefore, may well have been permeated by mysogynistic values and desires, yet it was (like any popular cultural discourse) also a realm of fissures and contradictions which offered spaces for negotiation to an array of interests – including those of women.

'THE NEGRO MAN-ABOUT-TOWN': BLACK MASCULINITY AND THE PLAYBOY ETHIC

The redrawing of sexual boundaries during the 1950s and early 1960s brought a new affirmation of sexual pleasure within American popular culture. Yet the 'liberation' wrought by these changes was largely the preserve of the white middle class. In contrast, the mores of black, urban communities became symbols of social pathology, while racism and economic inequality worked to exclude African Americans from the developing universe of hedonistic consumerism. The relative marginality of African Americans to the discourses of individuality, leisure and self-realization through consumption shows that the reach of postwar consumer culture was not nearly as pervasive as its advocates claimed. At the same time, however, the web of the consumer economy was gradually reaching out to black consumers and, as it did so, African American men were slowly brought into the fold of modern masculine identities.

The emergence of a consumption-driven economy during the 1920s and 1930s had depended on a largely white consumer market. Most African Americans were prevented from participating in the consumer spectacle by a combination of white racism and trenchant economic inequality. Forms of masculinity predicated on self-conscious displays of style, therefore, remained essentially a white domain. African American cultural forms such as jazz may have been championed by *Esquire* as a talisman of exciting 'otherness' but, for most of black America, active involvement in the world of narcissistic consumerism was out of the question. On occasions when minority ethnic groups did lay claim to displays of conspicuous consumption – as with the zoot suit phenomenon of the early 1940s – it was as a gesture of cultural defiance that provoked a wrathful response from many whites. Nevertheless, as the economic growth of wartime and postwar prosperity delivered improved incomes to many African Americans, black consumers were slowly linked to the commercial marketplace. And, as this took place, notions of black masculinity began to be reshaped to conform to the logic of consumer culture.

In the sphere of magazine publishing, for example, the dynamics of consumerism gradually registered on the way African American men were framed and addressed. Before the 1940s magazines geared to a black readership struggled on the margins of the commercial nexus and were predominantly concerned with establishing African Americans' rights as citizens and securing their access to jobs (Pendergast, 2000: 15). But, with the launch of *Ebony* in 1945, this began to change. Created by publisher John Johnson, *Ebony* was modelled after the hugely successful *Life* magazine, with lavish photo-spreads and optimistic articles on the accomplishments of black Americans. Yet, with its accent on entertainment and copy that was wedded to advertising, *Ebony* also offered a vision of the African American experience that embraced consumer culture as never before. And, through its engagement with modern consumerism, *Ebony* 'brought black men into the realm of modern masculinity' – the magazine's profiles of successful African American men giving special attention to their tastes and consumption patterns, while pictures of semi-clad African American women imitated the 'cheesecake' images that were a staple of *Esquire* (Pendergast, 2000: 209).

Ebony's inclusion of sexual images of black women was a subject of controversy. Since the late nineteenth century African American women activists had strived to challenge racist stereotypes of black women as sexually available objects of 'exotic' titillation. From this perspective, *Ebony's* representations of black women conspired with a heritage of racist sexual exploitation. On the other hand, some of *Ebony's* female readers endorsed the magazine's inclusion of 'cheesecake' pictures. Here, the sexualized representation of black women was read as a sign of racial progress, a challenge to notions of beauty dominated by images of white femininity (Meyerowitz, 1996: 18–21). This was a logic of racial 'equality' that also surfaced in the Playboy empire – the company proudly pointing to a black woman as one of the first Bunnies hired at its Chicago club, while in 1965 the first black Playmate was unveiled as a *Playboy* centrefold. The 'freedom' to appear as objects of sexual consumption was, however, a dubious privilege. Elsewhere, more explicit systems of prejudice also registered in the Playboy realm. Opened in 1961, the Miami and New Orleans Playboy clubs counted Jim Crow among their members, the clubs complying with segregationist policies in their refusal to hire black waitresses or admit black keyholders. The southern clubs were operated by franchise holders rather than the Playboy organization itself, yet the practice of segregation sat rather awkwardly alongside *Playboy*'s tacit support for the civil rights movement and Hefner's professed liberalism. To circumvent a public-relations disaster, the publisher bought back the southern franchises and opened the Miami club to African Americans, though in New Orleans the severity of local laws meant that the Playboy Club remained segregated until the passage of the Civil Rights Act in 1964.

More generally, white racism and the resilience of economic inequalities dictated that the playboy ethic of high-living fun remained out of reach for most African Americans. Even a seasoned Rat Packer like Sammy Davis often seemed more of a mascot rather than a full participant in the Clan's high-spirited antics, Davis frequently serving as the butt of racial jokes from Frank Sinatra and Dean Martin. Nevertheless, the success of *Ebony* – its circulation topping 300,000 within two years – showed that times were changing. By the late 1950s the idea of a black middle class was an established concept within social science, while advertisers were increasingly courting the disposable income of a growing number of African American white collar workers.[14] And, while *Playboy*'s appeal was tailored fairly exclusively to a white market until the late 1960s, other publishers were willing to follow *Ebony*'s lead in addressing African American men as stylish and upwardly mobile consumers. The foremost example was *Duke* magazine, launched in 1957. Based in Chicago, *Duke* was a *Playboy* imitator along the lines of *Nugget* or *Dude*, though in *Duke* the mix of 'cheesecake' pin-ups and narcissistic consumerism was expressly geared to 'the Negro man-about-town' (*Duke*, June 1957). The strength of racist stereotypes of black masculinity as 'wild' and sexually predatory, however, meant *Duke* had to exercise caution in appealing to its readers' sexual desires. For example, the magazine's centrefolds (the 'Duchess of the Month') avoided featuring white women, while *Duke* went to pains in emphasizing the 'normality' of African American men's sexual behaviour, arguing that 'at the bar and in the boudoir, Negroes are strictly old-fashioned . . . [and] still prefer everything straight in food, whiskey and love' (*Duke*, June 1957).

A short-lived experiment, *Duke*'s approach was ahead of its time. During the 1950s the black middle class remained a relatively small group and, although the success of *Ebony* showed that change was underway, a significant market of affluent black consumers was still some years off. Only in the late 1960s did the playboy ethic became an accessible option for African American men, advertisers and entre-preneurs gradually responding to the new consumer market created through rising black incomes.

*

In 1956 Ernest Dichter, the renowned marketing expert and motivational specialist, drew attention to the unique problems posed by patterns of economic growth in postwar America. 'One of the basic problems of this prosperity', averred Dichter, 'is to give people that sanction and justification to enjoy it and to demonstrate that the hedonistic approach to life is a moral one, not an immoral one' (cited in Jezer, 1982: 127). To sustain an economy increasingly dependent on consumer demand, a break had to be made with value systems that emphasized thrift and conservative reserve. Instead, the new economic imperatives of postwar America demanded a code of acquisitive consumerism and personal gratification. In the 1950s the burgeon-ing commercial youth market set the pace for this transformation, but it was the concomitant rise of a style-conscious and leisure-oriented middle-class faction that gave the new 'morality of pleasure as a duty' its most comprehensive expression. And, in legitimating the desires of the narcissistic consumer, the ascendance of this group's new 'ethic of fun' was intrinsic to the survival and regeneration of American capitalism. As Daniel Bell reflected in the late 1970s:

> Modern capitalism has been transformed by a widespread hedonism, that has made mundane concerns, rather than transcendental ties, the center of people's lives . . . Without the hedonism stimulated by mass consumption, the very structure of business enterprises would collapse. (Bell, 1979: 188–9)

Central to this transformation was the reconfiguration of middle-class masculinity. During the 1950s and early 1960s, family-oriented and production-focused models of manhood were increasingly displaced by masculine identities that placed a premium on individuality, the fulfilment of sexual desire and the pleasures of commodity consumption. This indulgent and style-conscious form of masculinity was not simply a fantasy constructed within popular texts like *Playboy*. In offering men a meaningful 'imagined identity', the playboy ethic 'spilled into' the realm of cultural practice. It influenced and informed men's relationship with the new world of consumerism, the young, upwardly mobile male eagerly buying into distinctive goods and signifiers that would mark him out as a hip, stylish and sexy man of the world. Yet this habitus was adaptive rather than rebellious. Rather than confronting or resisting the dominant social order, the 'young man of action and acquisition' pioneered lifestyles reconciled to the demands of a modern consumer economy. By popularizing and legitimating cultural attitudes that prioritized leisure-oriented consumption and individual gratification, the playboy ethic helped establish a middle-class moral code attuned to capitalism's dependency on the perpetual renewal of consumer markets.

By the end of the 1960s, however, postwar economic growth was running out of steam. Cold War ideologies of classless affluence were increasingly unsustainable as the persistence of inequality became evident and America entered a new phase of social and political conflict. Amid this turmoil, however, the ethos of hedonistic consumerism espoused by the new middle class not only survived but continued to prosper. Indeed, for all his neo-conservative cynicism, Daniel Bell was astute in outlining the paradox that saw the 'adversarial' styles and attitudes of the 1960s counterculture translated into 'the engine of modern capitalism':

> In the end, this is the cultural contradiction of capitalism: Having lost its original justifications, capitalism has taken over the legitimations of an antibourgeois culture to maintain the continuity of its own economic institutions. Capitalism is a very different social system now than it was one or two hundred years ago. (Bell, 1979: 188–9)

NOTES

1 For details of *Playboy*'s circulation during the mid-1950s see Ryan (1957: 12).

2 Meyerowitz (1996: 23–5) provides an account of the 1950s purity campaign.

3 The January 1957 edition of *Playboy* sold 687,593 copies, compared to *Esquire*'s sales of 778,190. Hefner seems to have derived wry satisfaction from usurping the magazine that was his original inspiration – *Playboy*'s January 1957 issue including a photo strip depicting its editor explaining over the telephone: 'I'm truly sorry Mr. Smart [then *Esquire*'s publisher], but at present our staff is at full capacity. Leave your name with the office boy and I'll call if something comes up'.

4 For wider discussion of Sinatra's capacity as 'an iconic hero' within American popular culture, see Mustazza (ed.) (1998).

5 Cohen (1997) provides a detailed consideration of the competing notions of masculinity constructed in Hollywood during the 1950s.

6 Popular retrospectives of the Rat Pack's high-rolling revelry exist in Levy (1998) and Quirk and Schoell (1998).

7 Once in office, however, JFK's relationship with Sinatra cooled. Warned by advisers that the singer's rumoured connections with the Mafia (Sinatra was a close friend of mobster Sam Giancana) could prove damaging, the President rapidly distanced himself from his former friend.

8   In some respects, this transformation is also detectable in the later Bond novels. *Goldfinger* (1959), for example, sees Bond trade in his classic Bentley for a more racy Aston Martin DB III, while in *Thunderball* (1961) a whole chapter (Chapter 14) deals with the controversy surrounding the correct way to mix a dry martini.

9   Warner Brothers also applied the formula to non-private-eye contexts, with *The Islanders* (1960–1), an adventure series revolving around charter pilots in the tropics, and *The Roaring Twenties* (1960–2), a series based around the exploits of two dashing journalists during the 1920s.

10 For further discussion of masculinity as the object of a spectatorial gaze, see Dyer (1982), Medhurst (1985) and Cohan and Hark (eds) (1993).

11 The concept of liminal zones as geographic spaces on the margins of conventional moral discipline is explored in Shields (ed.) (1991).

12 Highlights from the infamous *Bunny Manual* are reproduced in Scott (1998: 279–86).

13 For discussion of the construction of 'liberated' femininity in these texts see D' Acci (1997) and Miller (2000: 51–74).

14 An overview of the emergence of the concept of a black middle class is provided in Evans (1995).

Chapter 8
'Turn On. Tune In. Step Out': Counterculture, Nonconformity and the Masculine Consumer

Seldom has male fashion switched, twitched and disported itself with the urgency of today. Money and leisure are part of the reason; the suburban man wants – and can afford – bright togs to fit his weekend fun. A more energetic and pervasive influence is youth. Hipped on color and cacophony, whether it's psychedelic art or discothèques, young people dress to fit their milieu – and their elders are picking up the beat. 'It used to be that the son sneaked in to borrow his father's tie,' says James K. Wilson Jr., president of Hart Schaffer and Marx Clothes. 'Now the father is sneaking in to borrow his son's turtleneck.'

Pat Smith, 'Male Plumage '68', *Newsweek*, 25 November 1968.

'EVE OF DESTRUCTION'?: COUNTERCULTURE, CONSUMPTION AND CULTURAL TRANSFORMATION IN THE 1960S

By the time Tom Wolfe profiled the 'Pump House Gang', a clique of young and easy-living surfers from La Jolla, the 1960s surf scene was already mutating into something new. Reflecting on his 1965 article, Wolfe has recalled how the youths of California's middle-class beach communities were beginning to shift 'from the surfing life to the advance guard of something else – the psychedelic *head* world of California' (Wolfe, 1989: 15). During the early 1960s the youthful beach culture of playful adventure had been a beacon in America's cultural transformation – the image of young, affluent and carefree 'Beach Boys' (like the charismatic 'Murph the Surf' and his accomplices) crystallizing the wider rise of a middle-class, masculine identity configured around youthful leisure and the fulfilment of consumer desires. But by the mid-1960s Wolfe found a beach subculture in which the world of woodies, baggies and surf boards was giving way to a proto-hippie lifestyle of 'dropping-out', communal living and recreational drug use. Despite these shifts, Wolfe detected a marked continuity of ethos, the author arguing that the Pump House kid's 'so-called "dropping out" was nothing more than a still further elaboration of the kind of worlds that the surfers and the car kids . . . had been creating the decade before' (Wolfe, 1989: 15).
    Dramatic changes were certainly registering in the trappings of white, middle-class youth style. The teen culture of the late 1950s and early 1960s – whose affinity

with the values of hedonistic consumption had blazed a trail for the new ethics and lifestyles of middle-class America – was, by 1965, already looking like a tired anachronism. During the early 1960s the spectacle of fun-filled teenage consumption had arisen in conjunction with the wider climate of confident optimism that attended Kennedy's 'New Frontier' and its promise of inexhaustible economic growth and progressive social harmony. This ambience of national wellbeing, however, was transient. By the mid-1960s the American economy was beginning to stumble and notions of a blossoming universal prosperity were proving hard to sustain. Kennedy's assassination in 1963 was an ominous portent of the social and political strife to come. President Johnson's vision of the Great Society, with its commitment to 'abundance and liberty for all', endeavoured to revitalize faith in liberal idealism – yet the project steadily came apart at the seams as the continuing realities of class and racial inequalities became glaringly apparent. By 1965, then, the radiance of the 'Endless Summer' was dimming as liberal optimism crumbled in the face of racial violence, urban disorder and a spiralling sense of social discontent that, by the end of the decade, had become stridently politicized as the US sank into the mire of the Vietnam War. In such a context, the upbeat world of teenage good times looked increasingly incongruous. In its place there arose a middle-class youth culture suffused with a rhetoric of opposition and dissent – a shift exemplified by the success of 'Eve of Destruction', Barry McGuire's dystopic folk-rock anthem, which climbed to the top of the *Billboard* chart in September 1965.

Yet, as Tom Wolfe cogently observed, appearances could be deceptive. Rather than marking an abrupt shift in cultural gears, the 1960s counterculture actually emerged seamlessly from the hedonistic youth scene of the early 1960s.[1] Moreover, for all its bohemian and anti-establishment posturing, in many respects the developing counterculture actually reproduced (and extended) the ethos of personal gratification and indulgent consumption that had been at the heart of both the early 1960s youth spectacle and the wider middle-class 'ethic of fun' that had taken shape after the Second World War.

It has become a common axiom that the oppositional thrust of the 1960s counterculture was steadily co-opted by the forces of consumerism. What began life as an 'authentic' movement of grassroots radicalism and creativity is portrayed as being appropriated and incorporated into the cultural mainstream by a cynically exploitative commercial machine. Exemplary is Jackson Lears' argument that the forces of commodity consumption effectively neutralized the oppositional potential of the counterculture, the intervention of the consumer market reducing politics to questions of personality and style so that 'the rebellion of the 1960s lost its grasp of power relations and degenerated into a search for "alternative life-styles"' (Lears, 1989: 53).[2] Yet this linear narrative of authentic innovation subsumed by commercial incorporation is too simplistic. As Lears himself concedes, consumers are never merely the passive receptors of dominant cultural meanings, so that even the most commercialized cultural artefacts remain capable of reinterpretation and mobilization according to 'counter-hegemonic' interests (Lears, 1989: 54). Moreover, the forces of 'rebellion' never lie magically 'beyond' the influence of dominant institutions and ideologies. In the case of the 1960s counterculture, for example, its various elements were, from the outset, locked into a symbiotic relationship with the media, commercial entrepreneurs and market institutions. Rather than exploitatively preying on movements of countercultural 'authenticity', commercial institutions actually worked to galvanize and lend momentum to these movements – the counterculture only developing recognizable form and substance by being disseminated and popularized through the intercession of record companies, magazines, fashion retailers and a growing army of 'hip capitalists'. In these terms, rather than being a movement *against* dominant ideologies, much of the 1960s countercultural ferment can be seen as constituent in the broad *transformation* of the American middle class.

While the most politically conscious elements of the counterculture undoubtedly presented a profound challenge to the dominant order, the libertarian 1960s ethos of 'doing your own thing' was more *adaptive* than oppositional. It can be seen as articulating the core values of the new middle class – the emergent faction that distinguished itself through its scorn for conformity and its quest for individuality through 'new model lifestyles' (to coin Pierre Bourdieu's term). During the 1950s and early 1960s this faction had steadily coalesced as a distinct entity, drawing together notions of youth, affluence and hedonistic consumerism in a cultural configuration that challenged and gradually displaced the more traditional bourgeois mores of conservatism and puritanical reserve. This emergent cultural formation was, however, hardly radical. Finding its fullest expression in the concept of the playboy, the new middle-class 'ethic of fun' was largely geared to masculine desires, while the 'good life' of hedonistic consumption remained almost exclusively a white preserve until the late 1960s. Rather than radical, then, it is more accurate to see this new middle class habitus as a *pioneering* cultural force that engendered values, beliefs and ways of living that were tailored to modern consumerism's demands for a perpetually regenerating consumer market. The golden age of the playboy, however, was ephemeral. By the end of the 1960s the 'swinging bachelor's' claims to effortless cool were increasingly outflanked and undercut by the libertine excesses of the 'beautiful people' who were 'letting it all hang out'. And, as the image of the urbane playboy began to look hopelessly tired and 'square', the new middle class increasingly drew on the counterculture as a source for its expressive and distinctive consumer lifestyles. In this sense, then, the late 1960s were more a moment of cultural reconfiguration and adjustment than a calamitous 'eve of destruction'. The new American 'petite bourgeoisie' were certainly embracing a different set of tastes and styles, yet these remained underpinned by the ethos of hedonistic consumption that had become their cultural hallmark during the previous decade.

THE PEACOCK REVOLUTION: CONFRONTATION, STYLE AND THE 'ANTI-ESTABLISHMENT' CONSUMER

A sense of rupture with the past is invariably attended by a belief in cultural renewal through generational revolt. This was certainly the case in 1960s America, where the radical challenge of the New Left was inseparably entwined with notions of a generational breach with established political and cultural traditions. Influenced by the civil rights movement's campaign for racial equality, the New Left emerged on university campuses as a heterogeneous assortment of social and political groups whose goals and tactics were diverse and sometimes contradictory. During the early 1960s, however, most of these groups still placed their faith in the existing political system. When, for example, the Students for a Democratic Society (SDS) drafted their major document, the Port Huron Statement, in 1962, its aims and strategies were those of reformist humanism, the Statement calling for 'a participatory democracy' based on equality, non-violence and community. This humanistic idealism, however, steadily gave way to a more radical political stance as America's growing involvement in the Vietnam War came to preoccupy the SDS, the Berkeley Free Speech Movement and other New Left organizations. After 1965 many American universities were turned into centres of resistance to the war and the draft, a campaign which generated increasingly militant confrontations with university and civil authorities. At the same time a shift to more confrontational strategies also registered in the civil rights movement, as Black Power radicals became impatient with the non-violent tactics of the early 1960s.

The upsurge of political radicalism during the late 1960s was constituent in a wider set of social and political fissures that saw the 'expansive hegemony' of the preceding decades steadily unravel.[3] During the 1950s and early 1960s the scale of economic growth and the explosion of consumerism had sustained mythologies of universal prosperity which successfully mobilized popular support for the status quo. But these 'ideologies of affluence' proved impossible to sustain as the American economy lurched into stagnation. After 1966 rates of economic growth fell away as slowing productivity and creeping inflation were compounded by the fiscal burdens of the Vietnam War and the Great Society's reform programme. The early 1970s saw the economic downturn become even more pronounced, a dramatic rise in oil prices contributing to a steady climb in unemployment and a decline in incomes.[4] Economic deterioration, combined with the climate of political radicalism and a tide of urban disorders, presented a grave threat to social and political stability. In response, a more authoritarian state apparatus came into play. The violent attack by police on anti-war campaigners at the Democratic National Convention in Chicago in September 1968 pointed towards the increasingly coercive stance taken by the state at the end of the 1960s – a political shift that came to fruition under the Presidency of Richard Nixon.

Nixon's victory in the 1968 election was slim in terms of popular votes, yet he managed to touch a nerve in presenting himself as a spokesman for 'ordinary' America – a unifying force who could turn back the tide of disorder and return the US to domestic tranquillity. Trading on popular fears and apprehensions, Nixon garnered support for his tough line against the anti-war protests and urban unrest and in 1972 was re-elected with a huge mandate. Nixon's ascendance, then, signalled the emergence of a more authoritarian political state, but it also marked a reassertion of traditional petit bourgeois ideals – Nixon posing as the mouthpiece for a middle-class 'silent majority' who were fed up with 'big' government (especially in the areas of civil rights and social welfare), the decline of traditional values and a perceived slide into cultural permissiveness. Nixon's electoral success showed that the ethics of the traditional middle class (what he called 'the square virtues') were not dead and buried, but remained a force to be reckoned with. And in rallying popular support Nixon played heavily on fears of the cultural and political challenges posed by the civil rights movement, feminism, the counterculture and the political activism of 'campus bums'.

Nevertheless, while the mounting violence of the state was unmistakable, more generally the dominant response to the forces of dissent was ambiguous. In the media, for example, while there was certainly significant negative stereotyping of the counterculture and the anti-war protests, there was also more sympathetic coverage. While the political radicalism of the New Left was generally a subject of media hostility, the artistic expressions and aesthetic lifestyles of the counterculture were never universally condemned, but often provoked fascination – even a degree of admiration. In 1969, for example, *Life* magazine was breathtaken by 'The Phenomenal Woodstock Happening', the magazine's multi-page photospread describing in awe-struck tones how the event was 'less a music festival than a total experience, a phenomenon, a happening, high adventure, a near disaster and, in small way, a struggle for survival' (*Life*, 15 September 1969). A 1969 edition of *New Yorker* magazine, meanwhile, sold out when it featured a contribution from Charles Reich, the countercultural guru later developing the article into *The Greening of America* (1970), his clarion call for a 'new consciousness' that could bring peace and harmony to Western civilization. Rather than being reviled as an agency of social subversion, therefore, the counterculture was often received effusively – its expressive values and libertarian individualism finding a particular resonance with that faction of the middle class that, itself, espoused a creed of self-expression, distinction and personal 'liberation'.

The late 1960s was not the first occasion that the emergent faction of the American middle class had flirted with the cultural avant garde. The Beat movement that took shape in New York's Greenwich Village and San Francisco's North Beach during the late 1940s and 1950s had also been an object of fascination. As Barbara Ehrenreich observes, the Beats' rejection of convention and their virtues of masculine

independence, nonconformity and (often misogynistic) sexual expression found a degree
of affinity with the playboy ethos of hedonism and personal indulgence (Ehrenreich,
1983: 60). Indeed, during the late 1950s Playboy magazine (by then emerging as
the in-house journal for the new middle class) featured several contributions from
Beat luminary Jack Kerouac, together with 'The Beat Mystique' – a lengthy dissection
of the Beat phenomenon (Playboy, February 1958). However, while Playboy was
enthralled by the 'deep-freeze of coolsville' surrounding the Beat philosophy and
lifestyle, the magazine was suspicious of the movement's sullen nihilism and sloppy
anti-materialism. For editor Hefner, the Beats could be admired for defying the strictures
of conformity, but they lacked the spirit and verve of the playboy-set – the 'inverted
Beats' or 'Upbeats' – who 'searched for new answers and new opportunities in a
spirit that was positive in the extreme' (Playboy, January 1963). As Playboy executive
editor Ray Russell later explained:

> We liked the sort of freedom [the Beats] espoused . . . the liberated atmosphere,
> the artistic expression in poetry and prose. We were in favour of any kind of
> sexual liberation, as long as it was heterosexual lib. All that was positive. But
> we also felt that there was a lot in it counter to what we promoted in Playboy.
> The sandaled, dirty feet, unwashed aspects of the beats ran against the grain of
> the well-groomed, button-down, Aqua-Velva look our reader wanted. The anti-
> establishment attitude, lack of material ambition, or desire to get ahead, which
> typified the beats, was not what Playboy was all about. (cited in Weyr, 1978:
> 49)

In contrast, the developing countercultural scene of the 1960s offered a code
of optimism, excitement and stylishness more commensurate with the lifestyle
sensibilities of the new middle class. It was an affinity that advertisers adeptly played
upon. During the early sixties, in the wake of Madison Avenue's 'creative revolution',
it was already commonplace for advertisers to deploy images of 'youthfulness' as
an aphorism for excitement and 'hip' individuality. With the rise of the counterculture
in the late 1960s, the strategy further intensified. As one adman affirmed in a 1968
editorial for Merchandising Week: 'Everywhere our mass media push psychedelia
with all its clothing fads, so-called "way-out" ideas etc. Youth is getting the hard sell'
(cited in Frank, 1997: 120). To interpret this as a simple strategy of exploitation or
incorporation, however, would be misleading. Rather, the counterculture and consumer
capitalism were bound together in a mutually sustaining relationship, each nourishing
and energizing the other. Grounded in an ethos of self-fulfilment and immediate
gratification, the value system of the counter-culture was virtually tailormade for the
modern consumer market, while commercial muscle was vital in disseminating and
giving coherence to the counterculture's stylistic expressions. Among the narcissistic
and style-conscious new middle class, meanwhile, the fashions and attitudes of the
counterculture won special appeal. Indeed, rather than representing the antithesis of

the consumer society, the counterculture can itself be seen as a developmental phase in the evolution of the new, consumption-oriented petite bourgeoisie. As Thomas Frank explains, rather than representing the nemesis of advanced capitalism, 'the counter-culture may be more accurately understood as a stage in the development of the values of the American middle class, a colorful instalment in the twentieth century drama of consumer subjectivity' (Frank, 1997: 120).

The role of the counterculture in the affirmation and extension of a hedonistic consumer ethos became especially clear in the field of men's fashion. As Frank (1997: 193–9) shows, the late 1960s were a boom time for American menswear, sales climbing steeply to reach a high plateau by the end of the decade. And in this 'Peacock Revolution' the consumerist male was given full legitimacy. More than ever before it became possible for men to enjoy the pleasures of personal consumption without jeopardizing their claims to heterosexuality. As *Newsweek* observed in its survey of 'Male Plumage '68':

> Just ten years ago a man who dared challenge the supremacy of the three-button sack suit was promptly dressed down by his peers, often at the expense of his 'masculine image' . . . But a new dawn was soon to break over the soft, shapeless waistland [*sic*] of male attire . . . Now, no longer afraid of criticism, the American male is submitting his body to perfumes and his hair to stylists; wrapping himself in form-fitting suits of every shade and fabric; hanging pendants and beads from his neck; adorning his feet with brightly buckled shoes, and generally carrying on like a dandy straight out of the days of Beau Brummell. (*Newsweek*, 25 November 1968)

Above all, this 'new dawn' of masculine narcissism drew its energy and inspiration from the militant postures of the counterculture – sales campaigns drawing on 'radical' imagery and rhetoric as a guarantor of exciting nonconformity. 'Tune in. Turn On. Step Out', exhorted the sales pitch for Petrocelli sports coats, their 1968 slogan playfully reworking Timothy Leary's famous countercultural dictum. In a similar vein the H.I.S menswear firm launched their 'Anti-Establishment' fashion line in 1969 – the advertising copy for their 'anti-establishment stovepipe slacks' urging men to 'Belt a Conservative with a Stovepipe', while H.I.S promised to 'End the Draft' with their sheepskin 'anti-establishment polo coat'. In this way the iconography of radical youth served as an emblem of nonconforming individualism, an affirmation of a masculine identity that eschewed stodgy conservatism in favour of fashionable leisure, stylistic display and the pleasures of commodity consumption. As Ehrenreich perceptively argues, this was the moment at which models of hedonistic masculine consumerism were given their fullest expression, the new middle class relishing the opportunity to give free rein to its quest for 'hip' individuality and sensuous indulgence through distinctive patterns of consumption:

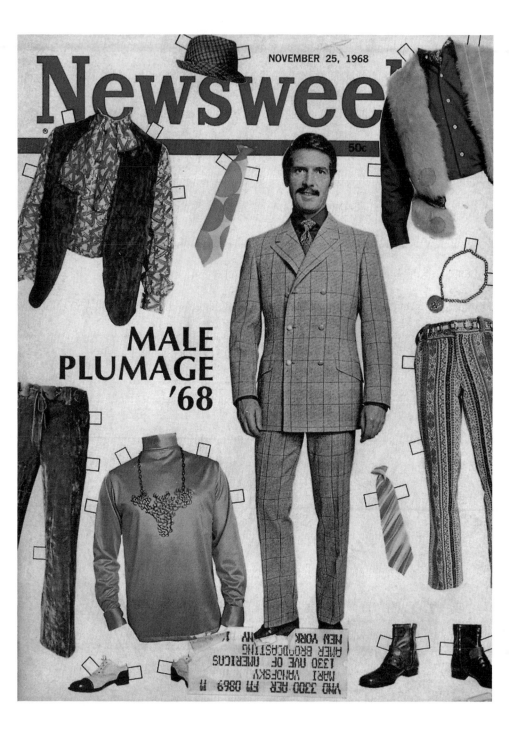

8.1 'Male Plumage '68'. (*Newsweek*, 25 November 1968 – *courtesy of Newsweek.*)

Never had the consumer culture been more congenial to men, more tempting, so that if there was a time to drop out, to abandon work and the material privileges of the middle class, this was not it. Uncounted thousands of middle-class, middle-aged men – men who would have been no more inclined to drop out than to drop acid at a business lunch – underwent a safer transformation; they grew out their sideburns, wore their shirts unbuttoned to display their beads or gold chains, and day-dreamed (like the hero of the movie '10') of long-haired young women with exotic sexual skills. (Ehrenreich, 1983: 115)

RADICAL CHIC, ZIPLESS FUCKS AND PSYCHEDELIC BUNNIES

Always a sharp-eyed cultural observer, Tom Wolfe was alert to the contorted racial dynamics of the late 1960s. When, in 1970, New York's cosmopolitan elite gathered at Leonard Bernstein's duplex apartment on Park Avenue for a fund-raising *soirée* with leaders of the Black Panther Party, Wolfe saw the episode as eminently symbolic – the event epitomizing the liberal avant-garde's attempt to cultivate an aura of 'radical chic' by identifying with what it fondly imagined to be the raw and vital 'authenticity' of cultural 'others' (Wolfe: 1970). This phenomenon was, of course, nothing new. Since the eighteenth century the themes and practices of Romanticism had invoked the image of the 'Noble Savage' as a captivating emblem of artistic and spiritual freedom. In the 1950s, meanwhile, in its esteem for all that 'straight' society considered deviant, the Beat movement eulogized the black hipster as a free-wheeling outsider unfettered by the conventions of white society.[5] The 'radical chic' of the late 1960s was a further step in the tradition, the counterculture appropriating black styles and argot as a marker of street-smart cool, while the Black Power movement was championed as an 'authentic' voice of anti-establishment rebellion.

In some respects this romanticization of a disenfranchised 'other' had a progressive impact – helping to engender white, middle-class support for the civil rights struggle. At the same time, however, this selective stereotyping of 'other' cultures as an 'authentic' force of dissent can be seen as implicitly racist. Alongside *Esquire* and *Playboy* magazines' reverence for jazz, and the 1950s craze for Polynesian cocktail kitsch, the counterculture's lionization of African American radicals (together with the late 1960s vogue for a *pot-pourri* of 'ethnic' fashions and trinkets) can be seen as exemplifying white America's long-standing love affair with notions of an 'exotic primitivism' that offers escape into a world of personal liberation and exciting 'difference'. Indeed, in these terms it was almost inevitable that H.I.S menswear chose to proclaim the arrival of 'Slack Power' in their 1969 'Anti-Establishment' fashion campaign.

In giving the hard sell to a pair of plaid slacks that (according to the advertising copy) 'had soul', the H.I.S campaign also pointed to the growing participation of

8.2 'Slack Power'. (Advertisement for H.I.S. anti-establishment post-grad slacks, 1969.)

African American men in the world of stylish and pleasure-oriented consumption. Moves in this direction were already visible by the 1950s (evidenced, for example, by the launch of magazines like *Ebony* and *Duke*), but it was only in the late 1960s that there existed a black middle class with a spending power sufficient to underpin African American men's entry into the playboy universe of commercial hedonism – manufacturers and advertisers more frequently framing black masculinity in terms of stylish and upmarket consumerism. By 1978, in fact, Thomas Weyr could confidently assert that '*Playboy*'s lifestyle appeals to blacks':

> They throng the clubs and have started some of their own patterned on them. Washington's Foxtrappe club is one. It has 4,500 members who pay $50 a year to frequent a renovated town house at 16th and R., drink in several bars, patronize a disco and use other facilities. (Weyr, 1978: 142-3)

The late 1960s and early 1970s also saw women increasingly brought into the fold of hedonistic pleasure. The 'single girl' culture of the early 1960s was, by the end of the decade, making way for an even more confident and sexually 'liberated' brand of femininity, a trend signposted by the proliferation of books and manuals geared to women's autonomous sexual fulfilment. Books such as the best-selling *How to Become the Sensuous Woman* by 'J' (1970), Nancy Friday's *My Secret Garden* (1973) and Shere Hite's *The Hite Report* (1976) jostled for shelf-space alongside block-buster fiction such as Erica Jong's *Fear of Flying* (1973) – a tale of a young woman's search for sexual independence through an anonymous 'zipless fuck', the novel selling over 3.5 million copies within two years of its publication. On the news-stands, meanwhile, 1973 saw the launch of both *Playgirl* and *Viva* – women's magazines that shamelessly aped *Playboy* in their mixture of glamorous high-living and recreational sex (though in this case the 'cheesecake' centrefold featured an Adonis-like 'Man of the Month').

The articulation of a femininity that was independent, aspirational and sexually autonomous was indebted to women's increasing education and employment, together with the profound impact of the Women's Movement. But it was also informed by the efforts of commercial interests that clamoured to cash-in on what was perceived as a lucrative, new market. Indeed, in some respects feminism itself became a hot commodity – presented as a cultural force that could be glamorously exciting in its refusal to conform. Indicative was the media's enthusiasm for Gloria Steinem who, since making her name as an investigative reporter in the early 1960s, had emerged as a leading light within American feminism. Steinem's success was indebted, at least partly, to her charismatic public persona. Wearing stylish aviator sunglasses, close-fitting jeans and t-shirts, and smiling and laughing in her press interviews, Steinem's aura combined confident independence with an intriguing sexual allure. For many women, this was an inspiring image, Steinem personifying a version of feminism in which it became possible to evade the confines of marriage and domesticity while retaining conventional qualities of sexual attractiveness and a guiltless enjoyment of consumerism. The same qualities also made her an ideal 'face of feminism' for the media – Steinem possessing 'star quality' in the way she challenged prevalent stereotypes of feminists as 'ugly, humorless, disorderly man-haters desperately in need of some Nair' (Douglas, 1994: 189). Indeed, in 1971 it was Steinem's appearance above all else that *Newsweek* foregrounded in its special feature on 'The New Woman', the magazine commenting on her 'incredibly perfect body' and 'long, blond-streaked hair falling just so above each breast' (cited in Douglas, 1994: 227).

Steinem's conspicuous public profile, then, signalled the rise of a new version of femininity in which a politically charged feminist consciousness sat comfortably alongside a consumption-driven lifestyle and an embrace of fashionable stylishness. In some senses this was a progressive cultural force, generating a 'user-friendly' version of feminism that could successfully appeal to large numbers of American women. At the same time, however, the kind of feminism personified in Steinem's 'celebrity' image could be interpreted as denoting 'safety rather than change' (Bradley, 1998: 167) – not so much a radical political challenge as a new variant of a 'commodity feminism' perfectly suited to the demands of consumer capitalism. As with all popular cultural phenomena, the contradictions and ambiguities were legion.

More widely, the sexual politics of the 1960s countercultural milieu were also fraught with inconsistencies. In many respects traditional gender roles were questioned and challenged – an experience that not only fed into the emergence of 'second wave' feminism during the late 1960s and 1970s, but which also prompted the beginnings of a critical engagement with traditional assumptions about masculine roles and identities. As Peter Filene argues, within the New Left there were 'young males who were practicing quite unmasculine ways of behaviour' by campaigning nonviolently in the civil rights struggle and 'imitating Ghandi and King by bending their heads and going limp beneath the fists and clubs of assailants' (Filene, 1986: 212). Ehrenreich, too, highlights an 'androgynous drift' within the counterculture as some men, at least, repudiated established masculine norms and experimented with more passive and benign forms of male identity (Ehrenreich, 1983: 107). Yet, for all the egalitarian sloganeering of the period, sexual inequality remained pronounced within the late 1960s cultures of dissent. Filene (1986: 196) notes that the New Left was largely a masculine monopoly, its leadership dominated by men, while the misogyny of many black radicals was crystallized in Stokely Carmichael's infamous quip that the position of women within the Black Power movement was 'prone' (though the radical leader conceded that, given a sufficient supply of envelopes, women might also be useful for 'the licking and the sticking') (cited in Green, 1999: 400–1). Much of the white counterculture was equally steeped in misogyny and machismo – 'sexual liberation' often amounting to little more than a reproduction of the traditional sexual division of labour and an intensification of the sexual exploitation of women.

Indeed, a telling index of the less than radical facets to the counterculture's sexual politics was the ease with which *Playboy* magazine felt it could align itself with the 'groovy' world of freakouts, psychedelia and free love.

For much of the 1960s Hugh Hefner seldom left the Playboy Mansion, instead immersing himself in his sybaritic wonderland and a whirl of endless parties. In 1968, however, he ventured into the outside world to see for himself the mayhem on the streets of Chicago during the Democratic Convention – only to be clubbed with a nightstick by one of Mayor Daley's finest. The incident has been interpreted by some as a catalyst in Hefner's life, with the editor drifting discernibly leftwards in his political outlook and worldview.[6] But even before 1968 Hefner's magazine had been a spokesman for many liberal causes. For example, while *Playboy* was always securely moored in the tastes and lifestyles of the new middle class, its *laissez-faire* morality made it a natural ally of the drug culture. In 1961 the first Playboy Panel had spotlighted the role of drugs in the jazz world and throughout the 1960s *Playboy* continued to cover the drug scene and defend the rights of drug users. As early as 1963, *Playboy* had introduced Timothy Leary to its readers and throughout the 1960s gave coverage to the drug guru and his causes. The Playboy Forum also served as a platform for arguments in favour of the reform of America's drugs laws, while the Playboy Foundation gave legal and financial help to convicted drug users and in the early 1970s Hefner used its funds to launch the National Organization for the Reform of Marijuana Laws (NORML).

Playboy also emerged as a forum for the liberal establishment's critique of the Vietnam War. At first, the magazine's stance on the war had been equivocal. In 1966 it had even launched 'Project Playmate' – army helicopters flying-in *Playboy* Bunnies for a morale-boosting visit to GIs serving in Vietnam.[7] Indeed, just as US troops had seen *Esquire* as a 'taste of home' during World War Two, servicemen in Vietnam cherished *Playboy* as a symbol of American culture, and Hefner was quite perceptive in his reflection that 'For the guy in Vietnam, *Playboy* was *the* magazine. It represented home and what the guys were fighting for' (cited in Weyr, 1978: 165). This was in spite of *Playboy*'s steady swing against American involvement in the war. As the mood of the country gradually changed, *Playboy* featured more frequent contributions from anti-war campaigners, including the likes of J.K. Galbraith, Senator William Fullbright and David Halberstam. At the same time, Hefner himself also took a more visible political role, being active in George McGovern's 1972 presidential campaign and throwing open both Playboy Mansions (by now Hefner also owned a magnificent spread in Los Angeles) for political fundraising events.

Nevertheless, for all its dalliance with radical causes and liberal politics, *Playboy*'s chief concern was always to shrug off responsibilities and live it up in a world of indulgent pleasure. In many ways, in fact, the magazine's lip-service to radicalism was a part of this – just one more credential in *Playboy*'s résumé of hip nonconformity. But *Playboy*'s real interests lay in carefree hedonism and stylish consumption, and in the counterculture the magazine found plenty to whet its appetite. Throughout the late 1960s and early 1970s *Playboy* drooled over the uninhibited sexual antics of the hippies and the 'tuned-in' fashions of the Age of Aquarius. The Summer of Love of 1967, for example, prompted a laudatory, ten-page photo-feature extolling the virtues of 'The New Wave-Makers' – 'those far-out and fanciful West Coast hippies, diggers and new leftniks who spark the action on today's youth scene' (*Playboy*, October 1967). The cover of *Playboy*'s Christmas 1967 edition, meanwhile, featured a suitably psychedelic cartoon of a smiling Bunny Girl (resplendent in lurid purple and orange), while bell-bottoms, cheesecloth shirts and faded denim all made frequent appearances in the magazine's fashion spreads as *Playboy* courted those 'freedom-seeking activists in the avant-garde of the sartorial revolution' (*Playboy*, May 1970).

Even student radicalism was a turn-on for *Playboy*. The cover of its 'Special Student Revolt Issue' depicted an attractive young woman tugging up her white 'Student Power' tee-shirt to reveal the unmistakable 'Bunny' logo painted on her naked midriff (*Playboy*, September 1969).[8] Admittedly, the issue included a thought provoking Playboy Panel on student unrest – with a particularly incisive contribution from Tom Hayden – though the previous year *Playboy* had already made clear its campus priorities in its 'Swinger's Guide to Academe'. Surveying the behaviour and attitudes of students at twenty-five universities, the guide provided a 'Campus Action Chart' rating institutions in terms of their extracurricular social life and the 'availability of women' (Berkeley scored well, but the University of Wisconsin carried the day, 'being clearly for those who are hedonistically ebullient'). Though tongue-in-cheek, the 'Swinger's Guide' was in some ways quite revealing about the prerogatives of both *Playboy* and its target audience. Rather than the fervour of radical politics or the cut-and-thrust of direct action, it was more the licentious side of campus life that exerted appeal:

> What every red-blooded male wants to know is, 'Where does my alma mater stand in the ranks of the sexual revolution? Is it in the vanguard or are there other schools that put fewer restrictions on life, liberty and the pursuit of heterosexual happiness?' (*Playboy*, September 1968)

THE DECLINE AND FALL OF THE PLAYBOY EMPIRE

Richard Nixon despised the worldview espoused by *Playboy*. The magazine's unbridled hedonism and liberal, intellectual pretensions were anathema to Nixon's straight-laced conservatism. Nixon frowned upon White House staff who read the magazine and, in 1970, lambasted the report of the President's Commission on Obscenity and Pornography (set up under Lyndon Johnson) which concluded there was little evidence that pornography was harmful and that the government should resist a drift into censorship. For the President the report itself was 'morally bankrupt', Nixon vowing that as long as he was in office there would be 'no relaxation of the national effort to control and eliminate smut from our national life' (cited in Miller, 1985: 214). However, although Nixon's trouncing of McGovern in the 1972 election suggested a groundswell of popular support for the President's 'square virtues', the new 'morality of pleasure as a duty' was here to stay. In fact, during the late 1960s and early 1970s, the credo was pushed even further amid the counterculture's 'no-holds-barred' celebration of sensory pleasure and immediate gratification. Unsurprisingly, then, this was a context in which the Playboy empire initially prospered.

The recession that began to bite at the end of the 1960s hardly touched *Playboy*. By 1969 net-earnings amounted to $7.5 million as sales rocketed, advertisers fell over themselves to buy page space and the Playboy clubs and hotels coined money. In November 1971, to maintain the incredible pace of expansion, Playboy Enterprises Inc. was floated on the stock exchange. Stock was quickly snapped up, profits surging as the magazine's circulation soared to a peak of over 7 million in September 1972. Results for the company's first fiscal year were equally spectacular, net earnings amounting to $10.6 million. Success continued into the following year, 1973 seeing net earnings reach $11.25 million while the net worth of the company shot up to $76.9 million (Weyr, 1978: 253). By the mid-1970s Playboy was a $200 million entertainment conglomerate – a triumph that was emblematic of the wider ascendance of the 'ethic of fun'.

But the bubble was already bursting. The fiscal report for 1974 showed that net earnings had slumped to $5.9 million – down a huge 48 per cent (Weyr, 1978: 258). Lacklustre film ventures had been a big liability, but this was not the only difficulty. Magazine circulation had slid down to 6.4 million, while the hotels, clubs and other concerns were all haemorrhaging cash – the Playboy corporation coming to rely on its London gambling operations (then under the redoubtable supervision of Victor Lownes) to stay afloat. Embarrassing scandals had not helped. *Playboy*'s gloss was tarnished by a federal drugs probe focused on the Mansion and amid the investigation Hefner's executive secretary, Bobbie Arnstein, had committed suicide. The key problem, however, was more fundamental – the Playboy empire was beginning to look passé.

Playboy and its 'swinging bachelor' archetypes had arisen amid the cultural transformations of the 1950s and 1960s. The success of the Playboy empire was a benchmark of the emergence of a new middle-class value system that eschewed puritanical reserve in favour of liberated consumerism. During the 1970s this ethos continued to take strides forward, drawing influence and inspiration from the libertine energies of the counterculture. But, against these new models of 'groovy' hedonism, the image and ethos of the 'swinging bachelor' looked sadly outdated and outmoded. The Rat Pack, for example, continued their boisterous antics but looked increasingly tired and 'square'. Their performances came to be exercises in nostalgia, a fond memorial to good times gone by. James Bond was also getting long in the tooth. In 1973 Roger Moore replaced Sean Connery as the silver screen 007, but the original film formula was looking antiquated. Instead, with Moore as Bond, the films changed direction and developed a more markedly comic inflection that parodied the playboy mythology and playfully debunked the earlier 007 escapades. *Playboy* also struggled to adapt, but was increasingly left behind by the pace of cultural change.

By the mid-1970s it was clear that the Playboy mystique was fading and in April 1976 'Playboy's Slide' was solemnly announced on the front page of the *Wall Street Journal*. The clubs had lost their air of classy sophistication and foundered in neighbourhoods beset by urban decay. The magazine, meanwhile, was outflanked by even brasher rivals. First came *Penthouse*. Launched in Britain in 1965 by publisher Bob Guccioni, *Penthouse* had been consciously modelled as a UK equivalent to *Playboy*.[9] In 1969, however, Guccioni decided to tackle *Playboy* on its home turf and launched his magazine onto the American market. It was an audacious challenge and at first *Playboy* disdainfully ignored the brazen newcomer. But, with its more explicit sexual content, *Penthouse* made *Playboy* appear old-fashioned and prudish by comparison and *Penthouse's* climbing circulation steadily bit into *Playboy's* sales. Other competitors, meanwhile, derided *Playboy* as an archaic and uptight institution of the establishment. *Hustler* took particular delight in baiting its opponent. Launched in 1974 by Larry Flynt, a thirty-year-old wheeler-dealer and owner of a chain of Ohio go-go clubs, *Hustler* deliberately shunned the 'classy', soft-focus ambience of *Playboy* and *Penthouse* in favour of a style that was defiantly tasteless. With a circulation that peaked at two million, *Hustler* was intentionally offensive and confrontational, pitching itself as rampantly transgressive in its contempt for bourgeois pretensions and taboos.[10] Of course, *Hustler* had a vested interest in heaping ridicule on its rivals but, by the late 1970s, *Hustler* was fairly astute in stigmatizing *Playboy* as a stumbling dinosaur. The older magazine and its publisher no longer had the lustre of rebellious nonconformity. Instead, they had become outmoded shibboleths of the cultural past:

> Hefner, once a champion of the hedonistic life, is no longer able to provide a good time for others. He's tied to the past; he's isolated; he fails to respond to his reader's current needs. His magazines are slick, but clearly outdated and often just dull. (*Hustler*, March 1976)

*

Faltering in the corporate doldrums, the late 1970s saw Playboy Enterprises embark on a programme of reappraisal and rationalization. In an effort to revive circulation the magazine moved away from its pursuit of upscale lifestyles and instead boosted its sexual content and imitated its rivals' explicit raunchiness. In the Playboy boardroom heads rolled, while a strategy of belt tightening and cost cutting saw a root and branch restructuring of the business empire. The least successful clubs and resorts were sold off and loss-making ventures like film production and book publishing were abandoned. Another body-blow, however, came at the beginning of the 1980s when Playboy, facing the loss of its gaming licenses, was forced to sell its lucrative British casinos. Another round of stringent cost cutting and realignment was inevitable. Assuming the presidency of Playboy Enterprises in 1982, Christie Hefner (the publisher's daughter) piloted a streamlining process which saw the closure of the remaining clubs and an increasing absorption in the proliferating pornography market – with growing dependence on video sales and the Playboy Channel, one of America's fastest growing cable TV services.

Paradoxically, the exponential growth of mass marketed pornography in the 1980s took place alongside the rise of a virulently reactionary and puritanical strain of conservatism. The secular and evangelical New Right first emerged in the mid-1970s and came into its own with the election of Ronald Reagan in 1980. With a political agenda that combined a faith in free market capitalism and a commitment to an authoritarian brand of law and order, in some senses the ascent of the New Right marked a resurgence of the Nixonian 'square virtues'. Indeed, the New Right held special contempt for the 'permissive' and 'cosmopolitan' liberalism of the 1960s which, it was argued, had laid the way for a wholesale breakdown in American morality by undermining traditional values of hard work, self-discipline and family loyalty. Nevertheless, while liberalism beat a bewildered retreat during the 1980s, the new middle class did not capitulate to the reassertion of conservative puritanism. Instead, a new faction of upwardly mobile Young Turks emerged to carry the torch of commodity consumption and individual gratification.

1984 was, according to a *Newsweek* cover story, the 'Year of the Yuppy '. The business shift from manufacturing and distribution to financial and information services had laid the way for a new generation of young, urban professionals who seemed to exist on 'a new plane of consciousness, a state of Transcendental Acquisition' (*Newsweek*, 31 December 1984). An obsession with entrepreneurship and materialism made the archetypal yuppy a conservative in political terms, but in cultural orientation he shared little in common with the puritanical crusaders of the New Right. Like earlier progeny of the new middle class, the yuppies conceived of themselves as freewheeling individualists and established their identity and status through their hedonistic tastes and dedication to commodity consumerism.[11] The heyday of the 'footloose bachelor' and 'vibrant youth', therefore, might have disappeared into the dim and distant past but the narcissistic, middle-class, male consumer – the 'young man of action and acquisition' for whom 'the name of the game is fun' – had become an enduring fixture in American culture.

NOTES

1   The hit 'Eve of Destruction' was, itself, indicative of these continuities. Though performed by folk-rocker Barry McGuire, the song was actually penned by P.F. Sloan who (as 'Flip' Sloan) had been one half of the Fantastic Baggies – a vocal surf duo that had collaborated with Jan and Dean and the Beach Boys in the early 1960s. Many other surf music stalwarts also moved into the folk-rock idiom associated with the nascent counterculture. For example, Gary Usher (formerly a key player in the surf and hot rod music scene) won critical acclaim as a producer with the Byrds, while the Beach Boys flirted with folk and progressive rock on the 1966 album *Pet Sounds* and the aborted *Smile* project of 1966/7.

2   Many other commentators have advanced a similar narrative of 'incorporation through commodification'. Abe Peck, for example, cites Columbia Records' in-famous advertising campaign 'But the Man Can't Bust Our Music' as evidence of a late 1960s shift 'from counter-culture to over-the-counter culture' (Peck, 1985: 164-5).

3   Drawing on the ideas of Antonio Gramsci, Chantell Mouffe uses the term 'expansive hegemony' to denote a moment of profound unity between rulers and ruled – a period in which a dominant class successfully deploys a set of ideological assumptions or 'articulating principles' in order to position itself at the head of a wide variety of social forces. See Mouffe (1981).

4   A more detailed account of the post-1966 economic downturn is provided in Gordon (1994).

5   The classic exposition of Beat veneration of Black subculture was provided in Norman Mailer's essay 'The White Negro' (Mailer: 1961). Polsky's (1971) survey of the New York Beat scene also highlighted the white avant-garde's admiration for the streetwise hipsters of the black ghetto.

6   Miller, however, is more circumspect, arguing that Hefner's views 'were no more radical after 1968 than they were before' (Miller, 1985: 174).

7   'Project Playmate' featured in a photospread in the May 1966 edition of *Playboy*.

8   In a similar vein, the centrefold Playmate for Christmas 1969 was a 'Radical Discovery' – a 'sometime scholar and full-time radical', she was 'an archetypal child of the rock age: always on the move, always ready to challenge authority – and always eager to have a good time' (*Playboy*, December 1969).

9   As Bob Guccioni explains, ' [*Playboy*] was doing extremely well in those days – it was outselling *Punch*, which was one of the better news-stand magazines in the UK. So, it occurred to me . . . that if [*Playboy*] were selling that well – as a magazine aimed at primarily *American* readers and very much a part of *American* culture – I figured that if one were to adapt the formula to an English publication, then it would sell at least as well if not better' (interview with author).

10 Kipnis (1992) provides a consumate assessment of *Hustler*'s contradictory and 'carnivalesque' discourse of transgression.

11 As Ehrenreich perceptively argues, the acquisitive yuppies of the 1980s actually shared a lot in common with the ostensibly anti-materialist counterculture of the 1960s:

> Like the sixties rebels, the yuppies were at the cutting edge of their class, a kind of avant-garde, charting a new direction and agenda. They were also, in their own way, rebels. Both radicals and yuppies rejected the long, traditional path to middle class success, but the defining zeal of the yuppies was to join another class – the rich. (Ehrenreich, 1990: 198)

Chapter 9
Conclusion: Cultures of Narcissism

His footsteps are the ones other men follow. His tastes are the ones other men acquire, his women the ones other men desire. Much about him has changed during *Playboy*'s 35 years: his clothes, his hair, his cars – accessories all. One thing, though, has remained the same through four decades: The man's style is born of a love for the best things in life.

'What Sort of Man Reads Playboy?', *Playboy*, Vol. 36, No. 1, January 1989.

MASCULINE CRISIS, DOMESTIC CONTAINMENT AND THE ETHOS OF 'PLEASURE AS A DUTY'

Apparently, the 1990s were a tough time to be an American man. According to a host of social commentators, masculinity was in 'crisis' – men intellectually and emotionally threatened by (and struggling to cope with) socio-economic upheaval and shifting patterns of gender relations. Looming large in this thesis of masculine crisis was Susan Faludi's florid portrait of 'the betrayal of modern man' (Faludi: 1999). Faludi's 'travels through a postwar male realm' depicted a generation of American men who had lost their sense of social relevance through an enervating combination of corporate downsizing, paternal neglect and the collapse of collective solidarities. For Faludi, the breakdown of traditional measures of masculinity had left American men angry and alienated, painfully betrayed by the disintegration of a male culture that had once guaranteed an authoritative and fulfilled manhood.

Notions of contemporary masculinity as being profoundly and uniquely 'under siege', however, can be misleading. As Lynne Segal observes, while particular groups of men may suffer through unemployment or social dislocation, structures of masculine power remain substantially secure:

> The perpetuation and tenacity of men's power in day-to-day gender relations is easily established. Men still have overwhelmingly greater access to cultural prestige, political authority, corporate power, individual wealth and material comforts, compared to women, in all parts of the world – whatever the costs, confusions and insecurities of individual men. (Segal, 1997: xi)

Moreover, recent perceptions of a bewildering 'masculine crisis' must be contextualized in a much longer narrative of gender anxiety. This book has shown that the development of modern masculine identities has been continually punctuated by a sense of insecurity and apprehension. As Michael Kimmel argues, it is possible to map out a history of 'gender crises' that 'occur at specific historical junctures, when structural changes transform the institutions of personal life such as marriage and the family, which are sources of gender identity' (Kimmel, 1987a: 123). As earlier chapters of this book testify, the late nineteenth century, the Depression era and the 1950s all witnessed their own moments of 'gender crisis' as both men and women struggled to redefine the meanings of masculinity and femininity amid periods of deep-seated social, economic and cultural transformation. Moreover, as Kimmel's (1997) expansive history of 'manhood in America' demonstrates, these moments of 'crisis' have invariably prompted both a mourning for men's 'lost' sense of potency and attempts to reassert traditional 'manly' qualities in the face of a perceived slide into 'femininity'. Often, this reaffirmation has entailed an emphasis on discipline and competition, or escapist fantasies and a longing for a return to the virile certainties of America's pioneering past. But 'masculinity' is always diverse and dynamic. Along-side appeals to 'traditional' male virtues of rough-hewn vigour and robust independence, there have also competed new articulations of masculine identity. In particular, this book has highlighted the emergence and subsequent ascendance of a style-conscious and desiring masculine subject – a masculine identity premised on youthful consumption, display and hedonistic leisure.

Beginning in the late nineteenth century, a masculine identity gradually took shape configured around codes of commodity consumerism and personal gratification. This avowedly pleasure-oriented and consumerist construction of American masculinity, moreover, was closely related to developments within the sphere of youth culture. From the bachelor subcultures of the postbellum metropolis, through the Jazz Age, to the 1930s heyday of *Esquire* magazine, constructions of 'youthful fun' and 'footloose bachelorhood' were complementary and interrelated, shifts in young people's tastes and value systems influencing and informing the wider rise of lifestyles grounded on leisure, pleasure and the satisfaction of consumer desire. Tracing its origins to the late nineteenth and early twentieth centuries, this model of masculinity was powerfully extended after the Second World War. During the 1950s and early 1960s, ideals of a masculinity formed around hedonistic consumerism intensified as the emergence of an advanced consumer economy brought with it a new middle-class formation that distinguished itself through a habitus prioritizing self-expression through style and distinctive patterns of consumption. In this class faction's new 'morality of pleasure as a duty' the archetype of the hedonistic masculine consumer found full expression.

Notions of postwar America as being overwhelmed by a paralysing culture of conformity are, as we have seen, a distorted caricature. Historians of Cold War 'domestic containment' are right to highlight the powerful ideological strategies that sought 'to unify, codify and contain – perhaps *intimidate* is the best word – the personal narratives of [the] population' (Nadel, 1995: 4). Yet it is misleading to conceive of these ideologies of conformity as all-pervasive, a comprehensive cultural force that went unchallenged until the mid-1960s and the emergence of 'a public discourse displaying many traits that would later be associated with "postmodernism"' (Nadel, 1995: 3). Instead, culture is *always* fragmentary and heterogeneous, inevitably ruptured by contradictions, inconsistencies and conflicts. America during the Cold War was no exception. Rather than abruptly splitting asunder during the 1960s, the ideologies of 'containment' were always fraught with tensions – not least in relation to concepts of gender. The much vaunted 'crisis in masculinity' of the 1950s, for example, saw a thoroughgoing critique of dominant ideals of sober and responsible manhood. Indeed, the image of the 'gray-flannelled', suburban breadwinner came to be perceived as the epitome of a stifling culture of regimentation and oppressive uniformity. In contrast, emergent models of masculinity held out the promise of individuality and freedom through their emphasis on personal consumption and immediate gratification. Here, the rise of a 'teenage' milieu predicated on commercial leisure and indulgent fun (given ultimate manifestation in the early 1960s Californian beach scene) operated in tandem with a burgeoning masculine universe of narcissistic style and sexual licence – these allied formations complementing and mutually informing one another as they challenged traditional middle-class mores of conservatism and puritanical reserve.

Coming to fruition in the 'playboy ethos' of the late 1950s and early 1960s, this emergent brand of middle-class masculinity drew together mythologies of youth, affluence and leisure in a powerful cultural configuration. With its emphasis on individuality, narcissistic style and conspicuous consumption, this was a middle-class value system adapted to the demands of the consumer economy – a new, commodity-driven bourgeois culture that could respond to modern capitalism's demand for an endlessly re-generating consumer market. Though ostensibly rebellious and anti-bourgeois, aspects of the 1960s countercultural ferment were actually constituent in this process of middle-class adjustment. Rather than radically *transgressive*, the bohemian ethos of individual freedom and libertine self-expression played a *transformative* role, further energizing the new middle class in its quest for lifestyles of hip nonconformity. As Ehrenreich argues, the real lure of the counterculture was its hedonism and, in its pursuit of pleasure, 'hippiedom did not so much counter the mainstream culture, as anticipate it, magnify it to transcendent proportions, and enrich it' (Ehrenreich, 1983: 113).

The rise of new lifestyles premised upon hedonism and conspicuous consumption inevitably collided and conflicted with the more conservative ideals of hard work, thrift and self-discipline traditionally associated with the American middle class. Indeed, both in the early 1970s and early 1980s conservative political triumphs seemed to announce a regeneration of the 'square virtues'. But, although the puritanical backlash was often severe, the cultural ethos of the new middle class remained alive and well. And, though the earlier archetypes of the 'footloose bachelor' and 'vibrant youth' were looking sadly dated, they were superseded by new, more à la mode, models of hedonistic consumption. The outward trappings of the 'playboy ethic' may have changed, but its values of personal gratification and hip consumerism were enduring.

The 1980s yuppy style of hectic excess took the 'playboy ethic' to dizzying heights, but ultimately the yuppy's unceasing aspirationalism proved too neurotic and angst ridden. Instead, the 1990s saw the yuppy's fevered profligacy eclipsed by a middle-class culture more subtle in its hedonism, but no less dedicated in its pursuit of style-conscious consumer lifestyles. For David Brooks (2000) this was embodied in the rise of the 'Bobos' – a new educated and liberal middle class whose habitus combined the social elitism of the bourgeoisie with a bohemian aesthetic vision (hence the epithet 'Bobo'). At the same time, after twenty years languishing in the dustbin of style, the original playboy élan also seemed set for a return. By the late 1990s Playboy share prices were up, magazine circulation was holding strong at between three and four million, a new Playboy casino (complete with Bunnies) had opened on the Greek island of Rhodes and there were plans for a new club in London's glitzy West End. More than this, however, Playboy was becoming fashionable again. Hugh Hefner was revered as an elder statesman of American good-time culture, making cameo TV appearances in everything from The Simpsons to Sex and the City, while a new generation of 'happening' Hollywood celebrities – Leonardo DiCaprio, George Clooney, Jim Carrey, Cameron Diaz – were spotted carousing at the Playboy Mansion. Playboy's resurgence was, no doubt, partly indebted to a wider vogue for retro-cool, a postmodern (and ironically coded) poaching from the stylistic past. Yet this vogue for tongue-in-cheek pastiche might, itself, be read as yet another quest for 'hip' distinctiveness – the latest articulation of the lifestyle sensibilities of the new middle class.

'THE MOST LIBERATING REVOLUTION OF ALL'?

For the prophets of masculine hedonism, the rise of a libertine ethos of personal gratification was an emancipatory step forward in American history. In the thirty-fifth anniversary issue of Playboy, for example, Hefner congratulated himself on his services to contemporary culture. 'In the prudish moral climate of the Fifties', the publisher reflected, 'Playboy unabashedly championed sexual liberation':

> Other magazines have shaped politics, dictated fashion, legitimized gossip. Playboy freed a generation from guilt about sex, changed some laws and helped launch a revolution or two. And did it while having fun – perhaps the most liberating revolution of all. So you may not think it immodest of us to say Playboy is the magazine that changed America. (Playboy, January 1989)

Others, however, are less enthusiastic. For the conservative Right, the rise of a value system that endorsed self-indulgence and sexual expression marked a malignant slide into an amoral and socially debilitating age of 'permissiveness'. On the Left, the same phenomena could be condemned as an example of free market capitalism at its worst – a cynical exercise in indoctrination, manipulation and exploitation. Critics from across the political spectrum, meanwhile, have lamented what they interpret as a modern climate of dissolute irresponsibility, shallow materialism and destructive self-absorption. Perhaps the most widely known expression of the thesis is Christopher Lasch's bestseller, *The Culture of Narcissism* (1979), and its barrage against what Lasch sees as a greedy and superficial society that has come to depend on hollow self-indulgence and frivolous consumerism. Others, too, have also elaborated accounts akin to this updated version of mass society pessimism. Faludi's chronicle of the modern masculine 'crisis', for example, avers that American men have become 'ruled by commercial values', joining women in an 'enslavement to glamour':

> The commercialized, ornamental 'femininity' that the women's movement diagnosed now has men by the throat. Men and women both feel cheated of lives in which they might have contributed to a social world; men and women both feel pushed into roles that are about little more than displaying prettiness or prowess in the market place. Women were pushed first, but their brothers have joined the same forced march. (Faludi, 1999: 602)

These critiques, however, are woefully monolithic in their approach, failing to allow for the full play of disparities and inconsistencies intrinsic to the consuming masculine subject. As Tony Bennett and Janet Woollacott have eloquently argued, popular culture is shot through with contradictions, always a site 'around which a constantly varying and always many faceted range of cultural and ideological trans-actions are conducted' (Bennett and Woollacott, 1987: 8). The 'ethic of fun' associated with the rise of the new middle class has been exemplary – simultaneously champion-ing capitalism's core values of possessive individualism, while challenging the hegemony of traditional bourgeois ideals. Indeed, in her original assessment of the 'playboy ethic', Ehrenreich acknowledged its prominent elements of sexism and commercial exploitation, yet also outlined an 'optimistic reading' that recognized in the narcissistic, male consumer a sense of questioning and a defiance of dominant expectations that was 'in step with feminism and with some broad populist impulse toward democracy' (Ehrenreich, 1983: 170). Nevertheless, we should not lose sight of the other end of the equation. Masculine identities and visual codes premised upon youthful hedonism and conspicuous consumerism certainly ruptured and displaced the traditional codes of a bourgeois masculinity rooted in ideals of hard work, thrift and puritanical conservatism. But, at the same time, they left wider power structures and systems of inequality essentially intact. Rather than a force for radical change, the imperatives of a leisure-oriented and hedonistic masculinity helped generate a middle-class culture acclimatized and better adapted to the demands of an advanced consumer economy. Ultimately, then, the playboy ethic was always more of a dry martini than a Molotov cocktail.

Bibliography

Abelson, E. (1992), *When Ladies Go A-Thieving: Middle-Class Shoplifters in the Victorian Department Store*, Oxford: Oxford University Press.

Adams, M. (1994), *The Best War Ever: America and World War II*, Baltimore: Johns Hopkins University Press.

Appleby, J. (1978), *Economic Thought and Ideology in Seventeenth-Century England*, Princeton: Princeton University Press.

Arendt, H. (1951), *The Origins of Totalitarianism*, New York: Harcourt Brace Jovanovich.

Austin, J. and Willard, M. (eds) (1998), *Generations of Youth: Youth Cultures and History in Twentieth-Century America*, New York: New York University Press.

Bagguley, P., Mark-Lawson, J., Sapiro, J., Urry, J., Walby, S. and Warde, A. (1990), *Restructuring: Place, Class and Gender*, London: Sage.

Bailey, B. (1988), *From Front Porch to Back Seat: Courtship in Twentieth Century America*, Baltimore: Johns Hopkins University Press.

Barber, L. (1999), 'Echo of the Bunny Man', *Observer Magazine*, 16 May: 18–23.

Bederman, G. (1995), *Manliness and Civilization: A Cultural History of Gender and Race in the United States, 1880–1917*, Chicago: University of Chicago Press.

Bell, D. (1960), *The End of Ideology: On the Exhaustion of Political Ideas in the Fifties*, New York: Free Press.

—— (1979), 'The New Class: A Muddled Concept', in B. Bruce-Briggs (ed.), *The New Class?* New Brunswick: Transaction.

Benjamin, W. (1983), *Charles Baudelaire: A Lyric Poet in the Era of High Capitalism*, trans. H. Zohn, London: Verso.

Bennett, T. and Woollacott, J. (1987), *Bond and Beyond: The Political Career of a Popular Hero*, Basingstoke: Macmillan.

Bensman, J. and Vidich, A. (1995a), 'Changes in the Life-Styles of American Classes', in A. Vidich (ed.), *The New Middle Classes: Life-Styles, Status Claims and Political Orientations*, London: Macmillan (originally published 1971).

Bensman, J. and Vidich, A. (1995b), 'The New Class System and Its Life-Styles', in Arthur Vidich (ed.), *The New Middle Classes: Life-Styles, Status Claims and Political Orientations*, London: Macmillan (originally published 1971).

Bentley, M. (1999), *Modern Historiography: An Introduction*, London: Routledge.

Bernard, J. (1961), 'Teen-Age Culture: An Overview', *The Annals of the American Academy of Political and Social Science*, Vol. 338, November: 1–12.

Berrett, J. (1997), 'Feeding the Organization Man: Diet and Masculinity in Postwar America', *Journal of Social History*, No. 30, Summer: 805–25.

Biskind, P. (1983), *Seeing Is Believing: How Hollywood Taught Us to Stop Worrying and Love the Fifties*, New York: Pantheon.

Blair, J. (1995) (3rd edn), *The Illustrated Discography of Surf Music, 1961–1965*, Ann Arbor: Popular Culture Ink.

Blair, J. and McParland, S. (1990), *The Illustrated Discography of Hot Rod Music, 1961–1965*, Ann Arbor: Popular Culture.

Bledstein, J. (1976), *The Culture of Professionalism: the Middle Class and the Development of Higher Education in America*, New York: Norton.

Blumin, S. (1985), 'The Hypothesis of Middle-Class Formation in Nineteenth-Century America; A Critique and Some Proposals', *American Historical Review*, Vol. 90, April: 299–338.

—— (1989), *The Emergence of the Middle Class: Social Experience in the American City, 1760–1900*, New York: Cambridge University Press.

Bly, R. (1990), *Iron John*, Reading, Mass.: Adison-Wesley.

Bourdieu, P. (1984), *Distinction: A Social Critique of the Judgement of Taste*, trans. R. Nice, London: Routledge.

Bradley, P. (1998), 'Mass Communication and the Shaping of US Feminism', in C. Carter, G. Branston and S. Allan (eds), *News, Gender and Power*, London: Routledge.

Brady, F. (1975), *Hefner*, London: Weidenfeld & Nicolson.

Breines, W. (1985), 'Domineering Mothers in the 1950s: Image and Reality', *Women's Studies International Forum*, Vol. 8, No. 6: 601–8.

—— (1986), 'The 1950s: Gender and Some Social Science', *Sociological Inquiry*, Vol. 56: 69–92.

—— (1992), *Young, White and Miserable: Growing Up Female in the Fifties*, Boston: Beacon Press.

Bremner, R. (1982), 'Families, Children, and the State', in R. Bremner and G. Reichard (eds), *Reshaping America: Society and Institutions, 1945–1960*, Columbus: Ohio State University Press.

Brenton, M. (1967), *The American Male*, London: Allen & Unwin.

Breward, C. (1999), *The Hidden Consumer: Masculinities, Fashion and City Life, 1860–1914*, Manchester: Manchester University Press.

Breazeale, K. (1994), 'In Spite of Women: *Esquire* Magazine and the Construction of the Male Consumer', *Signs*, Vol. 20, No. 1, Autumn: 1–22.

Brezinski, Z. (1956), 'Totalitarianism and Rationality', *American Political Science Review*, Vol. 50, No. 3: 751–63.

Brod, H. (ed.) (1987), *The Making of Masculinities: The New Men's Studies*, Boston: Allen & Unwin.

Brooks, D. (2000), *Bobos In Paradise: The New Upper Class and How They Got There*, New York: Simon & Schuster.

Brown, H.G. (1962), *Sex and the Single Girl*, New York: Bernard Geiss.

Bruce-Briggs, B. (ed.) (1979), *The New Class?* New Brunswick: Transaction.

Brunt, R. (1982), '"An Immense Verbosity": Permissive Sexual Advice in the 1970s', in Rosalind Brunt and Caroline Rowan (eds), *Feminism, Culture and Politics*, London: Lawrence & Wishart.

Buckley, C. (1994), *Cruising State: Growing Up in Southern California*, Reno: University of Nevada Press.

Burt, R. (1986), *Surf City / Drag City*, Poole: Blandford Press.

Butler, J. (1990), *Gender Trouble: Feminism and the Subversion of Identity*, London: Routledge.

——— (1995), 'Melancholy Gender/Refused Identification', in M. Berger, B. Wallis and S. Watson (eds), *Constructing Masculinity*, London: Routledge.

Buxton, D. (1990), *From The Avengers to Miami Vice: Form and Ideology in Television Series*, Manchester: Manchester University Press.

Carnes, M. (1989), *Secret Ritual and Manhood in Victorian America*, New Haven: Yale University Press.

Carnes, M. and Griffen, C. (eds) (1990), *Meanings for Manhood: Constructions of Masculinity in Victorian America*, Chicago: University of Chicago Press.

Cawelti, J. (1965), *Apostles of the Self-Made Man*, Chicago: University of Chicago Press.

Chandler, A. (1980), *The Visible Hand: The Managerial Revolution in American Business*, Cambridge: Belknap Press.

Chapman, J. (1999,) *Licence to Thrill: A Cultural History of the James Bond Films*, London: I.B. Tauris.

Chauncey, G. (1994), *Gay New York: Gender, Urban Culture and the Making of the Gay Male World, 1890–1940*, New York: Basic Books.

Chudacoff, H. (1989), *How Old Are You? Age Consciousness in American Culture*, Princeton: Princeton University Press.

Chudacoff, H. (1999), *The Age of the Bachelor: Creating an American Subculture*, Princeton: Princeton University Press.

Cipolla, C. (1980) (2nd edn), *Before the Industrial Revolution: European Society and Economy, 1000–1700*, New York: Norton.

Clark, C. (1989), 'Ranch-House Suburbia: Ideals and Realities', in L. May (ed.), *Recasting America: Culture and Politics in the Age of the Cold War*, Chicago: University of Chicago Press.

Clawson, M.A. (1989), *Constructing Brotherhood: Class, Gender and Fraternalism*, Princeton: Princeton University Press.

Cohan, S. (1996), 'So Functional for its Purposes: Rock Hudson's Bachelor Apartment in *Pillow Talk*', in J. Sanders (ed.), *Stud: Architectures of Masculinity*, Princeton: Princeton University Press.

——— (1997), *Masked Men: Masculinity and the Movies in the Fifties*, Bloomington: University of Indiana Press.

Cohan, S. and Hark, I. (eds) (1993), *Screening the Male: Exploring Masculinities in Hollywood Cinema*, London: Routledge.

Coleman, J.S. (1961), *The Adolescent Society; the Social Life of the Teenager and its Impact on Education*, Glencoe: Free Press.

Conekin, B. (2000) 'Fashioning the Playboy: Messages of Style and Masculinity in the Pages of *Playboy* Magazine, 1953–1963', *Fashion Theory*, Vol. 4, No. 4: 447–66.

Congdon-Martin, D. (1998), *Aloha Spirit: Hawaiian Art and Popular Design*, Atglen, PA: Schiffer.

Coontz, S. (1992), *The Way We Never Were: American Families and the Nostalgia Trap*, New York: Basic Books.

Corbin, H. (1970), *The Men's Clothing Industry: Colonial Through Modern Times*, New York: Fairchild Publications.

Cosgrove, S. (1984), 'The Zoot Suit and Style Warfare', *History Workshop*, No. 18: 77–91.

Cott, N. (1977), *The Bonds of Womanhood: 'Woman's Sphere' in New England, 1780–1835*, New Haven: Yale University Press.

Cox, H. (1965), *The Secular City*, Bloomsbury: SCM.

Craik, J. (1993), *The Face of Fashion: Cultural Studies of Fashion*, London: Routledge.

Dalley, R. (1996) (2nd edn), *Surfin' Guitars: Instrumental Surf Bands of the Sixties*, California: Surf Publications.

Davidoff, L. and Hall, C. (1987), *Family Fortunes: Men and Women of the English Middle Class, 1780–1850*, Chicago: University of Chicago Press.

Dawson, G. (1991), 'The Blond Bedouin: Lawrence of Arabia, Imperial Adventure and the Imaging of English-British Masculinity', in M. Roper and J. Tosh (eds), *Manful Assertions: Masculinities in Britain Since 1800*, London: Routledge.

Decker, J. (1997), *Made in America: Self-Styled Success from Horatio Alger to Oprah Winfrey*, Minneapolis: University of Minnesota Press.

D'Acci, J. (1997), 'Nobody's Woman? Honey West and the New Sexuality', in L. Spigel and M. Curtin (eds), *The Revolution Wasn't Televised: Sixties Television and Social Conflict*, London: Routledge.

D'Emilio, J. (1983), *Sexual Politics, Sexual Communities: The Making of a Homosexual Minority in the United States, 1940–1970*, Chicago: University of Chicago Press.

—— (1989), 'The Homosexual Menace: The Politics of Sexuality in Cold War America', in K. Peiss and C. Simmons (eds), *Passion and Power: Sexuality in History*, Philadelphia: Temple University Press.

D'Emilio, J. and Freedman, E. (1997) (2nd edn), *Intimate Matters: A History of Sexuality in America*, Chicago: University of Chicago Press.

Denning, M. (1987), *Cover Stories: Narrative and Ideology in the British Spy Thriller*, London: Routledge.

de Tocqueville, A. (1969), *Democracy in America*, Vol. II, trans. George Lawrence, London: Collins (orig. pub. 1840).

Dines, G. (1995), '"I Buy It For the Articles": *Playboy* Magazine and the Sexualization of Consumerism', in G. Dines and J.M. Humez (eds), *Gender, Race and Class in Media: A Text-Reader*, London: Sage.

—— (1998), 'Dirty Business and the Mainstreaming of Pornography', in G. Dines, R. Jensen and A. Russo (eds), *Pornography: The Production and Consumption of Inequality*, London: Routledge.

Doherty, J. (1988), *Teenagers and Teenpics: The Juvenilization of American Movies in the 1950s*, London: Unwin & Hyman.

Douglas, S. (1994), *Where the Girls Are: Growing Up Female with the Mass Media*, London: Penguin.

Dubbert, J. (1979), *A Man's Place: Masculinity in Transition*, Englewood Cliffs NJ: Prentice-Hall.

Dyer, R. (1982), 'Don't Look Now – The Male Pin-Up', *Screen*, Vol. 23, No. 3–4.

—— (1997), *White*, London: Routledge.

Edgren, G. (1994), *The Playboy Book: Forty Years*, London: Mitchell Beazley.

Edwards, T. (1997), *Men in the Mirror: Men's Fashion, Masculinity and Consumer Society*, London: Cassell.

Ehrernreich, B. (1984), *The Hearts of Men: American Dreams and the Flight From Commitment*, London: Pluto.

—— (1990), *Fear of Falling: The Inner Life of the Middle Class*, New York: Harper Perennial.

Ehrenreich, B. and Ehrenreich, J. (1979), 'The Professional-Managerial Class', in P. Walker (ed.), *Between Capital and Labour*, Boston: South End Press.

Eisenstadt, S.N. (1956), *Generation to Generation: Age Groups and Social Structure*, Glencoe: Free Press.

—— (1962), 'Archetypal Patterns of Youth', *Daedulus*, Vol. 9, Winter: 28–46.

England, R. (1960), 'A Theory of Midle Class Juvenile Delinquency', *Journal of Criminal Law, Criminology and Political Science*, Vol. 50, March/April: 535–40.

Erenberg, L. (1981), *Steppin' Out: New York Nightlife and the Transformation of American Culture, 1890–1930*, Chicago: University of Chicago Press.

Escobar, E. (1996), 'Zoot-Suiters and Cops: Chicano Youth and the Los Angeles Police Department During World War II', in L. Erenberg and S. Hirsch (eds), *The War in American Culture: Society and Consciousness During World War II*, Chicago: University of Chicago Press.

Evans, A. (1995), 'The Transformation of the Black Middle Class', in A. Vidich (ed.), *The New Middle Classes: Life-Styles, Status Claims and Political Orientations*, London: Macmillan.

Faludi, S. (1999), *Stiffed: The Betrayal of the American Man*, London: Chatto & Windus.

Fass, P. (1978), *The Damned and the Beautiful: American Youth in the 1920s*, Oxford: Oxford University Press.

Featherstone, M. (1991), *Consumer Culture and Postmodernism*, London: Sage.

Filene, P. (1986) (2nd edn), *Him/Her/Self: Sex Roles in Modern America*, Baltimore: Johns Hopkins University Press.

Fishman, R. (1987), *Bourgeois Utopias: The Rise and Fall of Suburbia*, New York: Basic Books.

Ford, L. (1994), *Cities and Buildings: Skyscrapers, Skid Rows, and Suburbs*, Baltimore: Johns Hopkins University Press.

Foreman, J. (1997), *The Other Fifties: Interrogating Mid-century American Icons*, Chicago: University of Illinois Press.

Foucault, M. (1979), *The History of Sexuality*, Vol. I, trans. Robert Hurley, London: Allen Lane.

Fox, R. and Lears, T.J. (eds) (1983), *The Culture of Consumption: Critical Essays in American History, 1880–1980*, New York: Pantheon.

Frank, T. (1997), *The Conquest of Cool: Business Culture, Counterculture and the Rise of Hip Consumerism*, Chicago: University of Chicago Press.

Freedman, E. (1974), 'The New Woman: Changing Views of Women in the 1920s', *Journal of American History*, Vol. 64, March: 398–411.

—— (1987), '"Uncontrolled Desires": The Response to the Sexual Psychopath, 1920–1960', *Journal of American History*, Vol. 74, No. 1, June: 83–106.

Friedenberg, E. (1959), *The Vanishing Adolescent*, Boston: Beacon Press.

—— (1965), *Coming of Age in America*, New York: Random House.

Friedrich, C. (1954), *Totalitarianism*, Cambridge, Mass.: Harvard University Press.

Frow, J. (1995), *Cultural Studies and Cultural Value*, Oxford: Oxford University Press.

Gabor, M. (1985), *The Illustrated History of Girlie Magazines*, London: Futura.

Gabor, M. (1996), *The Pin-Up: A Modest History*, New York: Evergreen.

Gaines, J. (1985), 'War, Women and Lipstick: Fan Magazines in the Forties', *Heresies*, 18–19.

Gans, H. (1965), 'Who's O-O-Oh in America', *Vogue*, 15 March: 108; 151.

Gelfand, M. (1982), 'Cities, Suburbs and Government Policy', in R. Bremner and G. Reichard (eds), *Reshaping America: Society and Institutions, 1945–60*, Columbus: Ohio State University Press.

Giddens, A. (1981) (2nd edn), *The Class Structure of the Advanced Societies*, London: Hutchinson.

Gilbert, J. (1986.), *A Cycle of Outrage: America's Reaction to the Juvenile Delinquent in the 1950s*, Oxford: Oxford University Press.

Gillet, C. (1983), *The Sound of the City: The Rise of Rock and Roll*, London: Souvenir.

Gingrich, A. (1971), *Nothing But People: The Early Days at Esquire: A Personal History, 1928–1958*, New York: Crown.

Goldman, R., Heath, D. and Smith, S. (1991), 'Commodity Feminism', *Critical Studies in Mass Communication*, No. 8: 333–51.

Goodman, P. (1960), *Growing Up Absurd: Problems of Youth in the Organized System*, New York: Random House.

Gordon, D. (1994), 'Chickens Home to Roost: From Prosperity to Stagnation in the Postwar US Economy', in M. Bernstein and D. Adler (eds), *Understanding American Economic Decline*, Cambridge: Cambridge University Press.

Gordon, M. (1980), 'The Ideal Husband as Depicted in the Nineteenth-Century Marriage Manual', in Pleck and Pleck (eds).

Gordon, R., Gordon, K., and Gunther, M. (1962), *The Split-Level Trap*, New York: Dell.

Gorn, E. (1986), *The Manly Art: Bare Knuckle Prize Fighting in America*, Itaca: Cornell University Press.

Green, J. (1999), *All Dressed Up: The Sixties and the Counterculture*, London: Pimlico.

Griswold, R. (1993), *Fatherhood in America: A History*, New York: Basic Books.

Haralovich, M. (1992), 'Sit-coms and Suburbs: Positioning the 1950s Homemaker', in L. Spigel and D. Mann (eds), *Private Screenings: Television and the Female Consumer*, Minneapolis: University of Minnesota Press.

Harrington, M. (1962), *The Other America: Poverty in the United States*, London: Macmillan.

Hechinger, G. and Hechinger, F. (1962), *Teen-age Tyranny*, New York: Morrow.

Hellmann, J. (1997), *The Kennedy Obsession: The American Myth of JFK*, New York: Columbia University Press.

Hersh, S. (1998), *The Dark Side of Camelot*, London: HarperCollins.

Higham, J. (1970), 'The Reorientation of American Culture in the 1890s', in J. Higham (ed.), *Writing American History: Essays on Modern Scholarship*, Bloomington: Indiana University Press.

Hoch, P. (1979), *White Hero, Black Beast: Racism, Sexism and the Mask of Masculinity*, London: Pluto.

Hochswender, W. and Gross, K. (1993), *Men in Style: The Golden Age of Fashion from Esquire*, New York: Rizzoli.

Hollingshead, A. (1949), *Elmstown's Youth: The Impact of Social Classes on Adolescents*, New York: Wiley.

hooks, b. (1991), *Yearning: Race, Gender and Cultural Politics*, London: Turnaround.

—— (1992), 'Eating the Other: Desire and Resistance', in b. hooks, *Black Looks: Race and Representation*, Boston: South End Press.

Horowitz, D. (1985), *The Morality of Spending: Attitudes Toward the Consumer Society in America, 1875–1940*, Baltimore: Johns Hopkins University Press.

—— (1998), *Betty Friedan and the Making of the Feminine Mystique: The American Left, The Cold War, and Modern Feminism*, Amehurst: University of Massachusetts Press.

Hounshell, D. (1984), *From the American System to Mass Production: The Development of Manufacturing Technology in the United States*, Baltimore: Johns Hopkins University Press.

Huyssen, A. (1986), *After the Great Divide: Mass Culture and Postmodernism*, London: Macmillan.

Jackson, K. (1985), *Crabgrass Frontier: The Suburbanization of the United States*, Oxford: Oxford University Press.

James, D. (1996), *Surfing San Onofre to Point Dune, 1936–1942*, San Francisco: Chronicle.

Jeffries, J. (1997), *Wartime America: The World War II Home Front*, Chicago: I.R. Dee.

Jeffreys, S. (1990), *Anticlimax: A Feminist Perspective on the Sexual Revolution*, London: Women's Press.

Jenkins, K. (1991), *Re-Thinking History*, London: Routledge.

Jezer, M. (1982), *The Dark Ages: Life in the United States, 1945–1960*, Boston: South End Press.

Johnson, P. (1984), 'Surf Music? What Do You Mean "Surf Music?"', *California Music*, No. 66: 33–51.

Jones, D. (1997), *Easy! The Lexicon of Lounge*, London: Pavilion.

Jones, L. (1980), *Great Expectations: America and the Baby Boom Generation*, New York: Coward, McCann and Geoghegan.

Kampion, D. and Brown, B. (1998), *Stoked: A History of Surf Culture*, Los Angeles: Evergreen.

Kann, M. (1991), *On the Man Question: Gender and Civic Virtue in America*, Philadelphia: Temple University Press.

Katz, E. and Lazarsfeld, P. (1955), *Personal Influence: The Part Played by People in the Flow of Mass Communications*, Glencoe: Free Press.

Keats, J. (1956), *The Crack in the Picture Window*, New York: Ballentine Books.

Keniston, K. (1967), *The Uncommitted: Alienated Youth in American Society*, New York: Delta.

Kervin, D. (1991), 'Advertising Masculinity: The Representation of Males in *Esquire* Advertisements', *Journal of Communication Enquiry*, Vol. 14, No. 1: 51–70.

Kerber, L. (1988), 'Separate Spheres, Female Worlds, Women's Place: The Rhetoric of Women's History', *Journal of American History*, Vol. 75, No. 1, June: 9–39.

Kimmel, M. (1987a), 'The Contemporary "Crisis" of Masculinity in Historical Perspective', in Brod (ed.).

—— (1987b), 'Pro-Feminist Men in Turn-of-the-Century America', *Gender and Society*, Vol. 1, September: 261–83.

—— (1997), *Manhood in America: A Cultural History*, New York: The Free Press.

Kipnis, L. (1992), '(Male) Desire and (Female) Disgust: Reading *Hustler*', in L. Grossberg, C. Nelson and P. Treichler (eds), *Cultural Studies*, London: Routledge.

Kirsten, S. (2000), *The Book of Tiki*, London: Taschen.

Kozol, W. (1994), *Life's America: Family and Nation in Postwar Photojournalism*, Philadelphia: Temple University Press.

Kraditor, A. (1968), *Up from the Pedestal: Selected Writings in the History of American Feminism*, Chicago: Quadrangle Books.

Lamont, M. (1992), *Money, Morals, and Manners: The Culture of the French and American Upper-Middle Class*, Chicago: University of Chicago Press.

Lanza, J. (1995a), *The Cocktail: The Influence of Spirits on the American Psyche*, New York: St. Martin's Press.

—— (1995b), *Elevator Music: A Surreal History of Muzak, Easy-Listening and Other Moodsong*, London: Quartet.

Lash, S. and Urry, J. (1987), *The End of Organized Capitalism*, Cambridge: Polity.

Latham, A. (2000), *Posing a Threat: Flappers, Chorus Girls, and Other Brazen Performers of the American 1920s*, Hanover, NH: Wesleyan University Press.

Lazar, W. (1967), 'Life Style Concepts and Marketing', in E. Kelly and W. Lazar (eds), *Managerial Marketing: Perspectives and Viewpoints*, Illinois: Homeward (originally published 1963).

Leach, W. (1984), 'Transformations in a Culture of Consumption: Women and Department Stores, 1890–1925', *Journal of American History*, Vol. 71, No. 2: 319–342.

Lears, J. (1989), 'A Matter of Taste: Corporate Cultural Hegemony in a Mass-Consumption Society', in L. May (ed.), *Recasting America: Culture and Politics in the Age of the Cold War*, Chicago: University of Chicago Press.

Lencek, L. and Bosker, G. (1989), *Making Waves: Swimsuits and the Undressing of America*, San Francisco: Chronicle.

Levenstein, H. (1993), *Paradox of Plenty: A Social History of Eating in Modern America*, Oxford: Oxford University Press.

Levy, S. (1998), *Rat Pack Confidential: Frank, Dean, Sammy, Peter, Joey and the Last Great Showbiz Party*, London: Fourth Estate.

Licht, W. (1993), *Industrializing America*, Baltimore: Johns Hopkins University Press.

Look (1958), *The Decline of the American Male – by the Editors of Look*, New York: Random House.

Lundberg, F. and Farnham, M. (1947), *The Modern Woman: The Lost Sex*, New York: Harper Brothers.

Lury, C. (1996), *Consumer Culture*, Cambridge: Polity.

Lynd, R. and Lynd, H. (1929), *Middletown*, New York: Harcourt Brace.

Macdonald, D. (1958), 'A Caste, A Culture, A Market', *New Yorker*, Part I, 22 November; Part II, 29 November.

Macleod, D. (1983) *Building Character in the American Boy: The Boy Scouts, YMCA and Their Forerunners, 1870–1920*, Madison: University of Wisconsin Press.

Mailer, N. (1961), 'The White Negro', in N. Mailer, *Advertisements for Myself*, London: Andre Deutsch.

Mangan, J.A. and Walvin, J. (eds) (1987), *Manliness and Morality: Middle Class Masculinity in Britain and America, 1800–1940*, Manchester: Manchester University Press.

Marchland, R. (1982), 'Visions of Classlessness, Quests for Dominion: American Popular Culture, 1945–1960', in R. Bremner and G. Reichard (eds), *Reshaping*

America: Society and Institutions, 1945–1960, Columbus: Ohio State University Press.

Marcuse, H. (1964), *One-Dimensional Man,* Boston: Beacon.

Marsh, M. (1988), 'Suburban Men and Masculine Domesticity, 1870–1915', *American Quarterly,* No. 40, June: 165–86.

—— (1989), 'From Separation to Togetherness: The Social Construction of Domestic Space in American Suburbs, 1840–1915', *Journal of American History,* No. 76, September: 506–27.

—— (1990), *Suburban Lives,* New Brunswick: Rutgers University Press.

May, E.T. (1978), 'The Pressure to Provide: Class, Consumerism and Divorce in Urban America, 1880–1920', *Journal of Social History,* Vol. 12, No. 2, Winter: 180–93.

—— (1980), *Great Expectations: Marriage and Divorce in Post-Victorian America,* Chicago: University of Chicago Press.

—— (1995), *Barren in the Promised Land: Childless Americans and the Pursuit of Happiness,* Cambridge: Harvard University Press.

—— (1999) (2nd edn), *Homeward Bound: American Families in the Cold War Era,* New York: Basic Books.

May, L. (1980), *Screening Out the Past: The Birth of Mass Culture and the Motion Picture Industry,* New York: Oxford University Press.

—— (ed.) (1989), *Recasting America: Culture and Politics in the Age of the Cold War,* Chicago: Chicago University Press.

Mazón, M. (1984), *The Zoot-Suit Riots: The Psychology of Symbolic Annihilation,* Austin: University of Texas Press.

McCall, L. (1992), 'Does Gender Fit? Bourdieu, Feminism and Conceptions of Social Order', *Theory and Society,* No. 21: 837–67.

McElvaine, R. (1993), *The Great Depression: America, 1929–1941,* New York: Times.

McGee, M. and Robertson, R. (1982), *The J.D. Films,* Jefferson: McFarland.

McInerney, J. (1996), 'How Bond Saved America – And Me', in J. McInerney, N. Foulkes, N. Norman and N. Sullivan (eds), *Dressed to Kill: James Bond, the Suited Hero,* New York: Flammarion.

McKendrick, N., Brewer, J., and Plumb, J.H. (1982), *The Birth of a Consumer Society: The Commercialization of Eighteenth Century England,* London: Europa.

McNair, B. (1996), *Mediated Sex: Pornography and Postmodern Culture,* London: Arnold.

McParland, S. (1992), *It's Party Time: A Musical Appreciation of the Beach Party Film Genre,* California: CM.

Medhurst, A. (1985), 'Can Chaps Be Pin-Ups?: the British Male Film Star of the 1950s', *Ten/8,* Vol. 8, No. 17: 3–8.

Merrill, H. (1995), *Esky: the Early Years at Esquire,* New Brunswick: Rutgers University Press.

Messick, H. and Goldblatt, B. (1974), *Gangs and Gangsters: The Illustrated History of Gangs from Jesse James to Murph the Surf*, New York: Ballantine.

Meyer, R. (1991), 'Rock Hudson's Body', in D. Fuss (ed.), *Inside/Out: Lesbian Theories, Gay Theories*, London: Routledge.

Meyerowitz, J. (1994), 'Beyond the Feminine Mystique: A Reassessment of Postwar Mass Culture, 1946–1958', in J. Meyerowitz (ed.).

—— (ed.) (1994), *Not June Cleaver: Women and Gender in Postwar America, 1945–1960*, Philadelphia: Temple University Press.

—— (1996), 'Women, Cheesecake, and Borderline Material: Responses to Girlie Pictures in the Mid-Twentieth-Century US', *Journal of Women's History*, Vol. 8, No. 3, Fall: 9–35.

Miller, D. and Nowak, M. (1977), *The Fifties: The Way We Really Were*, Garden City: Doubleday.

Miller, J. (2000), *Something Completely Different: British Television and American Culture*, Minneapolis: University of Minnesota Press.

Miller, R. (1985), *Bunny: The Real Story of Playboy*, London: Michael Joseph.

Mills, C.W. (1951), *White Collar: The American Middle Classes*, New York: Oxford University Press.

Mintz, S. and Kellog, S. (1988), *Domestic Revolutions: A Social History of American Family Life*, New York: Free Press.

Mitgang, H. (2000), *Once Upon a Time in New York: Jimmy Walker, Franklin Roosevelt and the Last Great Battle of the Jazz Age*, New York: Simon & Schuster.

Modell, J. (1987), 'Dating Becomes the Way of American Youth', in H. Graff (ed.), *Growing Up in America: Historical Experiences*, Detroit: Wayne State University Press.

—— (1989), *Into One's Own: From Youth to Adulthood in the United States 1920–1975*, Berkeley: University of California Press.

Moers, E. (1960), *The Dandy: Brummell to Beerbohm*, London: Secker & Warburg.

Moorhouse, H.F. (1991), *Driving Ambitions: A Social Analysis of the American Hot Road Enthusiasm*, Manchester: Manchester University Press.

Mouffe, C. (1981), 'Hegemony and Ideology in Gramsci', in T. Bennett, G. Martin, C. Mercer and J. Woollacott (eds.), *Culture, Ideology and Social Process*, London: Batsford.

Morris, G. (1993), 'Beyond the Beach: Social and Formal Aspects of AIP's Beach Party Movies', *Journal of Popular Film and Television*, Vol. 21: 2–11.

Mort, F (1988), 'Boys Own? Masculinity, Style and Popular Culture', in R. Chapman and J. Rutherford (eds), *Male Order: Unwrapping Masculinity*, London: Lawrence & Wishart.

—— (1996), *Cultures of Consumption: Masculinities and Social Space in Late Twentieth-Century Britain*, London: Routledge.

Muggleton, D. (2000), *Inside Subculture: The Postmodern Meaning of Style*, Oxford: Berg.

Mumford, L. (1961), *The City in History*, New York: Brace & World.

Mustazza, L. (ed.) (1998), *Frank Sinatra and Popular Culture: Essays on an American Icon*, Westport CT: Praeger.

Myerhoff, H. and Myerhoff, B. (1967), 'Field Observations of Middle Class "Gangs"', in E. Vaz (ed.), *Middle Class Juvenile Delinquency*, New York: Harper (originally published 1964).

Nadel, A. (1995), *Containment Culture: American Narratives, Postmodernism, and the Atomic Age*, Durham: Duke University Press.

Nasaw, D. (1993), *Going Out: The Rise and Fall of Public Amusements*, New York: Basic Books.

Nixon, S. (1996), *Hard Looks: Masculinities, Spectatorship and Contemporary Consumption*, London: UCL.

—— (1997a), 'Exhibiting Masculinity', in S. Hall (ed.), *Representation: Cultural Representations and Signifying Practices*, Milton Keynes: Open University Press.

—— (1997b), 'Circulating Culture', in P. du Gay (ed.), *Production of Culture/Cultures of Production*, Milton Keynes: Open University Press.

Olsen, G. and Rockoff, H. (1994) (8th edn), *A History of the American Economy*, New York: Harcourt Brace Jovanovich.

Osgerby, B. (2000), ' Muscular Manhood and Salacious Sleaze: The Singular World of the 1950s Macho Pulps', in N. Abrams and J. Hughes (eds), *Containing America: Cultural Production and Consumption in Fifties America*, Birmingham: Birmingham University Press.

Otfinoski, S. (1997), *The Golden Age of Rock Instrumentals*, New York: Billboard.

Packard, V. (1960a), *The Hidden Persuaders*, Harmondsworth: Penguin.

—— (1960b), *The Status Seekers: An Exploration of Class Behaviour in America*, London: Longman.

Palen, J. (1995), *The Suburbs*, New York: McGraw-Hill.

Palladino, G. (1996), *Teenagers: An American History*, New York: Basic Books.

Paoletti, J. (1985), 'Ridicule and Role Models as Factors in American Men's Fashion Change, 1880–1910', *Costume*, Vol. 29: 121–34.

Parker, R. (1982), *The Myth of the Middle Class: Notes on Affluence and Equality*, New York: Liveright.

Parsons, T. (1949), 'The Social Structure of the Family', in R. Anshen (ed.), *The Family: Its Functions and Destiny*, New York: Harper Row.

—— (1954), 'Age and Sex in the Social Structure of the United States', in T. Parsons, *Essays in Sociological Theory*, Glencoe: Free Press (originally published 1949).

—— (1955), 'The American Family: Its Relation to Personality and the Social Structure', in T. Parsons and R. Bales (eds), *Family, Socialization and the Inter-action Process*, Glencoe: Free Press.

Peck, A. (1985), *Uncovering the Sixties: The Life and Times of the Underground Press*, New York: Pantheon.

Peiss, K. (1986), *Cheap Amusements: Working Women and Leisure in Turn-of-the-Century New York*, Philadelphia: Temple University Press.

Pells, R. (1985), *The Liberal Mind in a Conservative Age: American Intellectuals in the 1940s and 1950s*, New York: Harper Row.

Pendergast, T. (2000), *Creating the Modern Man: American Magazines and Consumer Culture, 1900–1950*, Columbia: University of Missouri Press.

Peterson, T. (1956), *Magazines in the Twentieth Century*, Urbana: University of Illinois Press.

Pleck, E. and Pleck, J. (eds) (1980), *The American Man*, Englewood NJ: Prentice-Hall.

Polsky, N. (1971), *Hustlers, Beats and Others*, Harmondsworth: Pelican.

Potter, D. (1954), *People of Plenty: Economic Abundance and the American Character*, Chicago: University of Chicago Press.

Potter, J. (1974), *The American Economy Between the World Wars*, London: Macmillan.

Pumphrey, M. (1987), 'The Flapper, The Housewife and the Making of Modernity', *Cultural Studies*, Vol. 1: 179–94.

Quirk, L. and Schoell, W. (1998), *The Rat Pack: Neon Nights with the Kings of Cool*, New York: Avon.

Reiman, R. (1992), *The New Deal and American Youth: Ideas and Ideals in a Depression Decade*, Athens: University of Georgia Press.

Reisman, D. (1950a), *The Lonely Crowd: A Study of the Changing American Character*, New Haven: Yale University Press.

—— (1950b), 'Listening to Popular Music', *American Quarterly*, Vol. 2, Winter: 359–71.

—— (1958), 'The Suburban Sadness', in W. Dobriner (ed.), *The Suburban Community*, New York: G.P. Putnam.

Reiss, S. (1999) (2nd edn), *Touching Base: Professional Baseball and American Culture in the Progressive Era*, Westport: University of Illinois Press.

Roosevelt, T. (1900), *The Strenuous Life: Essays and Addresses*, New York: Century.

Roper, M. and Tosh, J. (eds) (1991), *Manful Assertions: Masculinities in Britain Since 1800*, London: Routledge.

Rosen, M. (1973), *Popcorn Venus: Women, Movies and the American Dream*, New York: Coward, McCann & Geoghegan.

Rostow, W.W. (1960), *The Stages of Economic Growth: a Non-Communist Manifesto*, Cambridge: Cambridge University Press.

Rotundo, E.A. (1983), 'Body and Soul: Changing Ideals of American Middle-Class Manhood, 1770–1920', *Journal of Social History*, No. 16, Summer: 23–38.

—— (1987), 'Learning About Manhood: Gender Ideals and the Middle-Class Family in Nineteenth-century America', in J. Mangan and J. Walvin (eds).

—— (1993), *American Manhood: Transformations in Masculinity from the Revolution to the Modern Era*, New York: Basic Books.

Rowbotham, S. (1977) (3rd edn), *Hidden From History: 300 Years of Women's Oppression and the Fight Against It*, London: Pluto.

Rupp, L. (1982), 'The Survival of American Feminism: The Women's Movement in the Postwar Period', in R. Bremner and G. Reichard (eds), *Reshaping America: Society and Institutions, 1945–60*, Columbus: Ohio State University Press.

Ruth, D. (1996), *Inventing the Public Enemy: The Gangster in American Culture, 1918–1934*, London: University of Chicago Press.

Rutsky, R.L. (1999), 'Surfing the Other: Ideology of the Beach', *Film Quarterly*, Vol. 52, No. 4, Summer: 12–23.

Ryan, M. (1981), *Cradle of the Middle Class: The Family in Oneida County, New York, 1790–1865*, New York: Cambridge University Press.

Salisbury, H. (1967), 'The Suburbs', in Edmund W. Vaz (ed.), *Middle-Class Juvenile Delinquency*, New York: Harper & Row (originally published 1958).

Santelli, R. (1997), 'Catch a Wave: An Informal History of New Jersey Surfing', in K. Grover (ed.), *Teenage New Jersey, 1941–1975*, Newark: New Jersey Historical Society.

Savage, M., Barlow, J., Dickens, P. and Fielding, T. (1992), *Property, Bureaucracy and Culture: Middle Class Formation in Contemporary Britain*, London: Routledge.

Savran, D. (1992), *Communists, Cowboys, and Queers: The Politics of Masculinity in the Work of Arthur Miller and Tennessee Williams*, Minneapolis: University of Minnesota Press.

Schiffer, N. (1997), *Hawaiian Shirt Designs*, Atglen PA: Schiffer.

Scott, K. (1998), *The Bunny Years*, Los Angeles: Pomegranate Press.

Scranton, P. (1991), 'Diversity in Diversity: Flexible Production and American Industrialization, 1880–1930', *Business History Review*, Vol. 65, Spring: 27–90.

Segal, L. (1997), (2nd edn), *Slow Motion: Changing Masculinities, Changing Men*, London: Virago.

Segal, L. and McIntosh, M. (eds) (1992), *Sex Exposed: Sexuality and the Pornography Debate*, London: Virago.

Seward, R. (1978), *The American Family: A Demographic History*, Beverley Hills: Sage.

Shi, C. (2001), 'Mapping Out Gender Power: A Bourdieuian Approach', *Feminist Media Studies*, Vol. 1, No. 1: 55–9.

Shields, R. (ed.) (1991), *Places on the Margin: Alternative Geographies of Modernity*, London.

Simmons, C. (1989), 'Modern Sexuality and the Myth of Victorian Repression', in K. Peiss and C. Simmons (eds), *Passion and Power: Sexuality in History*, Philadelphia: Temple University Press.

Sinfield, A. (1994), 'Un-American Activities', in A. Sinfield, *Cultural Politics – Queer Reading*, London: Routledge.

Skeggs, B. (1997), *Formations of Class and Gender*, London: Sage.

Sklar, K. (1973), *Catherine Beecher: A Study in American Domesticity*, New Haven: Yale University Press.

Skolnick, A. (1991), *Embattled Paradise: The American Family in an Age of Uncertainty*, New York: Basic Books.

Smith, D. (1995), 'Recent Change and Periodization of American Family History', *Journal of Family History*, No. 20, Autumn: 329–46.

Smith, R. (1990), *Sports and Freedom: The Rise of the Big-Time College Athletics*, New York: Oxford University Press.

Snowman, D. (1977), *Kissing Cousins: An Interpretation of British and American Culture, 1945–1975*, London: Temple Smith.

Sorokin, P. (1956), *The American Sex Revolution*, Boston: Sargent.

Spectorsky, A.C. (1955), *The Exurbanites*, New York: Lipincott.

Spigel, L. (1992a), 'The Suburban Home Companion: Television and the Neighbourhood Ideal in Postwar America', in B. Colomina (ed.), *Sexuality and Space*, New York: Princeton Architectural Press.

—— (1992b), *Make Room for TV: Television and the Family Ideal in Postwar America*, Chicago: University of Chicago Press.

—— (1997a), 'White Flight', in L. Spigel and M. Curtin (eds), *The Revolution Wasn't Televised: Sixties Television and Social Conflict*, London: Routledge.

—— (1997b), 'From Theatre to Space Ship: Metaphors of Suburban Domesticity in Postwar America', in R. Silverstone (ed.), *Visions of Suburbia*, London: Routledge.

Starr, K. (1973), *Americans and the Californian Dream, 1850–1915*, New York: Oxford University Press.

—— (1990), *Material Dreams: Southern California Through the 1920s*, New York: Oxford University Press.

—— (1985), *Inventing the Dream: California Through the Progressive Era*, New York: Oxford University Press.

—— (1997), *The Dream Endures: California Enters the 1940s*, New York: Oxford University Press.

Stearns, P. (1990) (2nd edn), *Be a Man! Males in Modern Society*, New York: Homes & Meir.

Steele, T. (1984), *The Hawaiian Shirt: Its Art and History*, New York: Abbeville.

Strasser, S. (1989), *Satisfaction Guaranteed: The Making of the American Mass Market*, Washington: Smithsonian.

Taylor, E. (1989), *Prime-Time Families: Television Culture in Postwar America*, Los Angeles: University of California Press.

Tester, K. (ed.) (1994), *The Flâneur*, London: Routledge.

Toop, D. (1999), *Exotica: Fabricated Soundscapes in a Real World*, London: Serpent's Tail.

Trader Vic (1946), *Trader Vic's Book of Food and Drink*, New York: Doubleday.

U.S. Bureau of Census (1975), *Historical Statistics of the United States: Colonial Times to 1970*, Washington: USGPO.

Valant, G. (1987), *Vintage Aircraft Nose Art*, Osceola WI: Motorbooks.

Vaz, E. (ed.) (1967), *Middle-Class Juvenile Delinquency*, New York: Harper & Row.

Veblen, T. (1953), *The Theory of the Leisure Class; an Economic Study of Institutions*, New York: Mentor Books (originally published 1899).

Walkowitz, J. (1992), *City of Dreadful Delight*, London: Virago.

Warner, S. (1962) *Streetcar Suburbs: The Process of Growth in Boston, 1870–1900*, Cambridge MA: Harvard University Press.

—— (1972) *The Urban Wilderness: A History of the American City*, New York: Harper & Row.

Warren, C. (1987), *Madwives: Schizophrenic Women in the 1950s*, New Brunswick: Rutgers University Press.

Weeks, J. (1985), *Sexuality and Its Discontents: Meanings, Myths and Modern Sexualities*, London: Routledge.

Weeks, J. (1989) (2nd edn), *Sex Politics and Society: The Regulation of Sexuality Since 1800*, London: Longman.

Weisblat, T. (1994), 'What Ozzie Did for a Living', *The Velvet Light Trap*, No. 33, Spring: 14–23.

Weisman, L.K. (1992), *Discrimination By Design, A Feminist Critique of the Man-Made Environment*, Chicago: University of Illinois Press.

Weiss, J. (2000), *To Have and to Hold: Marriage, the Baby Boom and Social Change*, Chicago: University of Chicago Press.

Weyr, T. (1978), *Reaching for Paradise: The Playboy Vision of America*, New York: Times.

White, K. (1993), *The First Sexual Revolution: The Emergence of Male Heterosexuality in Modern America*, New York: New York University Press.

White, T. (1994), *The Nearest Faraway Place: Brian Wilson, the Beach Boys and the Southern Californian Experience*, New York: Henry Holt.

Whyte, W. (1956), *The Organization Man*, New York: Simon & Schuster.

Williams, L.R. (1998), 'Sex and Consciousness: Pornography and Censorship in Britain', in P. Cobley and A. Briggs (eds), *The Media: An Introduction*, London: Longman.

Wilson, E. (1985), *Adorned in Dreams: Fashion and Modernity*, London: Virago.

Wilson, S. (1955), *The Man in the Gray Flannel Suit*, New York: Simon & Schuster.

Winkler, A. (1986), *Home Front USA: America During World War II*, Arlington Heights: H. Davidson.

Wittner, S. (1974), *Cold War America: From Hiroshima to Watergate*, New York: Praeger.

Wofford, H. (1980), *Of Kennedys and Kings: Making Sense of the Sixties*, Pitttsburgh: University of Pitttsburgh Press.

Wolfe, T. (1965), 'The Kandy-Kolored Tangerine-Flake Streamline Baby', in T. Wolfe, *The Kandy-Kolored Tangerine-Flake Streamline Baby*, New York: Farrar, Strauss & Giroux.

—— (1970), *Radical Chic & Mau-Mauing the Flak Catchers*, New York: Farrar, Straus & Giroux.

—— (1989), 'Introduction', in T. Wolfe, *The Pump House Gang*, London: Black Swan.

Wright, G. (1983), *Building the Dream: A Social History of Housing in America*, New York: MIT Press.

Wyllie, I. (1954), *The Self-Made Man in America: The Myth of Rags to Riches*, New Brunswick: Rutgers University Press.

Wylie, P. (1955) (revised edn), *Generation of Vipers*, New York: Rinehart.

Zelditch, M. (1955), 'Role Differentiation in the Nuclear Family: A Comparative Study', in T. Parsons and R. Bales (eds), *Family, Socialization and the Interaction Process*, Glencoe: Free Press.

Index

Information in notes is indexed in the form 84n8, ie. note 8 on page 84.